THE TREE OF LOVE GIVES SHADE TO ALL

Proverbs, Maxims, Idioms and Exhortations

Otha Richard Sullivan

Copyright © 2012 Otha Richard Sullivan
All rights reserved.

ISBN-10: 061562295X
EAN-13: 9780615622958

Dedication

Special dedication to my parents, Benjamin Franklin and Iola Sullivan, and to my devoted niece, Debra Barnes McGee.

Acknowledgements

I am grateful to all the individuals who provided proverbs and sayings they recalled growing up, hearing their parents and elders use them to teach them about life. My utmost gratitude extends to Dr. Betty Nyangoni, Esther Keith, Henrietta Lawrence, Eric Coburn, Barbara King McKinley, Richard Burger, Dr. Virginia Lloyd, Frenchy J. Hodges, Gustina Atlas, LaDonna Campers, Calvin Dalrymple II, and the late Andrew Rudolph, Betty Colden and Marlene Bingham.

About the Author

Dr. Otha Richard Sullivan has been in public education for more than thirty years, serving as a teacher, counselor, administrator, and Ombudsman.

Dr. Sullivan has written several articles on career opportunities, education and African American History. He is the author of *African American Inventors, African American Women Scientists and Inventors,* and *African American Millionaires,* published by John Wiley & Sons, Inc. He is the co-author of Black Stars in the Civil War.

Dr. Sullivan currently lives in Detroit, Michigan.

Foreword

The seeds for this book began in 1983 while employed as an educational administrator at Lorton Prison in Lorton, Virginia. More than forty, bright-eyed and believed we could save the world individuals boarded a bus each day on the fringe of Capitol Hill in Washington, D.C. to teach, guide and administer educational programs for prison inmates. While riding the shuttle bus along Interstate 95 from Washington, D.C. to Lorton, Virginia, we passed the time by telling stories about one's childhood, its richness and strengths and how elders and parents instilled lessons in us by using mother wit, father wit, proverbs, maxims, idioms, aphorisms and traditional sayings. These lessons imparted values, spirituality, morality, character, respect for self and others. These teachings taught us invaluable orientation to how to become effective citizens, self-sufficient and successful individuals. African American elders passed down these proverbs from generations that began during slavery. They were quite committed to teaching us lessons that would help us overcome adversities, discrimination and a need to demonstrate excellence.

One of the sayings I shared with my colleagues, which I often heard my parents and elders use was, "Take care of the high chair, so you do not have to worry about the electric chair." This saying taught the importance of teaching children values and morals that would engender character and prevent them from committing crimes that would lead to incarceration. Parents strongly believed in teaching their children lessons that would help them avoid trouble. I suppose the daily reminder of working with strong, able-bodied individuals behind bars, who seemed to be content to have "three slops and a cot," spurred us to identify and discuss the lessons elders taught us to prevent failure and incarceration. We believed that somehow the lessons of the past were sorely missing in the lives of these young men.

We desperately sought to understand what could have gone wrong in a couple of decades in so many African-American households and communities that led to the need for not just one prison, but nine facilities for African American males in the District of Columbia. This sad state of affairs was evident throughout the country where African American males warehoused. We sought answers to the reasons for this phenomenon. We pondered the question of why is the incarceration of African American youth and adults so incommensurate to other individuals. What parental lessons were lacking in their childhood that led to the imprisonment of these men? We all agreed it was not a children problem, but an adult problem. We realized that the teachings, values and culture from which these men came were antithetical to those of parents and elders.

The daily trips became a setting for sharing old sayings and African American proverbs. Each person on the bus, who wished to participate, would write the first saying that came to mind on a slip of paper, shared with each other. We recognized there were common, strong, and colorful threads of experiences and teachings that we mutually shared in one's background. All of us were products of homes where parents vigorously inculcated teachings that emphasized spirituality, self-respect, achievement, moral reasoning, persistence, sacrifice, and strategies to be empowered in the broadest sense of the word. Parents taught us the same lessons their parents taught them and handed down from generation to generation. These teachings enabled elders and ancestors overcome adversities, biased rules, Jim Crow laws and other restrictions that denied African Americans first-class citizenship.

Each of us who worked at the prison felt blessed to have strong kinship bonds of parents, grandparents, aunts, uncles and a village of elders who taught the importance of a strong religious orientation, self-respect, a tenacious emphasis on education, and a respect for all elders in the community. We were products of the real village where everyone sought to teach, reinforce and evaluate growth and development.

While each of us hailed from different geographical areas of the country, socioeconomic levels and educational backgrounds, a sense of family and kinship evolved from the common teachings and proverbs of men and women who believed that they were responsible to love, support and raise healthy children to be contributors to the world. We were all products of parents and a community of elders who took their responsibility as adults as a mandate to teach children to become the best they could be.

Otha Richard Sullivan

This book presents expressions, proverbs, idioms, aphorisms and maxims that elders used to teach lessons to their children and those who lived in the community. Every adult viewed themselves as individuals who were parents, mentors and strong role models responsible for all children in the village. They firmly believed in the African proverb: "It takes a whole village to raise a child."(This saying comes from the Igbo culture.) There is an urgent need to return to the old landmark of the teachings of elders and ancestors. Many individuals have lost sight of the way elders taught invaluable lessons. They based their teachings in the Biblical admonition in Proverbs 23:10: "Do not remove the old landmark." Elders believed that the teaching of ancestors were applicable to today's youth. A gospel song, *Let us All Go Back to the Old Landmark*, written by Rev. William Herbert Brewster. The choir sang this song in the churches of my youth. This song appealed to us to understand that when faced with confusion, lack, and poverty in lives, "we can move forward if we return to the place and time when we knew who we were and what we were doing and start again to overcome adversities."

I recall several individuals who were a part of the village who taught me invaluable lessons about life. There was Reverend Chatman who cut my hair and taught me impeccable grooming skills. I learned how to type and the importance of grammar from Mr. Rutherford, a neighbor who was a poet and orator. He taught me the importance of speaking Standard English and insisted that I know how to conjugate verbs and use proper subject-verb agreement. There was Mrs. Tatum, a domestic, who introduced me to the proper way to dine, how to set a table and how to use silverware. I learned how to speak well from Miss Ratliff, my first grade teacher who always corrected my grammar. There was Reverend Mays, pastor of the Sweet Pilgrim Missionary Baptist Church in my hometown. He taught me to abide by the Ten Commandments and honor my mother, father and every elder. I learned the importance of compassion from Miss Ceola and Mister Diego, my next door neighbors, who insisted that I assist homebound senior citizens in the community with their chores. My grandfather Joseph Booth taught me the importance of saving money and helped me open my first Christmas savings account. He introduced me to books, African American History, African American inventors and African American newspapers. Miss Lillie McLaurin who owned the only African American newsstand on Mobile Street in Hattiesburg, Mississippi introduced me to the joy of reading and an appreciation of diverse cultures. My elders taught me how to dream and fulfill dreams of becoming a professional from the African American doctor and dentist in the neighborhood. My uncle Marvin Booth, an agricultural economist, taught me the personal satisfaction of farming and beauty in growing flowers. Uncle Perry Sullivan, an elementary school teacher, taught me the importance of elocution, proper manners and etiquette.

The large village of church members at Mt. Zion Missionary Baptist Church introduced me to the Bible and the importance of always regarding it as the "good book." They taught me how to read, comprehend, interpret and apply scripture. It was the older deacons in the church who oriented me to the importance of spirituality, which gave me a clear picture of God's law and how to apply it to my life. Every parent and elder in the community taught me the basic rules of behavior for spiritual and moral living. All of my teachers taught and reinforced the importance of education. Education was the only anecdote to freedom. They committed themselves to always informing me that I would complete high school, attend college and share my education with youth as a way of paying it forward.

Many of the sayings in proverbs come from villages in Africa. Many of the African American sayings were about family life and how to rear children and how to be effective parents. These proverbs have helped many generations of children and adults on how to be family members and a credit to elders and ancestors.

As children, we knew the reality that white people discriminated against African Americans, which permeated society. Elders and parents told us that we could overcome adverse conditions with a thorough preparation to be the best we could be. Consequently, we understood that in order to compete, take a rightful place in society and be recognized for abilities and talents we had to be two times smarter than any white person. . They stressed that one's appearance had to be immaculate. Speech had to be articulate, and behavior must surpass that of other groups. They taught us to disregard the outside world's perception and stereotypes. White people held perceptions we were inferior. Elders constantly reminded us the African American roots planted in individuals were ingenious and "made a way out of no way." We did not "faint in the day of adversity" for this would be offensive to one's ancestors.

We believed parents had the formidable responsibility in teaching values, appropriate decorum and the development of character. I recall my childhood in south Mississippi during the 1940s and 1950s was a rich experience, filled with parental involvement. We were fortunate to have two parents in the home. We had surrogate parents in the form of every elder and adult in the immediate neighborhood. Consequently, all elders regarded themselves as an extension of one's family. They felt responsible for reinforcing the teachings of parents and had the right to discipline us as surrogate parents. Their unwavering commitment and dedication to healthy development provided a grapevine of communication to parents and teachers about one's behavior outside the home.

These African American proverbs and gems of wit and wisdom are from the rich African heritage. Many of these gems come from slaves who lived and worked on plantations. The proverbs offer wisdom, direction, guidance, education, comfort and lessons to assist individuals through the formidable challenges of living. These sayings have lasted for many years, and they are effective ways to teach values. They represent a strong bridge that connects all African Americans.

This book is an attempt to share the richness of these sayings with all individuals. It is a personal appeal to parents and elders to continue to use them while teaching children and youth to overcome challenges they face, and be the best they can be. They are succinct and powerful lessons and say more than a lengthy sermon. This homespun wisdom called "isms" in my family. They are skillful in using a few words to teach life's lessons. African-American proverbs speak to child rearing, provide lessons for identity rather than confusion; encourage individuals to seek knowledge and enlightenment; offer succor in the face of adversity; deliver moral teachings in a world filled with temptation; promote the development and use of common sense in life's myriad of experiences; and connect generations with a legacy of wisdom. We must never lose the spirit and richness of proverbs. They are the daughters of experience.

Dr. Sullivan presents a number of topics and some narratives about his experiences of growing up in Mississippi. These experiences are quite similar to others raised in the South at the time. A list of African American proverbs, sayings, exhortations, aphorisms and maxims used to teach valuable lessons to children, follow some narratives. Some sayings, proverbs, and idioms are literal, while others are not.

The Tree of Love Gives Shade to All

This book attempts to share how to improve the state of youth. It is an appeal to parents to take responsibility for their children and be accountable for their actions. The problems and struggles many of today's youth face, and the serious circumstances and conditions in which they are living are caused by the absence of effective parents and positive role models to teach youth values that will help them become more productive, healthy and prosperous individuals. I recognize that many individuals are in denial about the cause of the difficulties so many youth face. . Hopefully, the rich history of overcoming past and present struggles will help parents, elders, and others become diligent in developing strategies, and provide healthy environments and stimulation for today's youth. We, and only we, can change the mayhem and loss of lives affected by the negative conditions and environments with which so many youth face. This book seeks to share some lessons and strategies for today's struggles.

Contents

A

Ability	7
Action	7
Adults	7
Adversity	9
Advice	15
Age	15
Ambition	17
Anger	19
Appearance	21
Appreciation	25
Art	25
Attitude	27

B

Beauty	29
Beliefs	29
Blame	29
Blessings	31
Books	33
Business	35

C

Caution	37
Chains	41

Challenges	41
Change	45
Character	45
Children	45
Clothes	51
Communication	53
Compassion	59
Complexion (Colorism)	61
Corruption	65
Courage	65
Criticism	69

D

Death	71
Debt	73
Deceit	75
Decisions	75
Despair	77
Destruction	77
Devil	77
Discord	79
Distrust	83
Dreams	85

E

Education	87
Effort	95
Epiphany	97
Equality	99
Evil	101
Experience	101

F

Failure	105
Faith	107
Family	109
Farming	111
Fathers	113
Fear	115
Flowers	115
Fly	119
Folly	123
Food	123
Fool	125
Forethought	125
Forewarning	127
Forgiveness	127
Friendship	127

G

Generosity	131
Gifts	131
Goals	135
God	139
Goodness	143
Gossip	143
Gratitude	145
Greetings	145
Grief	145

H

Happiness	147
Hatred	147

Healing	151
Health	153
History	153
Home	155
Honesty	157
Hope	157
Hugs	161

I

Identity	163
Ignorance	171
Illness	173
Independence	173
Industry	173
Injustice	173
Integrity	175
Intelligence	175

J

Jealousy	177
Joy	177
Judge	177
Justice	179

K

Kindness	181
Knowledge	183

L

Laughter	187
Leadership	187

Lessons	187
Lies	189
Life	189
Limitations	195
Loss	197
Love	197
Luck	201

M

Marriage	203
Mediocrity	207
Meekness	209
Men	209
Mentoring	211
Mistakes	213
Money	215
Mothers	216

O

Obstacles	223
Opportunity	223

P

Pain	225
Past	225
Patience	227
Payback	231
Peace	231
Politics	231
Potential	233
Poverty	233
Prayer	239

Pressure	241
Pride	241
Priorities	241
Privilege	245
Promise	247
Purpose	247

R

Reason	249
Relationships	249
Religion	251
Reputation	253
Responsibility	253
Roles – boys -girls	255

S

Sacrifice	257
Secrets	259
Self-acceptance	259
Self-esteem	261
Self-sufficiency	263
Sex	267
Shame	269
Sharing	269
Silence	271
Sin	271
Sloth	271
Sorrow	273
Stereotypes	275
Success	281
Superstitions	283

T

Talk	285
Thief	285
Time	285
Toughness	287
Travel	287
Trouble	289
Trust	291
Truth	291

V

Valediction	295
Violence	295
Virtue	299
Vision	299
Voting	299

W

Wealth	303
Weapons	303
Wisdon	305
Women	305
Words	307
Work	307

Z

Zeal	311

Introduction

More than 147 years have passed since the Emancipation Proclamation was signed by President Abraham Lincoln. The Proclamation did not free all American slaves. Emancipation only applied in parts of the South where the Union had not conquered. Lincoln wrote, "I do order and declare that all persons held as slaves within said designated states and parts of states as henceforward shall be free." The states where slaves were emancipated were Arkansas, Texas, Louisiana, Mississippi, Alabama, Florida, Georgia, South Carolina, North Carolina and Virginia. The Emancipation Proclamation did not cover some 500,000 slaves in the slave-holding border-states (Missouri, Kentucky, Maryland or Delaware) which were Union states.

Since the Emancipation Proclamation, African Americans have made great advancements in economics, education, labor, law, politics, inventions, family, and housing. One of the greatest achievements in our history is the 2008 election of an African American, Barack Obama, as president of the United States of America. This phenomenal achievement served notice to all African Americans that they can reach the highest level of office in this country. It is also a testament to the reality that one's race, ethnicity, or socio-economic level does not limit a person's possibility for achieving eminence in any profession. Clearly, this milestone is a credit to the tremendous struggles, sweat, toil and tears of our elders who always taught their children that they could achieve in the face of adversities and discrimination. Our ancestors and elders also had high expectations for their children and constantly told them, "You must be two times better academically and morally than any white person to be recognized and succeed in the elusive American dream of equality."

We must be mindful that the election of Barack Obama was not the bright new dawn of post-racial American History and racial tension did not end with the election of Obama. The expectations, demands, and barriers he faces as president are greater than any white president in our history. While he has made tremendous gains as president in implementing his pre-election issues, a myriad of politicians and citizens have been critical of his presidency and refuse to give him credit for his domestic and foreign policy accomplishments. I am reminded of my parents' teachings of more than 60 years ago that I, as an African American, had to be two to three times smarter than white people to get ahead in life. They also told me that no matter the number of degrees and achievements I receive, racism will still be evident in this country, which would attempt to deny me the respect, equality and opportunities of white people.

Political racism has reared its repugnant head and caused some leaders to call President Obama names that they never would have attributed previous presidents. The Birthers (conspiracy theorists who reject the legitimacy of the United States citizenship of President Obama), right wing zealots, and tea party individuals have questioned his faith as a Christian and resorted to labeling him a Muslim, an anti-Semite, a terrorist and other stereotypes that demean him. Disrespect of our president was demonstrated when GOP Representative Joe Wilson yelled out "You lie" during Obama's health care speech. Arizona Governor Jan Brewer showed contempt when she shook her finger under the president's nose when he visited Arizona. In a speech in Janesville, Wisconsin, Rick Santorum, former senator of Pennsylvania and GOP presidential hopeful, called President Obama a "Government N*gger." Newt Gingrich, a former congressman from Georgia and speaker of the House and GOP presidential contender in the 2012 election, referred to President Obama the "food stamp president." Senator Harry Reid (D. Ariz.) showed his bias when he type-casted President Obama as "light-skinned" with no Negro dialect unless he wanted to have one." Senator Grassley tweeted that President Obama is stupid.

Vitriolic statements continue to be directed at President Obama from politicians, citizens and religious leaders. Wealthy GOP super PAC donor Foster Friess in a television interview on April 12, 2012, said, "Now that they (Rick Santorum and Mitt Romney) have trained their barrels on President Obama, I hope his teleprompter is bulletproof." Musician Ted Nugent denounced President Obama and his top advisers as "evil" and urged the National Rifle Association members to help "chop off their heads off in November, 2012." Peoria Roman Catholic Bishop Daniel Jenky compared Obama's policies to Stalin and Hitler The list of rants continues from Obama's detractors.

President Obama has been called arrogant and angry by some whites. They refuse rather than accept Mr. Obama as an equal. These individuals have resorted to the term "arrogant," an expression that has been historically used by racially bigoted southern whites to refer to African Americans who are intelligent, articulate and confident. These individuals refuse to accept this African American man as an equal and an individual who is a scholar, mover and shaker. While negative attacks have been directed at President Obama, some biased individuals and right wing politicians have hurled offensive comments at First Lady Michelle Obama. These types of negative criticisms have never been made of former first ladies. Representative Jim Sensenbrenner of Wisconsin in a church fundraiser in his district referred to Mrs. Obama as having a large butt. Mike O'Neal, the speaker of the Kansas Legislature, referred to Mrs. Obama as "Mrs. Yomama." Walt Baker, the CEO of the Tennessee Hospitality Association, said "Mrs. Obama resembles a chimpanzee." He forwarded this racist email to 12 prominent Nashville citizens. Others have referred to the First Lady as an angry black woman. These individuals refuse to give credit to the educational achievements, the sterling careers and professional experience of Mrs. Obama whose education far surpasses that of recent first ladies. She holds a degree from the prestigious Princeton University and a law degree from Harvard University, one of the best schools in this country. Mrs. Obama's detractors never commented on the educational or professional experiences of former First Lady Nancy Reagan who received an English and drama degree at Smith College or that Barbara Bush dropped out of Smith College or that Pat Nixon received a Bachelor of Science degree in merchandising or Betty Ford studied dance at the Calla Travis Dance studio or that Laura Bush received a Bachelor of Science degree in education and a Master's degree in library science.

Our youth must be taught the special lessons of our ancestors and elders who overcame formidable challenges and oppression. We must hold fast to these powerful teachings to assist our children and youth to rise above negative conditions and circumstances. In the absence of these teachings, countless African Americans will be mentally enslaved due to their economic, social, health educational status and lack of guidance.

While there has been countless research and excuses presented on the causes for the plight of some African Americans, the reality is that too many parents and adults are in denial about their conditions and lack strategies to overcome negative circumstances, opting to blame others for their conditions of poverty. Although these circumstances are relevant, I am convinced that many of the negative conditions of some African Americans is directly related to the lack of effective parents, children having children, the absence of accountability among some parents, a dearth of confident parents, the lack of discipline for children, the shortage of a strong work ethic, a dependency on outside sources for support, the absence of positive role models in the family and community, the modicum of blame placed on external sources for social, economic and physical conditions, the failure of youth to complete high school, the absence of spirituality and morality, unimportant priorities, and a failure to develop and demonstrate respect for self and others. Children are like sponges and what they experience in their environment soaks into them and becomes their norm for behavior, values, and priorities.

Our children and youth cannot be taught successful skills by parents who say, "Do as I say and not as I do." Children cannot become successful when they live in an environment where low expectations are the norm. Children cannot value the importance of work when they never see any adults going to work. Children cannot develop appropriate conflict resolution skills when they witness reactive responses to conflict. Children cannot learn the importance of moral values when parents and other adults are immoral in their behavior and actions.

Sadly, too many African Americans are living in spiritual and financial poverty, which is exacerbated by many difficulties that lead to deferred dreams and death at an early age. All too often, some African Americans do not know and apply the history of the difficulties their ancestors experienced and the manner in which they overcame adversities. Our youth must know their history and how their ancestors survived and triumphed during formidable challenges and inequities.

Our strength in overcoming obstacles is rooted in determination, persistence, hard work, faith and a belief that we are worthy of life's riches. I am convinced that freed slaves did not faint in the day of adversity and sought to be strengthened by their desire to overcome the physical chains and shackles they faced during slavery. They held fast to the scripture of Isaiah 54:17: "No weapon that is formed against thee shall prosper and every tongue that rise against you in judgment you shall condemn. This is the heritage of me, says the Lord." This firm belief in this scripture undergirded the teachings and beliefs of our elders and parents who sought to lift them and their children above the daily apartheid conditions they faced.

Although my great-great grandfather, Levin Booth, was born a slave in South Carolina in 1789 and sold on the auction block of Charleston, and taken to a plantation in Taylorsville, Mississippi, he died a successful businessman in the community of Oakahay in Covington County, Mississippi.

In 1870, the first time African Americans were enumerated by name on the U. S. Census, Mississippi had a population of 827,922 of which 382,896 were white and 444,201 were African American. Other data included name, age, sex and color, occupation, value of real estate owned, value of personal property owned, place of birth and the ability to read or write. In 1860, there were 204 slave owners in Covington County, Mississippi where my ancestors were slaves. Slaves comprised 35.5 percent of the county's population of the population of 2,845 free whites. While some slave owners had an average of four slaves, William Speed and John Knight had respectively sixteen and twenty-two slaves.

Tracing my ancestors back through slavery was incredibly challenging as slaves were only enumerated by age and sex. Through an extensive review of slave inhabitants in Covington County, Mississippi, I was able to view the 1870 U. S. Census, the first time African Americans were enumerated by name. Using my maternal ancestors' ages in 1870, I viewed the 1860 slave records and found that my great-great grandfather Levin Booth, my great-great grandmother and great grandfather were owned by John Reddoch. I recall my parents referred to land on which my maternal grandfather lived was formerly Reddoch land. At the time, this revelation had no meaning for me until many years later when I was finally able to associate that land with the place where my ancestors were slaves.

Based on the 1860 U. S. Census, Mississippi had a population of 791,396. The free population was 354,700 and the slave population was 436,696, which was 55.1 percent of the population.

Reviewing the 1870 Census, I found that my great-great grandfather owned more than a hundred acres of land and was able to read and write. He fared much better economically and educationally than many of the whites in the community. According to the 1870 U. S. Census, my great-great grandfather had real estate valued at $100, the equivalent of about $1,695 in 2012, and personal property of $126, the equivalent of about $2,136 in 2012. I am convinced that this achievement was a huge testimony to this man's industry and fortitude to achieve and overcome tremendous obstacles. Our ancestors were endowed with a strong will, faith, and an ability to survive the many years of slavery. Their yearning for success was instilled by their elders who always taught them by example that they were a child of God and deserved the same rights as others. They were the embodiment of faith which allowed them to believe in freedom and claim better conditions.

My great-great-grandfather Levin Booth applied for a homestead in 1878 under the Homestead Act passed and signed by President Abraham Lincoln on January 1, 1863. Booth applied for his homestead of 80.75 acres in 1878 and received a patent for the land in 1883. He was required to pay $18 in fees. This patent was assigned to my great-great grandfather after he lived on the land for 5 years, built a home, improved the land and farmed the land.

The only way we can change the devastating conditions and hopelessness of some of our youth is to be effective adults and parents who teach children essential values to become successful. We must be committed to be a part of that village. Failure to be effective parents and adults assure that our children will never overcome the social, physical, emotional, and financial poverty some individuals face today.

The teachings of our elders of years gone by are important today as they were many years ago. These lessons and sayings, which seemed to be simple words, were quite powerful in teaching youth to overcome formidable challenges. The proverbs, idioms, sayings, and exhortations covered every area in life. The profound expressions helped youth to become the best they could be. These teachings are significant today as adults, children and youth face present struggles.

ABILITY

. A great pleasure in life is doing what people say you cannot do.

. He/she can't cut the mustard. — One is unable to complete a task.

. Paddle your own canoe.

ACTION

Our ancestors and parents encouraged us to be about the business of actions, rather than just talking.

. Actions speak louder than words. (Some people talk a lot but don't take action)

. Bullets don't have eyes.

. It isn't anything to it but to do it.

It is important to take action.

. Only those who do nothing make no mistakes. Those who do nothing don't make mistakes.

. Talking about fire doesn't boil the pot. One cannot get a pot or pan boiling without starting the fire.

ADULTS

Our ancestors were positive role models who took their responsibilities seriously. Today's adults must rise to the enormous duties of taking care of their children and teaching values that will help them succeed. Marian Wright Edelman,

Chairman of the Children's Defense Fund, speaking on continuing Dr. Martin Luther King's work wrote: "We do not have a children problem. We have an adult problem. It's adults' responsibility to make a better life for their kids. When I was growing up in Bennettsville, South Carolina, the outside world told me as a black girl that I wasn't worth anything. But I didn't believe it because my parents said it wasn't so. My preacher said it wasn't so. My teachers said it wasn't so. So I knew it wasn't so." I recall this same type of teachings growing up in Mississippi. Our parents, elders, teachers, and every adult in the community told us we had the ability to achieve. They reminded us on a daily basis that we were capable of competing with anyone and anywhere. They also instilled the important lesson that we had to be two to three times smarter, moral, and spiritual than others to take a special place in life. We must employ these same teachings with today's youth. They must be taught that they are special individuals with limitless opportunities. They need to hear this message on a regular basis by their parents and elders.

Our children need parents and elders who are present in their lives to teach moral and spiritual lessons. Children whose parents are absent and are negative role models pass on counterproductive behaviors to them. Edelman addressing the incarceration of African American youth and adults wrote, "Black children are nearly nine times and Latino children are three times as likely as White children to have an incarcerated parent. Blacks constitute one third and Latino one-fifth of the prisons in America, and 1 in 3 Black men, 20 to 29 years old, is under correctional supervision or control. Of the 2.3 million in jail or prison, 64 percent are minorities; of the 4.2 million persons on probation, 45 percent are minority; and of the 800,000 on parole, 59 percent are minority. Our youth need to know that their punishments for crimes are always disproportionate to others.

. A good example is the best sermon.

. Being a role model is the most powerful form of educating.

. To be in your children's memories tomorrow, you have to be in their lives today.

. Your children will become what you are….So be what you want them to be.

ADVERSITY

Our elders constantly encouraged us to view adversities as opportunities to grow spiritually, morally and economically. Although, our ancestors were enslaved physically for many years, their minds were always free to think of freedom and deliverance. They believed in the instruction of Ecclesiastes 7;14; "In the day of prosperity be joyful, but in the day of adversity, consider; God also hath set the one over against the other, to the end that man should find nothing after him." Adversities are the afflictions that test our spiritual strength. We are never given more than we can bear. Each affliction provides strategies to deal with life's challenges and overcome them.

We all have faced or will be confronted with adversities in our life. These adversities are the teachers that instill strength, wisdom, and provide effective strategies to cope with difficult circumstances. The manner in which we deal with adversities determines how healthy and prosperous we will become. Adversities are tools by which God fashions us for better things. When we look at adversity with vision and the light of truth, we learn invaluable lessons that help us change our thoughts, beliefs and actions. We must understand that we are all a diamond in the rough. We come to know and understand that adversity is the powerful way of polishing the precious diamond in us. We get to know the lesson in the Chinese proverb: "The gem cannot be polished without friction, nor man perfected without trials."

. A crooked cornstalk can still have straight ear. — We can't judge the quality of things by its shape.

. A day of sorrow is longer than a month of joy. — Our grief lasts longer than joy.

. A day without sunshine is like night. — Life has its challenges.

. A dry well teaches us the worth of water.

. Adversity introduces a man to himself.

The Tree of Love Gives Shade to All

. A mule can tote so much goodness in his face that he doesn't have any left for his hind legs.

. Appreciate the unexpected.

. Clouds gather before a storm.

. Come hell or high water. — A difficult situation or obstacle will be overcome.

. Concern should drive us into action and not into depression.

. Crosses are ladders which lead to heaven. — Those who bear no oppression bear no crown.

. Don't let anyone out pick you in your own field.

. Don't trouble trouble until trouble troubles you. — Don't go looking for trouble.

. Even the biggest brook runs dry sometimes. — Everyone runs through a period of drought.

. Every cloud has a silver lining.

. Every dog has its day. — Everyone gets a chance eventually.

. Everything is not always peaches and cream. — Life is not always filled with joy.

. Folks on the rich bottomland stop bragging when the river rises.

. Grin and bear it. — Be joyful in difficult times.

. Hard times will make a monkey eat cayenne pepper.
   We will eat some things we dislike during hard times.

. He/she is down in the dumps. — Feeling sad or depressed

. He that endures is not overcome. — Those who persist overcome.

. If it is not one thing, it's another. — One thing goes wrong and another challenge emerges.

. If you can't bear any cross, you'll have no crown. — We never progress without struggles.

. If you can't stand the heat, get out of the kitchen. — If you are not up to the challenge, stop.

. I have been in sorrow's kitchen and I licked the pot clean.

. In trying times, don't quit trying. — Always make effort in the midst of trials.

. It's a mighty bad wind that never shifts.

. It's hard to make clothes for a miserable man.

. It rains, and every man feels it someday. — Everyone experiences difficult times.

. I wish you enough rain to appreciate the sun more.

. Keep a stiff upper lip. — Keep the faith in hard times.

. Life isn't about waiting for the storm to pass. It's about learning to dance in the rain.

. Life has its little ups and downs.

. Life is short and full of blisters.

The Tree of Love Gives Shade to All

- Mellow nuts have the hardest rind. — The best things in life are often difficult to achieve.

- Misfortunes make us wise. — We acquire special knowledge from difficulties.

- Mountain, get out of my way. — We must remove obstacles in our lives.

- No man is more unhappy than the one who is never in adversity; the greatest affliction is never to be afflicted.

- No one would ever have crossed the ocean if he could have gotten off the ship in a storm.

- Nothing can suffice a person except that which they have not.

- Nothing dries as quickly as a tear.

- Rainfall falls on every rooftop. — We all experience some adversities.

- Rolling stones gather no moss.

- Roll with the punches. — Accept what is dealt to you.

- Sorrows catch meddlers.

- Sunshine comes behind the storm. — Brighter days follow trials and tribulations.

- The best way out of difficulty is through it. — Don't let challenges impede your progress.

- The deeper you dig, the richer the soil.

- Take it in stride.

- Take it on the chin.

- The longest day is sure to have its nights. — During difficult times, we often face long nights.

- There but the grace of God go I.

- There is never a road without a turn.

- There is no sweet without sour. — Life has its good and bad moments.

- The sun isn't going to shine in your door always. — Every day is not filled with joy.

- The very time I thought I was lost, my dungeon shook and my chains fell off. When individuals feel there is no way out of difficulties, we can find ways to overcome them.

- Time is a great healer. — Time does heal wounds and heartaches.

- Tough times don't last, tough people do. — Persistence is important in difficult times.

- Turn your stumbling blocks into stepping stones. We often stumble before we succeed.

- What is bitter to endure may be sweet to remember.

- When I dig another out of trouble, the hole from which I lift him is the place where I bury my own.

- When it rain it pours.

- When things go wrong, don't go with them.

The Tree of Love Gives Shade to All

. Where there is a will there is a way.

. Without danger we cannot get beyond danger.

. Worrying never changes anything.

. You can't be a true winner until you have lost. — Failure can lead to success.

. You have to put up with the rain to get the rainbow. — Success comes from difficulties.

. You have to take the fat with the lean. — It is important to deal with the good and the bad.

. You need to have it together to hold it together. — Strength is necessary when facing difficulties.

. You should not give up at the end. — It is important to never give up.

. You win some and you lose some.

ADVICE

. Fall on deaf ears. — Helpful information is ignored or disregarded.

. If you wish good advice, consult an old man. Old people have a lot of experience.

. Never give advice unasked. — Beware of giving advice when none is requested.

. Never offer advice. A wise man doesn't need it, and a fool doesn't consider it.

AGE

. Act your age and not your shoe size. — Stop behaving immaturely.

. Age is a very high price to pay for maturity. — Some people age but don't mature.

. Age and treachery will triumph over youth and skill.

, Age is mind over matter. If you don't mind, it doesn't matter.

. Age is only a number. — Age is relative. It is a state of mind.

. As you grow older, you stand for more and fall for less.

. A woman who will tell her own age will tell anything.

. Eat coconuts while you have teeth. — Be aware of your ability.

. Everyone wants a long life, but no one wants to get old. — Some people fear getting old.

- God, God Almighty, old age is not a disease. — Reaching old age is a blessing.

- He/she is long on the tooth. — An elderly person

- He/she is over the hill. — A person has reached old age.

- I might wear out, but I won't rust out. — Age may bring infirmity.

- Might be old, but I am not cold. — Being old doesn't mean being lame.

- Nothing gets old but clothes. — Have a positive attitude toward aging.

- Older than the hills

- Old gray mare and what she used to be. — Old age brings some limitations.

- Old kindling wood is easy to catch fire. — Old pieces of wood burn easily.

- The eyebrow is older than the beard.

- There is no fool like an old fool. — Older people should possess wisdom.

- There's snow on the mountaintop, but there is fire below.
  Age is one thing, but ability is another thing.

- The older the moon, the brighter it shines.
  An older person is likely to give better advice based on experience.

- You can't teach old dogs new tricks.
    People who are accustomed to doing things in a particular way will not abandon their habits.

- Youth looks forward and age backward.

- Wrinkles are the service stripes of life. — Our face shows our struggles and triumphs.

AMBITION

None of us is born to be mediocre. Each of us has the energy and personal power to achieve. It is important to teach our children at the earliest age that they must do their best in all of their efforts. Poet Nikki Giovanni once wrote, "Mediocrity is safe." Countless individuals accept mediocrity for it is an easy route to take in life. There are no risks. Many individuals accept the average and substandard and believe they are not entitled to more. Mediocrity causes individuals to be critical of their circumstances, always conveniently using their plight as reasons for not doing better. They tend to blame others for their conditions.

Historically, African Americans have regarded mediocrity as a barrier to freedom, justice, and racial progress. In fact, mediocrity has been viewed by our people as "a sin and a shame." We can teach excellence by demonstrating excellence. We cannot expect children to learn this attribute in a vacuum. It must be taught and modeled for them.

. A bend in the road is not the end of the road unless you fail to make the turn. When faced with detours, it is important to know alternate routes.

. Adversity tries virtue. — During difficulties, our virtues are often tested.

. Afflictions are the best blessings in disguise. — We learn from our adversities.

. All things are less dreadful than they seem.

. Always have more than one iron in the fire. — Plan your life with a number of options.

. Every man thinks his own burdens are the heaviest. When we go through trials, we often think our situation is worse than anyone else.

. Every path has a puddle.

. Hard times make a monkey eat red pepper when he doesn't care for black.

. He who does not advance will recede. — Achievement is important to progress in life.

The Tree of Love Gives Shade to All

. He/she will have a long row to hoe. — It will be a difficult task or assignment.

. If it is to be it's up to me.

. If you aim at nothing, you'll hit it every time.

. If you fall, you don't have to wallow. — Don't stop when you fail. Get up and go forward.

. Jump at the sun, you may not land on the sun, but at least you'll be off the ground.

. Keep your eyes on the prize. — Keep your focus on your goals.

. Perseverance brings success. — Never stop trying to reach your goals.

. Sometimes when we are afraid of the future, we cling to the past. It is easier to languish in the past than work toward the future.

. Stretch your mind and fly. — Dare to dream, persist and reach new heights in life.

. That's one up and coming woman (man) — He/she possesses the ability to achieve success.

. The difficulties of life are intended to make us better not bitter.

. What God's got for a man, he'll get it.

. When things go wrong, don't go with them. When we fail, we need to rise and go forward.

. With each sunrise, we start anew. — Every day has special opportunities.

. You can't keep a good man down.

. You've got to play big to win big. — Success requires persistence, discipline and hard work.

 ANGER

Our elders used the Bible to teach children and others about how to deal with anger. I recall my Grand-father teaching me the importance of never demonstrating anger and malice toward others. He used the Biblical scripture in Ephesians 4:31-32: "Let all bitterness and wrath and anger and clamor and slander be put away from you, along with all malice; Be kind to one another, tenderhearted, forgiving another as God in Christ forgave you." We were taught that harsh words bring no reward. Respectful words bring honor to all.

. An angry person is seldom reasonable, a reasonable person is seldom angry.

. An eye for an eye only ends up making the whole world blind.

. Anger is only one letter short of danger. — Anger can cause problems.

. Anger of the mind is poison to the soul.

. Anger makes dull men witty, but it will keep them poor. Anger leads to poverty and lack.

. Control your attitude; otherwise your attitude will control you.

. Don't let a little dispute injure a great friendship. — Respect disagreements as lessons.

. Every mad man thinks all other men are mad. — Angry people think others are angry.

. Fit to be tied.

. Fly off the handle.

. Go off the deep end. — Become angry or emotional.

- Harsh words bring no reward. Respectful words bring honor to all. Be kind to others.

- Have a bone to pick with someone. — Annoyed and want to talk with someone.

- Hot under the collar.

- Jump down someone's throat. — Shout at a person in an angry manner.

- Keep your shirt on

- Love is an endless act of forgiveness. — The expression of real love is to forgive others.

- Mad as a mule chewing on bumblebees.

- Madder than a wet hen

- Not the fastest horse can catch a word spoken in anger.

- Overcome an angry person by restraining your anger. — Don't respond to anger with anger

- Rake someone over the coals. — Scold someone severely.

- Skin someone alive — Punish someone severely.

- The best cure for a short temper is a long walk, — Take time to think before you act.

APPEARANCE

We can never become healthy individuals and find the special peace of mind that comes from an appreciation and acceptance of the physical features that God gave us. When we feel insecure about the texture of our hair, the color of our skin, and our unique physique, we believe we are unattractive and less than others whose physical attributes we admire. Some individuals spend more time buying and using beauty products, keeping hair and nail appointments and seeking corrective measures to their physical appearance, than spending time on filling their hearts and minds with positive thinking, beliefs, opinions and commitments.

While it is important to project an attractive appearance, true beauty exudes from an individual's pride, confidence and spirituality. We are victimized when we permit others to define beauty for us. Cosmetics, hot comb, relaxer, Indian Remy hair, hair color, skin bleaching cream cannot make a person beautiful. Real beauty is inward and expresses itself externally.

Our elders stressed appropriate appearance. We were taught that cleanliness is next to Godliness. The family's clothes were always spotless. Washing clothes was a trying operation. The wash day usually occurred on Saturdays and took most of the day to complete the job. I recall my mother would use three galvanized steel tubs called "wash tubs," which were situated side by side. One was used for washing and the other two for rinsing clothes. In the first pot, lye soap made from lye and fat was used to soap the clothes. The clothes were rubbed by hand along a "wash board" made of a corrugated metal surface mounted on a wooden frame. After carefully scrubbing the clothes, they were placed in the rinse pots and then placed in the black wash pot. This pot was about eighteen inches in diameter and rounded on the bottom. It held about 15 gallons of water. Mother would use a wooden stick to push the clothes up and down. The final process was to wring out the clothes and place them on a clothes line. After clothes finished drying, they were pressed using a smoothing iron. The washtubs were quite useful at the time as we used them to take a bath in them with water heated from a wood burning stove.

Our parents and elders always told us, "Beauty is as beauty does." This quality was reinforced by our teachers, parents, and everyone in the community. I recall daily inspections by my teachers at Grace Love Elementary School before class began. They stood like sentries outside the classroom and meticulously inspected each child with their sharp eyes and nose, looking carefully at teeth, hair, fingernails, clothing, and shoes. With their olfactory glands, they were able to identify every child whose hygiene was malodorous or wholesome. A child's worst nightmare was to be directed to step aside by the teacher for inappropriate appearance or poor hygiene. The teacher talked to the child about proper hygiene and appearance. By the next day, appearance and hygiene had changed for the better. While our parents and teachers earned meager pay, they demanded that each child be clean and appropriately dressed. It did not matter to the teacher or parent if the child wore a home-spun shirt, fashioned from flour and fertilizer sacks, or an outfit made of fine fabrics, it was mandatory that a child be clean.

. A fair face may hide a foul heart. — Looks can be deceiving.

. A little piece of tin, but hard to bend. — A person can be small in stature but strong in ability.

. All hat, no cattle. — When someone talks big, but cannot back it up.

. All that glitters is not gold. — We cannot judge the quality of something by appearance.

. Beauty is in the eyes of the beholder. — Different people see beauty in various ways.

. Beauty is only skin deep. — Physical beauty is superficial.

. Beauty is only skin deep and ugly is to the bone.

. Cleanliness is next to Godliness. — A person is clean, good and spiritual.

. Clothes don't make the man. — You cannot cover up inadequacies.

. Cute as a button

. Cutting off a mule's ear doesn't make it a horse.
    We cannot change individuals by altering their physical appearance.

. Don't buy a pig in a poke. — Caveat emptor: Let the buyer beware.

. He/she is a bag of bones — One is very underweight.

. He/she is dressed to a tee. — Well dressed with attention to detail.

. He/she is dressed to the nines. — A person dressed flamboyantly, dressed well.

. He/she is easy on the eyes.

. He/she is sharp as a tack, and rusty as a nail. — A person is well dressed and foul smelling.

. He looks like he got beat with an ugly stick.

. It must be jelly. Jam doesn't shake like that.

. Looks are a dime a dozen and they fade away.   Beauty fades in time

. Looks won't do to split rails with. — Appearance cannot get a job done.

. Never depend too much on the blackberry blossoms.

. Pretty is as pretty does. — Judge people by their behavior and not appearance.

. Ripe apples make the tree look taller.

. Seeing is believing — One can only believe what they experience personally.

- She looks like homemade sin. — An unattractive female

- Stepping like a rooster in deep mud.

- Sunflowers aren't so mighty pretty in the dark.

- The bigger you are, the harder you fall. — One's size does not win the fight.

- Thin as a rail. — Skinny person

- The wheat crop can't fool you when it comes to the thrashing.

- Ugly man doesn't fool with the looking glass.

- You can't judge a book by its cover. — Appearance does not imply the content.

- You can't tell much about a chicken pie until you get through the crust.

- You look like something the cat dragged in.

 APPRECIATION

We were always encouraged to be grateful for all things. We were mandated to start each day with a special acknowledgement of the Almighty, for it was He from whom all blessings flowed.

. Appreciate the unexpected.

. Bring me my flowers while I am still alive.

. Don't bite the hand that feeds you. — Don't harm someone who helps you.

. He knows what side his bread is buttered on. Knowledge from where help comes

. If you don't have the best of everything, make the best of everything you have.

. No duty is more urgent than that of returning thanks.

. Take what you can get until you get what you want. — Appreciate what you have.

. Thanks cost nothing. — Show gratitude for kindness.

. The blacker the berry; the sweeter the juice

 ART

Art surrounds our life. It is an expression of life itself. It can be the creative finger paintings of a child to the crude drawing of a person and the wonderful work of Romare Bearden, art draws us into a magical medium of communication. Art is everywhere and invites us to stop and take note of creativity and special wonders that touch us each day. Bearden once wrote, "We look too much to museums. The sun coming up in the morning is enough." It inspires, provokes thoughts and criticisms; creates images of the past and the present; and invites us to share in its special pleasures.

Our elders and parents instilled in us an appreciation for art. We were introduced to the magnificent quilts that our mothers and grandmothers made. They shared with us how our ancestors did woodcarvings and made art from recycle materials they found. Our mothers created fashionable garments from flour and fertilizer sacks for family members. We were taught that creativity was a healthy way to spend leisure time and a way to create helpful objects with little investment other than time.

An appreciation of art teaches and encourages us to look at life in its representation of individuals, events, and diverse cultures. Leonardo da Vinci wrote, "Art is the queen of all sciences communicating knowledge to all the generations of the world." Art invites us to communicate with a special talent that emerges in individuals and appreciate the freedom to express and share their feelings of faith with others.

There is an artist in all of us just waiting to emerge. Art is a positive outlet to express our deepest emotions of joy, happiness, pain, and long suffering. While we have been oriented to look for art in a museum or gallery, it surrounds us in the formation of land, the rising and setting of the sun, the budding of trees, flowering of plants and changes of seasons. Art is as healing and helpful to our hearts and minds.

. Art is everywhere.

. Art is how the heart can only show its true feelings.

. Art is the tree of life.

. Art washes from the soul the dust of everyday life.

. Life is a work of art designed by the one who lives it.

. Life is very nice, but it lacks form. It's the aim of art to give it some.

. The creation of beauty is art.

 ATTITUDE

Our elders often told us that our attitude determines our altitude in life. Having a positive attitude was not an option for children.

. Attitude is everything.

. Get up on the wrong side of the bed. — A person is having a bad day.

BEAUTY

Real beauty is not found in the outward appearance of an individual.

. Beauty may have fair leaves but bitter fruit.

. Beauty without virtue is a curse.

. Modesty has more charm than beauty. — Modesty is more precious than beauty.

BELIEFS

Our beliefs were instilled by our elders and parents. These beliefs were deeply rooted in Christianity.

. Eye itching mean company must be coming

. It's bad luck all year if a woman is your first visit on New Year's.

. It's good luck to eat black-eyed peas and hog jowl on New Year's.

. Right hand itching means you are going to receive some money.

BLAME

The greatest cop-out in life is to blame others for our unhealthy social, emotional, financial and physical health. People who blame others tend to overemphasize themselves while underemphasizing the negative effects of their behavior and actions. When we blame others, it relieves our feelings of personal culpability. It allows us to rise above the other person to a position of righteous superiority. This negative behavior causes denial and separates us from the problem and the responsibility of working toward a solution.

There are many individuals who choose poverty by blaming others for their circumstances. Individuals who blame others for their actions, reactive behavior, circumstances, social, emotional and physical being will not enjoy prosperity and good health. They spend their time trying to find excuses for their actions, believing that the world owes them something. They fight work, are irresponsible, lack industry, and are the first to criticize others, and live a life of denial. Dr. George Washington Carver once said, "Ninety-nine percent of the failures come from people who have the habit of making excuses."

Blame is an infectious disease that destroys the mind and impairs one's thinking, leading to a life of lack and poverty in the broadest sense.

. Don't find fault, find a remedy.

. Don't lay it on the cow when the milk gets sour. — Take care of things to preserve the quality.

. The bad workman blames his tools. — Refuse to accept responsibility for one's actions.

. When you blame others, you give up your power to change. Blame keeps individuals powerless

. You should not blame or praise yourself.

BLESSINGS

Our life has been blessed from the time of conception to delivery and throughout our journey in this life. These blessings, which are a promise from God, enable us to be creative in our thoughts and deeds and experience health, peace, goodness, joy, happiness, love and abundance. We can greatly enhance our emotional, physical, and financial health by identifying our special blessings on a daily basis.

I have begun a daily journal of blessings where I list the special blessings. At the end of the week, I review the journal and find that each day is much the same except each day is noted with more abundant blessings. Each day upon awakening, I write in my journal: Blessing number (1) Thanking God for breath in my body, being of a sound mind, and having the activity of my limbs. Blessing number (2) Feeling eternally blessed to have good health, to move my limbs and walk with energy to the kitchen and put on the coffee pot. Blessing number (3) the ability to bathe myself, dress myself and drive myself to work. Blessing number (4) have a job where I can teach youth strategies to empower themselves through education. The list of blessings is noted in the journal throughout the day. I have found that there is no blessing so trivial that I neglect to write it in my journal.

What are your blessings? Have you taken the time to etch them in your mind or write them on a piece of paper? If not, treat yourself to this special, proactive activity of counting your blessings on a daily basis. I have found that keeping a blessing journal keeps me positive in a world that is filled with too much pain, suffering, lack, crime, inhumanity and other Godless behavior. It enables me to be in touch with the real source of my strength, the root of the love that fills me with a special energy and the recognition that each day is a special gift, a birthday, an anniversary, a time for celebration and a time to decrease the number of negative conditions.

Each day, I understand that everything in life is holy. Above all, the journal keeps me steadfast in praising God from whom all blessings flow. Try writing down your blessings and you will be surprised how your personal happiness and abundance increases. When you count your blessings, you will refuse to have fear, worry and other negative conditions, which threaten your health and prosperity.

. Blessed are they who can laugh at themselves, for they shall never cease to be amused.

. Count your blessings.

. God bless the child that's got his own.

. Great blessings come from heaven.

. Blessed are they who can laugh at themselves, for they shall never cease to be amused.

. When life gives you a hundred reasons to cry; show life that you have a thousand reasons to smile.

. With each sunrise, we start anew. — Every day offers new opportunities.

BOOKS

Mary McLeod Bethune once wrote, "The whole world opened to me when I learned to read." Books have removed the shackles of slaves, introduced individuals without formal education to ideas for invention, taken readers on wonderful adventures to lands far from their home, enlightened men, women and children to the amazing contributions of individuals from cultures throughout the world and provided immense pleasure to billions of people around the world.

A walk through the homes of America provides an idea of how some individuals spend their leisure time and an awareness of the things they value. A visitor is greeted with the blaring of a wide flat-screened television in the living room with individuals sitting around watching, not talking, only saying "shut up" if one dares to speak while a favorite program is viewed. Compact Disc players, DVDs, and various tapes dot every room. Books are in short supply or nonexistent. A library card is about as available as a Rolls Royce on a sharecropper's farm in Belzoni, Mississippi. Pencils, pens, writing paper and other educational tools seem to be about as extinct as an outhouse in New York City.

Posters of athletes, rap singers and popular models cover the walls while the "must have" clothing of designers is hooked on walls with some prominence. At the same time, there are several pairs of expensive Nike or Air Jordan gym shoes and knock off Gucci, Louis Vuitton and designer bags prominently placed among the entertainment media.

Sadly, many adults and children are impoverished in their lack of knowledge of African American History. They do not know the fact that Harriet Tubman was an abolitionist and not a rap singer from Compton, California or that Leontyne Price was an opera singer and not a character on *The Days of Our Lives*. I might add that while some of the children are not proficient in spelling in school, most of them can spell with 100% accuracy the names of fashion designers such as Versace, Tommy Hilfiger, Gucci, Louis Vuitton, Coogi, Triple Goose Down, Ralph Lauren, Nautica and Coach. Designer clothing and shoes have become a fashion accessory and status symbol for many who use them to present a false sense of self-worth and affluence.

Some children are not introduced to books and don't read books, an essential skill for success and upward mobility. Reading skills are essential in mastering all subject matter. Nonreaders are more likely to drop out of school, be incarcerated, and unemployed.

Our youth need to have the same priority of stampeding to the library to check out books, as some do at the launch of the $180 New Nike Air Jordan XI Concord shoes. While these shoes are quite expensive, the reality is the cost to produce these gym shoes is less than $7. Books would provide education on how to become producers rather than consumers. Unfortunately, many of today's youth will always be consumers and never producers, which will lead to self-sufficiency and a way out of poverty. Sadly, most of these youth's priority is to own a pair of these shoes. They have no knowledge that they were made in Asian sweat shops. They don't have a clue that the workers are paid from $43 to less than $100 per month. Workers are paid an average wage of .20 to .40 an hour and are required to work in conditions that are unsafe and hazardous to the lives of the workers.

The youth has no social consciousness that many of these workers have lost their lives in producing clothing and shoes for America. They need to be advocates that no person should be without their human rights. The conditions in many of these sweat shops are deplorable. African Americans should be particularly concerned about the plight of these workers as our history shows that many of our ancestors were treated in the same manner. They worked long hours for low wages and were denied their human rights. While it is a choice of a consumer to buy any products they desire, it is important to know that the clothing, shoes and other products they purchase and enjoy are made by individuals who basically are treated and paid like slaves. As consumers rather than producers, these individuals are also in a state of bondage.

Our children will continue to fail and have negative priorities about what is important in life. We handicap children for a lifetime and relegate them to poverty forever when they don't read. Children at the earliest age are introduced to standardized tests that select, identify, sort and label them into educational categories that predestine them to failure for a life time due to their lack of reading skills. If children are not able to read, they are disproportionately placed in special needs classes and given labels that define them for a lifetime.

As parents, we must invest in books and other educational materials. We need to introduce books to children at the earliest age. Children need to see adults reading and recognize the joy they receive from reading. The pleasure of reading is never appreciated if we, adults, do not value books. We can improve our children's success by reading to them and instilling the importance of reading and falling in love with books. The reading scores of our children by third grade determine if a child is going to be a success or failure in life. It appears that some states have begun to use the third grade reading scores to determine the number of prisons and detention facilities.

Dr. Benjamin Carson, noted surgeon, in *Gifted Hands*, wrote, "Through the use of books I had the whole world at my feet, could travel anywhere, meet anyone and do anything." We must invest in books for our children. They cost a mere pittance when compared to the electronic equipment, designer clothing, the latest gym shoes and inconspicuous consumptions of other material things. Our youth need to know that there is a tremendous wealth gap between black and white Americans. More of some African Americans' assets are tied up in cars, clothes, and jewelry, conspicuous consumption that says I am prosperous by what I drive, wear, and the bling that adorns my body

. A good book on your shelf is a friend that turns it back on you and remains a friend.

. Books give not wisdom where was none before.

. Book lovers never go to bed alone. — A good book keeps one company.

. Condense soup, not books. — Read the entire book to gain knowledge.

BUSINESS

Our elders taught children and youth to be about the business of learning how to become self-sufficient.

. Black is beautiful, but business is business. — Business is not based on relationships.

. Business neglected is business lost. — A neglected business will not prosper.

- Don't mix business with pleasure.
    There is a time for business and a time for pleasure.

- Fair exchange isn't highway robbery.

- I am just minding my own business.

- I laugh and joke, but I don't play. — Be serious in business.

- It takes six months to take care of your business and six months to leave other people's business alone.

- Live together like brothers and do business as strangers.

 # CAUTION

. A leopard doesn't change its spots.

. A man wrapped up in himself makes a very small package.

. All who snore are not sleep. — Don't mistake an action for the real thing.

. A man that pets a live catfish isn't crowded with brains.

. A mule can be tame at one end and wild at the other.

. A pig has enough arithmetic to take the shortest cut through a thicket.

. A pullet can't roost too high for an owl.

. A woman who will tell her age will tell anything.

. A snake may change his skin, but he's still a snake.

. Barking dogs seldom bite.

. Better safe than sorry.

. Black snake knows the way to the hen house

. Buzzards aren't circling in the air just for fun. — When buzzards circle, it is a sign of death.

. Choose the hills wisely on which you must do battle.

. Cockroach can never justify himself to a hungry chicken.

- Damned if you do, and damned if you don't. A person is between a rock and a hard place.

- Dogs don't bite at the front gate.

- Don't buy a pig in a poke — It is important to inspect your purchase.

- Don't cross the bridge before you get to it.

- Don't chain your dog with sausages.

- Don't change horses in the middle of the stream.

- Don't fling away the empty wallet

- Don't have too many irons in the fire.

- Don't jump out of the frying pan into the fire.

- You don't look back; something may be gaining on you.

- Don't put the cart before the horse

- Don't spill the beans.

- Don't waste all your buck shots on one bird.

- Elephant in the room

- Empty vessels make the most noise.

- Every man has his price.

- Friendly as fire ants

- Get out while you are ahead.

- Haste makes waste.

- Honey is sweet but bees sting.

- Hungry rooster doesn't cackle when he finds a worm.

- I don't cotton to that.

- I don't have a dog in that fight.

- If you can't beat them, join them.

- If you can't run with the big dogs, you'd better stay on the porch.

- If you play with fire, you will get burned.

- If your coattail catches a fire, don't wait till you can see the blaze before you put it out.

- It is best to be cautious and avoid extremes.

- Keep your hands on the plow.

- Keep your head about you.

- Leave well enough alone.

- Look before you leap.

- Monkey should know where he is going to put his tail before he orders trousers.

- Never burn your bridges behind you.

- Nothing is as easy as it looks.
- Nothing ventured, nothing gained.
- Oil and water don't mix.
- Speech is silver, silence is golden.
- Take the bull by its horns.
- The bush has ears. The wall has a mouth.
- The palm can always follow the vine.
- There is not much difference between a hornet and yellow jacket if they're in your clothes.
- Walk with a crooked stick until you can find a straight one.
- Watch out when you get all you want and fattened hogs aren't in luck.
- What costs nothing is worth nothing.
- When it takes a half a hoecake to catch a catfish, leave him alone.
- Where there is smoke - there is fire.
- Whoever heard of a mouse making a nest in a cat's ear?
- You cannot make a silk purse out of a sow's ear.
- You don't drown by falling in water. You drown by staying there.
- You don't have a snow ball's chance in hell.

CHAINS

Our people knew about chains and shackles. They taught their children to refuse to be enslaved mentally.

. You can take the chains off arms, but not off minds.

CHALLENGES

Our elders faced formidable challenges. They always found ways to overcome obstacles. They believed in the Biblical admonition of "If you faint in the days of adversity, your strength is small." We all face challenges in our daily lives. These challenges give us an opportunity to overcome obstacles and learn from them.

. The palm can always follow the vine.

. Damned if you do, and damned if you don't. — A person is between a rock and a hard place.

. Keep your hands on the plow. — We cannot produce without effort.

. A pig has enough arithmetic to take the shortest cut through a thicket.

. A pullet can't roost too high for an owl.

. By the yard, it is hard, by the inch, it's a cinch.

. Compared to my problems, yours don't amount to a pimple on a mosquito's ass. Problems are relative as to the degree of difficulty.

. Don't bite off more than you can chew. — Be aware of your strengths and weaknesses.

- Don't count your chickens before they hatch. — Never depend on production.

- Don't cry over spilt milk. — Don't regret what cannot be undone.

- Don't limit your challenges. Challenge your limits.

- Don't make a mountain out of a mole hill.

- Hard times make a monkey eat red pepper when he doesn't care for black.

- He is a jack of all trades and master of none.

- Hungry rooster doesn't cackle when he finds a worm.

- I am moving south where the weather suits my clothes.

- If at first you don't succeed, try and try again.

- If it'd been a snake, it would have bit you.

- If it isn't broke, don't fix it.

- If you can't beat them, join them.

- If you don't grab for yourself, then nothing is going to help you. You are the master of your fate.

- It's easy as Sunday morning.

- It takes a heap of licks to strike a nail in the dark.

- Keep a stiff upper lip.

- Learn from your mistakes.

- More than enough is too much.

- Nothing is as easy as it looks

- Nothing ruins a duck but its bill.

- Pullets can't roost too high for the owl.

- Quit while you are ahead.

- Take the bull by its horns.

- There's more than one way to skin a cat.

- Two heads are better than one.

- Walk with a crooked stick until you can find a straight one.

- When the tree has fallen, even a goat may climb it.

- Where there is a will, there is a way.

- We will cross that bridge when we come to it.

- Who never climbed, never failed.

- You can't get blood from a turnip.

- You cannot unscramble eggs.

- You have got to know where you're going before you can get there.

- You win some. You lose some.

CHANGE

. Change the joke and slip the yoke.

. Change your mind and you change your life. Change comes from introspection and direction.

. In order to change, we must be sick and tired of being sick and tired.

. Never swap horses crossing a stream.

CHARACTER

. A person shows what he is by what he does with what he has.

. Character is a diamond that scratches every stone. — Character is a precious attribute.

. Character is a victory, not a gift.

CHILDREN

Our ancestors viewed all children as precious resources. Every elder played a significant role in the development of all children. They viewed all children as being a part of building a better world. Our elders corrected children as in the teachings of Proverbs 13:24: "He that spares his rod hates his son; but he that loves him chastens him betimes." Our elders used proverbs to teach African Americans how to overcome hundreds of years of slavery and Jim Crow. Unfortunately, today's youths have little or no knowledge of African American proverbs. They are not taught the contributions of African Americans. Sadly, many of these youths are reared in homes by single mothers who do not have the special "village" of elders who can teach special lessons about life and challenges.

Our parents and teachers stressed moral education and a respect for laws and authority. Our elders admonished their sons and daughters, "Take care of the high chair so you don't have to worry about the electric chair." The electric chair was symbolic of the most extreme punishment for some crimes. Our parents used the Ten Commandments as their guide to teach children moral education. Parents believed that their children were their responsibility and were a tangible product of the lessons they taught and reinforced. The most difficult experience for a parent at the time was to have a son or daughter arrested for any crime.

Our parents and elders recognized the enormous task in raising children. They were cognizant that their actions and behaviors taught their children how to function in the world. They understood that children are products of their experiences, environments, and observations. Children were like sponges and they absorb everything around them. Consequently, our parents worked hard to be positive role models and examples of appropriate behavior.

Some of the teachings of parents during my childhood are as relevant today as they were in the past. The parenting skills are listed below:

· Make a conscious decision to have children and be prepared emotionally, financially to support them.

· Invest time and effort in teaching children morals, values, and appropriate behavior.

· Set limits with children.

· Provide unconditional love for children.

· Involve children in church and religious activities.

· Always set high expectations and never accept mediocrity.

· Encourage communication and language development.

- Introduce children to books at the earliest ages and spend time reading with them. Instill the importance of learning to read well as it is the key to success.

- Set effective moral standards of behavior by being positive role models.

- Acquire health insurance to protect the physical growth and development of children

- Set positive eating habits by providing nutritious meals.

- Invest in early childhood education by involving children to educational opportunities in the community.

- Teach the importance of self-respect and respect for others.

- Limit access to television and other distractions and choose positive, educational activities.

- Teach the importance of manners and being polite.

- Teach children the importance of taking care of their bodies and regarding their bodies as their special temple.

- Teach children the importance of compassion and kindness to others.

- Teach responsibility by assigning appropriate age tasks.

- Limit the purchase of material things.

- Provide an environment that is safe, free from physical, sexual and emotional abuse.

- Be an advocate for your children.

- Provide children with basic needs and not the most expensive material things.

- Acknowledge your child's achievements and behavior.

- Teach values such as honesty, patience, forgiveness, respect and generosity.

- Use respectful language; respect a child's feelings, opinions and individuality.

- Provide consistent, structured and fair discipline.

The statistics for the likelihood of African American males going to state or federal prison are alarming. Based on the Bureau of Justice and current rates of first incarceration, an estimated 32% of black males will enter State or Federal prison during their lifetime, compared to 17% of Hispanic males and 5.9% of white males.

. Act like you got some raising.

. A hard head makes a soft behind.

. Child, don't you raise your voice at me. Don't you ever forget I brought you into the world and I will take you out.

. Children are what they are made.

. Children should be seen and not heard.

. Chip off the old block.

. Don't bite at everything you see. — Be careful what you choose to latch onto.

. Every crow thinks his crow is the blackest. — Every parent is proud of his child.

- He's a chip off the old block.

- He is cut from the same cloth.

- He is knee high to a grasshopper.

- He that corrects not youth controls not age.

- I didn't raise any fish.

- It is a wise child that knows its own father.

- It is your little red wagon and you're going to have to pull it.

- I raised her since she was knee high to a duck.

- I tell my children that children and groceries both have expiration dates. When they become a certain age, they are leaving this house.

- It is your little red wagon. You are going to have to push or pull it.

- Jaybird doesn't rob its own nest. — Don't take from your family and give to another family.

- Just because everybody is doing it, doesn't mean it is right.

- Keep your drawers up and your knees shut.

- Like father, like son.

- Mama doesn't play.

- Mothers raise their daughters and let their sons grow up.

- My mama didn't raise any fools.

The Tree of Love Gives Shade to All

- Rise and shine!

- Speak when spoken to; answer when called.

- Sticks and stones may break my bones, but names will never hurt me.

- Stop sticking your nose in grown folks' business.

- Straighten up and fly right.

- Take care of the high chair so you don't have to worry about the electric chair.

- That child has a face that only a mother could love

- The laughter of children is an international language.

- The Lord doesn't like little pitchers with big ears.

- The son disgraces himself when he blames his father.

- This child has to learn that every day is not Christmas.

- To be in your children's memories tomorrow, you have to be in their lives today.

- You are beginning to smell yourself.

- You are getting too big for your britches.

- You aren't too old for your wants to hurt you.

- You don't believe fat meat is greasy.

- You have got to crawl before you walk.

. Your mother didn't raise you in a dog house.

. You talk back to me girl. I will knock you back into next week.

. You weren't born with a silver spoon in your mouth.

CLOTHES

We were always taught that our clothes should always be neat for cleanliness was next to Godliness. What we did not have in clothing, we made up in cleanliness. I am convinced that many of today's youth do not have role models at home, individuals who should be teaching them about their appearance and appropriate apparel. Many boys and girls find their role models in hip hop musicians and rappers.. Some males wear pants sagging and showing their underwear.

Larry Plant, singing about sagging pants: "Pants on the ground, looking like a fool with your pants on the ground." The style of sagging was popularized by hip-hop artists in the 1990's and is adapted from the prison system where belts are prohibited to prevent suicide among inmates or injury to others. Our youth enslave themselves when they walk around with their pants below their behinds. Consequently, some African American youth have regressed in the great strides that were made in the past.

Our elders, men and women who were adults and positive role models, taught us that our clothes should always be neat. What we did not have in clothing, our appearance reflected self-respect. "First impressions count" was taught as a mantra" by our parents and elders. During segregation, we occasionally shopped at local department stores but were not able to try on clothing. We had to guess our sizes as there was no return policy for African American customers. I recall that when my parents bought me shoes, they traced my feet around a piece of paper and presented it to the salesperson. Quite often the shoes did not fit properly and were taken to a shoe shop to be stretched.

The Tree of Love Gives Shade to All

The clothing industry is a multi-billion dollar business throughout the world. Some people regard clothing as the most important thing about their being. To them, clothes make the person. No amount of clothing can disguise a person's feeling of insecurity, unhappiness, and discontent. Those who over compensate by wearing expensive designer clothes cannot hide their true feelings.

Marian Wright Edelman, in *Save Our Children: They are Our Most Precious Resource* wrote, "Nobody ever asked what kind of car Ralph Bunche drove or what kind of designer suit Martin Luther King, Jr. bought." Unfortunately, many of today's youth put more emphasis on clothing than they do in reading, writing, and mathematics. Quite often these are the very children whose parents are unable to afford expensive clothing and struggle to meet their most basic needs.

We must teach our children at the earliest age that material things do not make the person. They need to understand that the most important thing about clothing is it should be clean and pressed. Growing up in Mississippi, I wore outfits fashioned from bleached flour and fertilizer sacks. I believed that this was the most popular clothing as every other child wore the same type of clothing. While we may have desired new clothing, the convenience of indoor plumbing, and a Sears-built home, there was little time to spend time wishing as the farm work, schoolwork, and homework assignments were our priorities. The only store bought shirt I wore was the one I traveled in on the train to college.

. Clothes don't make the man.

. Dressed up like a dog's dinner. — One who is extremely dressed.

. He/she is dressed to kill. — Well dressed.

. He/she is sharp as a tack. — Well dressed.

COMMUNICATION

We were taught to speak clearly and watch what came out of our mouth for the tongue was the source of most discord. Our tongue can be one of the most serious problems when we spew out things that are unkind and unhelpful to others.

Actions speak louder than words.

. A diplomat is one who thinks twice before saying nothing.

. A dog that will bring a bone will carry one. — Be careful of those who bear bad news for they will carry news.

. A good listener is a silent flatter.

. All bark and no bite. — Someone threatens but is not willing to fight.

. A man has two ears and one mouth that he may hear much and speak little.

. An empty wagon makes a lot of noise.

. A penny for your thoughts

. A pullet always tells where she lays her first egg.

. Ask me no questions and I'll tell you no lies.

. A slip of the tongue isn't any strain on the backbone.

. A still tongue makes a wise head.

. A tattling woman can't make the bread rise.

- Believe some of what you see, and none of what you hear. Be careful what you give credibility.

- Better be silent than talk ill.

- Beware of fast talkers. — Be leery of fast talkers.

- Bite your tongue.

- Call a spade a spade.

- Come again.- What did you say?

- Does a one-legged duck swim in circles?

- Dog doesn't get mad when you say he's a dog.

- Don't let your mouth overload your tail.

- Don't put the cart before the horse. — Don't reverse the order of things or events.

- Every ass likes to hear their bray. — Someone likes to talk.

- Every goodbye is not gone. Every shut eye is not asleep.

- Flog a dead horse.

- Hearsay is half lies. — You can't believe hearsay.

- Her tongue knows no Sundays. — A person never stops talking.

- He speaks out of both sides of his mouth. — He/she cannot be trusted.

- He speaks with forked tongue.

. Honey hush!

. Hush your fuss!

. I am selling it like I bought it. — Repeating what is said to someone without checking facts.

. I cooked his goose. — I made a person shut up.

. I do declare.

. If you can't say anything nice about a person, don't say anything at all.

. If you talk the talk, you've got to walk the walk.

. Is the cat got your tongue? — Can you talk?

. It is easier said than done.

. It is like talking to a brick wall.

, It's many a slip between the cup and the lip.

. It will be hell to tell the captain. — It will be difficult to tell the boss.

. I wasn't born yesterday.

. I won't touch that with a ten foot pole. — I will not deal with that situation.

. Just between you, me and the gatepost.

. Least said soonest mended.

. Left hand does not know what the right hand is doing.

The Tree of Love Gives Shade to All

. Lend me your ear.

. Let me pull your coattail. — Give a word to the wise.

. Liquor talks mighty loud when it gets loose from the jug.

. No news is good news.

. Now, doesn't that take the cake?

. Out of sight and out of mind.

. Pay it no mind.

. Pick up your ears. — Listen carefully.

. Preaching to the choir

. Put that in your pipe and smoke it.

. Put your foot in your mouth. — Saying something foolish, tactless and without thought.

. Run that by me one more time. — Would you repeat that?

. See and be blind; hear and be deaf. — Don't repeat what you see or hear.

. Shoot the breeze. — Make relaxed, casual conversation.

. Shut mouth doesn't catch flies.

. Some things are better left unsaid. — Silence is often the best response.

. Speaking "off the cuff"

- Speak softly and carry a big stick.

- Speak of the Devil and he is bound to appear.

- Speak when you are spoken to.

- Stop beating around the bush. — Refuse to speak directly about an issue.

- Talk is cheap.

- Talking to you is like singing a love song to a hog.

- Talk out of the back of your head.

- That dog won't hunt.

- That's all she wrote.

- That takes the cake.

- The most effective answer to an insult is silence.

- The walls have ears.

- Think before you speak.

- Turn a blind eye. — Refuse to acknowledge something that is real.

- We can all sing together but we can't talk together.

- What eyes don't see, the mouth can't talk about.

- When all is said and done, more is said than done.

- When coon takes water, he is fixing to fight.

The Tree of Love Gives Shade to All

. When no one is willing to listen to you, think.

. Who speaks sows; who listens reaps.

. You can read my letters, but you sure can't read my mind.

. You can see a lot by listening.

. You can't get a word in edge wise.

. You can't make heads or tails of it.

. Your guess is good as mine.

. You hit the nail on the head.

. You run your mouth and I will run my business.

COMPASSION

The meaning of compassion is the ability to recognize the suffering of others and take actions to help them. Our ancestors believed in compassion and always reached out to others to overcome adversities in their lives. Survival often depended on the entire community helping others when their crops suffered drought, when their homes were destroyed by natural disasters and when neighbors did not have enough food to feed their families.

Our Christian faith teaches us that Jesus was involved in ministries of compassion. His ministry was filled with many acts of compassion. Christ healed people who were physically sick, delivered people who had spiritual oppression, fed people and performed miracles to feed people. In Psalm 103, verse 8, we are taught "The Lord is compassionate and gracious, slow to anger and abounding in love." In Second Corinthians 1:3-5: we are taught, "Praise be to God and Father of our Lord Jesus Christ, the Father of compassion and the God of all comforts, who comforts us in all our troubles so that we can comfort those in any trouble with the comfort we receive from God."

For the past several years, our country has witnessed numerous disasters that have displaced people and cause them to lose all of their possessions. There was Hurricane Katrina in New Orleans, which devastated sections of the city. The Ninth Ward especially suffered from the storm. People were displaced from their homes that were destroyed by the mighty floods. Individuals showed compassion by opening their homes to the homeless, provided assistance to clean up areas, donated money to help individuals buy food and other necessities. These acts of compassion demonstrated the benevolence of people who sought to ease their suffering. Recent tornadoes have blanketed the South causing death, mayhem and loss of homes. Again, strangers from throughout the country have rallied to help those in need by donating goods and services.

We should not wait for a disaster as large as Hurricane Katrina or tornadoes to reach out to others and show our compassion. We can express our compassion on a daily basis by identifying those who are suffering emotional, physical or financial hardships. We can visit the sick neighbor who is immobile and clean the house. We can take the time to mow the lawn of an elderly neighbor. We can prepare a meal for a homebound neighbor or offer to provide respite time for a family member who needs a break from caring for a family member.

. A kind and compassionate act is often its own reward.

. He who takes no care of little things will not have the care of great ones.

. Make no judgment where you have not compassion.

. Nobody cares how much you know unless they know how much you care.

. People will forget what you said. People will forget what you did. But people will never forget how you make them feel.

. The smallest good deed is better than the grandest intention.

COMPLEXION

African Americans come in a rainbow of skin tones. The first distinction made on skin color is historically based in slavery. U.S. Census enumerators listed individuals as black, mulatto or white on census data from 1870 through 1930. Much of their designation was based on the complexion of blacks. There was a difference made between African Americans based on skin color during slavery. Light skinned slaves were generally permitted to work in slave owners' home, while darker-skinned slaves were restricted to working from sunup to sundown in the fields of cotton, tobacco and other agricultural crops. House slaves lived very close to whites in the "big" house, often living in closets, attics, or corners of the big house. They served as nannies, coachmen, and house servants. These slaves were considered to be kinder, gentler and more acceptable than darker-skinned blacks by slave holders. It appears that slaveholders believed that darker-skinned slaves were better physically to work in the fields. Their lives were somewhat different when it came to privileges accorded to house slaves and field slaves. Field slaves were issued less food, were regarded as not as intelligent as the house slaves. House slaves became aware of the distinctions made between them and darker-skinned slaves and believed that their white blood made them superior.

Discrimination among African Americans continued to exist after slavery based on skin color. According to Yvonne Bivins of Forrest County, Mississippi, in her research of the multiracial societies in Forrest County and Jones County, Mississippi, mulattoes were told to "Keep to their own kind," which meant socializing with individuals who were similar in skin color. Several communities were established for "White Negroes" after the Civil War throughout the Piney Woods of South Mississippi. The communities of Six Town, Soso, Sheeplow and Kelly Settlement were formed for "White Negroes."

Kelly Settlement gets its name from John Kelly who was an early petitioner in the Mississippi Territory. He purchased 540 acres on the Leaf River near the present-day town of Hattiesburg. His son, Green Kelly, was reported to have several intimate liaisons with a slave named Sarah. Sarah bore children for Kelly. These off-springs of Kelly were categorized as mulattos and quadroons. According to Bivins, when Green Kelly died, he bequeathed parcels of land for his white and mulatto off-springs. The mulatto children were given land on the Monroe Road section of Hattiesburg, Mississippi and the white children were given land on the Eatonville Road, a short distance from the Monroe Road area.

My maternal ancestors who were mulattoes were given special privileges that were denied to darker-skinned blacks. My mother who was light-skinned, a mulatto, fell in love with my father, a dark-skinned man. His ancestors were always considered pure blacks and field slaves. My grandfather was vehemently opposed to this proposed union as he believed her darker-skinned boyfriend was not desirable, and would destroy his family's bourgeois social status and bloodline. After my father received a marriage license, my grandfather threatened him and demanded that he return the license. He did not. My grandfather demanded every preacher to refuse to conduct a marriage ceremony. He felt that my mother was considering marrying a man who was beneath her social status. My grandfather always required his sons and daughters to marry others who had the same light-skinned complexion. My mother, dressed in a polka dot dress and tennis shoes, eloped with my father and was married by the only preacher in the county who refused to be threatened by my grandfather. After their marriage, my mother was shunned by her parents for more than five years.

It was quite common at the time for mulattos to seek other mulattos to marry to keep their skin color. Parents often traveled to "White Negro" communities to find desirable mates for their sons and daughters. In some cases, the mates chosen were relatives. Some oral historians in Mississippi also share that mulattos in some areas did not want their children to attend school with dark-skinned African Americans. At some point, special schools were established for mulatto children only. One such school was founded in Jones County at Gitano, Mississippi. While it was proposed as a private Seventh Day Adventist School, it only welcomed and accepted light-skinned relatives.

The special privileges accorded house slaves were prevalent after slavery in educational opportunities and other special privileges. Light-skinned blacks were generally enrolled in private colleges such as Howard University, Morgan State University, Fisk University, Atlanta University, Wilberforce University and Hampton Institute. These students were enrolled in a liberal arts curriculum, which prepared them for careers as doctors, lawyers and other professional careers. Darker-skinned blacks were enrolled in state-supported vocational and agricultural institutions at Tuskegee Institute and historically black land-grant colleges in the South where they were trained to work in menial jobs.

The distinction of color among some African Americans and opportunities afforded them continued to exist as late as the 1950s. During the last semester of my junior year of high school in 1959, I applied to Fisk University in Nashville, Tennessee. Fisk University was named in honor of General Clinton B. Fisk of the Tennessee Freedmen's Bureau. Founded on January 9, 1866 and incorporated as Fisk University on August 22, 1867 with the mission "To provide the highest standards, not of Negro education, but of American education at its best." As an applicant to Fisk, I was asked to attach a current photo to the lengthy application form. The application listed several categories that were used to assess my pedigree and suitability for admission such as my parents' educational level, occupation, family income, number of automobiles and the quality of furnishings in my home. Although I was to become the salutatorian of my graduating class with excellent grades and good SAT scores, I was not accepted. While I am sure I passed the "brown bag" and "comb" test, most likely my application was rejected due to my parents' socio-economic level and their lack of a college degree. Several predominantly white universities admitted me and I was not required to attach a photo or designate my race or list the material trappings in my home. While I have no proof of the reason I was denied admission, I believe I was denied admission because my complexion was not acceptable and comparable to the Fisk student family. At the time, there was a "brown bag" test used to discriminate against other blacks. Also, there was a "comb test" used to determine the texture of one's hair. Evidently, from my photo, admissions people felt that I would not be able to pass the comb test,

The "brown bag" test continued to be a measure of one's potential for social position and employment. I recall as a child that Mississippi department stores and general stores advertised for "colored" help. In the classified ad for elevator operators and other menial jobs where African Americans were in view of whites, there was a requirement that applicants must be fair-skinned African Americans. When men and women were hired for these "brown bag" qualified jobs, they appeared to be proud and felt more self-esteem than dark-skinned blacks. Dark-skin blacks were relegated to jobs where they were not visible to the public.

It appears that the "brown bag" test is alive today when we look at the news anchors on television stations. Cosmetic makers tend to hire more light-skinned blacks as models. The movie industry also tends to hire and support lighter skin actors.

. All God's children got good hair.

. Beauty is only skin deep.

. Black is beautiful.

. Heads that are filled with wisdom have little space left for conceit.

. Laundry is the only thing that should be separated by color.

. Prejudice is being down on something you're not upon.

CORRUPTION

. A bribe will enter without knocking.

. He that has to do with what is foul, never comes away clean.

. One scabbed sheep will mar a whole flock.

. Who greases his way, travels easily.

COURAGE

Our history is filled with courageous individuals who sought to change bad situations for African Americans. Crispus Attucks, an American slave, merchant seaman and dock worker displayed considerable courage when he fought for America's independence. He was the first person shot to death by redcoats during the Boston Massacre in Boston, Massachusetts. Harriet Tubman's life is a monument to courage and determination. She freed herself from slavery and played a significant role in liberating other slaves.

Our elders, who were emancipated from slavery, demonstrated courage as they began a life after freedom. I recall my grandfather sharing the story that slaves who were freed from the plantations in Covington County, Mississippi farmers faced incredible odds in starting their life after slaves were emancipated. Former slaveholders believed freed slaves would not be able to survive on their own and would go running back to their former slaveholders for assistance. Our ancestors did not believe their perceptions and worked hard to remain free people. Our elders did not permit adversities to prevent them from starting a new life. They settled on land in the Hopewell Community, the highest point in Covington County, Mississippi. Whites referred to the area surrounding the ridge as "N*gger Ridge." Former slave masters believed this land was infertile and would not grow crops to help the freed slaves survive. The land turned out to be some of the richest land in the county. Our ancestors planted and harvested bountiful crops of vegetables, cotton and fruit.

There were difficult challenges our ancestors faced as they started their new life. Having left plantations and farms with only the tattered clothes on their backs, they had to build houses, farm the land, make clothing, and find ways to survive. They did not permit fear to get in the way of success and worked together as a community to build houses, cultivate the land, and start a small school under the shade of oak trees to teach children and adults to read and write. They shared their skills in agriculture, tool making, and construction with their neighbors to help them become self-sufficient. Their courage, determination, and persistence enabled them to overcome adversities and moved forward as freed persons.

Former slaveholders were not pleased with the emancipation of African Americans. A Yazoo planter shares the thoughts of whites about emancipation: "I think God intended the 'N*gger' to be slaves. Now since man has deranged God's plan, I think the best we can do is keep them as near to a state of bondage as possible. My theory is feed them, clothe them well, and if they don't work,whip them well." This attitude would lead to another form of peonage when sharecropping became prevalent in the country.

When the civil war ended, the United States Congress passed four statutes known as *Reconstruction Acts*. The former Confederate States were required to fulfill these acts to be readmitted to the Union. Tennessee was excluded from this requirement as it had ratified the Thirteenth Amendment to the United States Constitution and had been readmitted to the Union. To ensure that southern states provided equal rights to African American, five military districts were established from 1865 to 1877 to suppress violence against African American and white voters.

Reconstruction provided freedmen with equal rights under the Constitution. African Americans were able to vote and take political office. They were also to be treated fairly in jobs and courts. Some public schools were established. The *Freedmen's Bureau* bill became law. This Bureau was created to provide clothing, food, fuel and offer advice in negotiating labor contracts. Constitutional amendments known as the *Reconstruction Amendments* were adopted. The Thirteenth Amendment abolished slavery was ratified in 1865. Citizenship to African Americans was guaranteed in the Fourteenth Amendment, which was ratified in 1864. The Fifteenth Amendment, passed in February, 1870, guaranteed African Americans the right to vote.

The Reconstruction period in the South brought some temporary changes to the lives of African Americans. By 1877, when President Rutherford B. Hayes assumed office, he removed troops from the capitals of the Reconstruction states, which gave former confederate states full control. When conservative democrats were back in power and gained control, laws and codes were established to deny African American rights they were given during Reconstruction. Southern states instituted literacy tests that mandated that a person had to read in order to vote. African Americans were required to pay a poll tax of $2 to vote, which posed a hardship on some African Americans. A spate of Jim Crow Laws was created to separate facilities through the south for African Americans and whites.

These laws regarding separate facilities were supported by the U. S. Supreme Court in the case of Plessy v. Ferguson in 1896. In 1890, the State of Louisiana passed the "Separate Car Act" law, which mandated separate accommodations for African American and whites on railroads. On June 7, 1892, Homer Adolph Plessy, a freeman purchased a first-class ticket at the Press Street Depot in New Orleans and boarded the "whites only" car of the East Louisiana Railroad. Plessy refused to move to the "colored only" car and was arrested, convicted and sentenced to pay a $25. Plessy argued that his rights were abridged under the Thirteenth and Fourteenth Amendments in the case of *Homer Adolph Plessy v. the State of Louisiana.* The local judge in the case ruled that Louisiana had the right to regulate railroad companies that operated within state boundaries. The lower court's decision was appealed to the Supreme Court of Louisiana, which upheld the decision.

The decision of the Louisiana Supreme Court was appealed to the U. S. Supreme Court. The Court in its landmark decision upheld the constitutionality of state laws requiring racial segregation in public facilities under the doctrine of "separate but equal." This ruling would stand until the Supreme Court's decision in Brown v. Board of Education in 1954.

Freed slaves faced many restrictions with the adoption of Black Codes by Southern states. Mississippi adopted Black Codes, which was a way to deny freedom and opportunities of ex-slaves and maintain the old order. These codes included: all freedmen who lived and cohabited together as husband and wife were considered legally married; every black person could be arrested and carried back to his or her legal employer who quit the service of his or her employer before the expiration of his or her term of service; freed African Americans could not inter-marry; could not own or carry a firearm or Bowie knife; and any black could be arrested for vagrancy.

. A man of courage never wants weapons. — Courageous individuals do not need weapons or armor.

. Courage is the power to let go of that which is familiar. Dare to dream and rise above circumstances.

. Courage is the right disposition toward fear. Courage thwarts fear

CRITICISM

. If you have to criticize, do it lovingly.

DEATH

Our elders regarded death as something inevitable, which led to a better place. Our ancestors and elders did not view death as an end, but a beginning as Sojourner Truth said in 1883, 'I'm going home like a shooting star.'

What would you say to a loved one on his death bed? What are the things you wished you had said or done to the loved one who died suddenly? Death tends to bring out the good stuff of condolences, an outpouring of sympathy and human kindness. We prepare meals for family members and neighbors, and collections are taken to purchase flowers. We cease with the business of life, taking off from work to pay our last respects. Tears are shed, hearts ache, and quite often guilt reign supreme, feelings of remorse over the things that could have been done to express their love and compassion while the person lived.

In death, there is a steady flow of presentations, tributes, and honors, attesting to the character and value of the departed soul. They are unable to experience the healing power of flowers, the quiet language of love they speak, and relate to the magnificence of their fragrance.

If we would put on our funeral clothes of love daily, we would love more and express the Commandments of God. We should not wait for the death of a loved one to show our love and appreciation, two powerful agents in living and sharing a fuller and healthier life. It is important to express kindness, understanding, patience, and goodness with others each day as if it were the last. We need to give friends, family members, and others flowers while they can smell them and enjoy the special joy they bring. Prepare special meals that can be enjoyed and shared in love and thanksgiving. Call up loved ones and just say, "I thought of you today and want you to know how special you are. I love you."

. All death is sudden to the unprepared.

. All the buzzards will come to the mule's funeral.

. A man lives his funeral every day. — A person is known by the life he lives before death.

. Ax the trunk, the tree dies.

. Days are numbered

- Dead is dead.

- Death doesn't see any difference between the big house and the cabins.

- Death is sleep's older brother.

- Everybody wants to go to heaven, but nobody wants to die.

- He/she is dead as a door knob.

- He would be a good one to send for death.

- If you want to see how much folks are going to miss you, stick your finger in the pond and Then pull it out and look at the hole.

- One has only to die to be praised.

- People are dropping like flies.

- She gave up the ghost.

- Six feet of earth make all men equal

- The bitterest tears shed over graves are for words left unsaid and deeds left undone.
    Those who grieve the most are generally those who failed to do anything for the person while he lived.

- The graveyard is the cheapest boarding house.

- The quicker the death; the quicker heaven

- To live in hearts we leave behind is not to die

- We all get to go when the wagon comes.

- You might as well die with the chills as with the fever.

- You never know the length of a snake until its death.

DEBT

Our elders emphasized the importance of never being in debt to anyone. I recall my grand-father cautioned us about being in debt. He cited scripture about debt: "The rich rule over the poor - and the borrower is servant to the lender." (Proverbs 22:7) Our ancestors believed that debt can lead to bondage and cautioned family members to not be indebted to anyone.

Many of our elders were former sharecroppers. The institution of sharecropping was another means to keep African Americans indebted to white land owners. The land owners provided seed, implements, provisions, and basic shelter for blacks. Blacks planted and harvested the crops, which was mainly cotton. The white land owners sold each year's cotton harvest and computed each African American family's share of the proceeds. They deducted food, clothing and other necessities that were provided to sharecroppers. While this process was supposed to be fair, many blacks ended up in debt and these debts were carried over to the following year and caused sharecroppers to be relegated to poverty.

Each year, sharecroppers found they were deeper in debt. During the off season, sharecroppers were forced to buy clothing, food and other supplies on credit at plantation commissaries. The prices at the commissaries were exorbitant for shoddy goods. Debts continued to pile up as sharecroppers were stuck in an endless cycle of debt.

. Buying on credit is robbing next year's crop. — Avoid borrowing on anticipated results.

. Buying on the installment plan makes the months shorter and the year longer.

. He/she is heads over heels in debt.

. He who gets in for a penny will soon be in for a pound.

. If one wants to get out and stay out of debt, he should act his wage. Live within your means.

- It is better to go to bed hungry than to wake up in debt. Debts last longer than hunger.

- It's like robbing Peter to pay Paul. — A person uses another person's money to pay someone else.

- Never owe a dime and you will never owe a dollar. People who borrow find themselves in more debt.

- Out of debt and out of danger. — A person who is out of debt is out of danger.

- Punctual pay gets willing loan. — Pay your bills on time and you will get credit

- The man in debt is a swimmer with his boots on. People in debt sink financially.

- Who pays beforehand is served behindhand — Pay upfront than later.

DECEIT

. A liar is sooner caught than a cripple.

. Butter wouldn't melt in your mouth.
   Someone who looks innocent. They are capable of doing unpleasant things.

. He/she is a snake in the grass.

. He that hears much hears many lies. — A busybody is the recipient of many lies.

. One may smile and smile, and be a villain still. — Smiles can be deceiving.

. Something is nasty in the woodshed. — Someone has a dark secret.

. Something isn't clean in the milk.

. Speak with a forked tongue.

. Steal someone's thunder.

. Sweep something under the rug. — A person hides or ignores something.

DECISIONS

I recall my parents using the caution of Aesop, "Look before you leap." They admonished us to think before making a decision. We all have had the experience of making a decision without fully thinking about it or relying on the special life of the Infinite Presence in us to guide us in our decision making. Some individuals are quick to divorce themselves from individuals whom they view and treat as imperfect. We must know that none of us is perfect. We often refuse to forgive others for their human frailties and choose to judge others and burn bridges and refuse to improve our interpersonal relations with others. When we decide to terminate relationships based on mistakes or refuse to forgive others, we do ourselves a great disservice.

The Tree of Love Gives Shade to All

There are times that we make decisions on relationships without thinking about the value and potential of the relationship. Negative thoughts and opinions quite often encourage us to destroy marriages, relationships, change jobs and alienate family members. When we do this, we are just as guilty as the individual that we judged.

. Deer in the headlights

. Freedom is the opportunity to make decisions

. Get out while the getting is good.

. Good plans shape good decisions. — The best decisions are directly related to effective planning.

. If you can't run with the big dogs, you'd better stay on the porch.

. It is not hard to make decisions when you know what your values are. Values shape good decisions.

. Spirit is willing but the flesh is weak.

. Take it or leave it.

. The ball is in your court.

. The cake is not worth the candle.

. Wash your hands of something.

. You can't un-ring a bell.

DESPAIR

As Alexander Dumas wrote, "Only a man who has felt ultimate despair is capable of feeling ultimate bliss." Our elders believed despair was a part of life to reach blessedness.

. Been down so long, down don't worry me. — Adversity is not a stranger to me.

. He is a glutton for punishment. — One who does a lot of things that most people find unpleasant.

DESTRUCTION

. Despair is always destructive. — Desperation leads to destruction.

. He/she is going to hell in a hand basket. — A person is on a course for destruction.

DEVIL

Many teachings centered on the evil forces of the devil and how diligence always outdoes the devil.

. An idle mind is the devil's workshop.

. Don't swap the devil for a witch.

. Devil tempts, but he is no force.

. Even the devil was an angel in the beginning.

The Tree of Love Gives Shade to All

- Go not to hell for company. — Don't follow those who are headed to hell.

- If Satan says I don't have grace, I'll take him back to the starting place.

- If you don't want to trade with the devil, keep out of his shop. Stay out of evil situations.

- Old Satan couldn't get along without plenty of help. Many people are food for the devil.

- Old Satan loves a big crowd.

- Religious contention is the devil's harvest.

- Satan isn't scared of long sermons.

- Satan loads his cannons with big watermelons.

- Tell the truth and shame the devil.

- What goes under the devil's back has to come under his belly.

DISCORD

"Don't have anything to do with foolish and stupid arguments, because you know they produce quarrels." (2 Timothy 2:23)

. A chip on his shoulder.

. Acting like a bat out of hell

. Acting like a chicken with its head cut off. — Act in a frenzied manner.

. A knife cuts both ways.

. A liar will steal. A thief will kill.

. Better a tooth out than always aching.

. Beware of Greeks bearing grits.

. Black snake knows the way to the hen house.

. Bury the hatchet. — Let bygones be bygones.

. Contempt is the sharpest reproof.

. Crow and corn can't grow in the same field.

. Devil is in the detail.

. Don't beat a dead horse to death. — To force an issue that is already settled.

. Don't hate the player, hate the game.

. Don't lay it on the cow when the milk gets sour.

The Tree of Love Gives Shade to All

. Don't let your mouth overload your hips. — Be careful of talking too much.

. Don't publish people's defects

. Dress someone down.

. Drive a person up a wall. — Irritate or annoy someone.

. Even a worm will turn. — Even the simplest of animals will be defensive.

. Evil knows where evil sleeps.

. Eyes are bigger than your stomach. — When a person wants more than is good for them.

. Faulty individuals are most prone to find fault.

. Give a man enough rope, he will hang himself.

. Have a bee in your bonnet. — Being upset.

. Have an axe to grind. — One has a dispute with someone.

. He drinks so much he staggers in his sleep.

. He/ she is selling wolf tickets.

. Hold your feet to the fire. — Hold someone accountable and make good on a promise.

. I don't have a dog in that fight. — I don't have a reason to be a part of that battle.

. If you live with dogs, you learn to howl. — We emulate our conditions.

- I smell a rat. — Detecting someone is betraying another person.

- It pesters a man dreadful when he gets mad and doesn't know who to cuss.

- It takes two to tangle.

- I wouldn't give you air if you were in a jug.

- Like a bat out of hell.

- Let sleeping dogs lie. — Forget the past.

- Live by the sword, you die by the sword.

- Never bring a knife to a gunfight.

- Never declare war unless you mean do battle. — Don't start something that you fail to finish.

- Nervous as a long tailed cat in a room full of rocking chairs

- Never take a shirt from a naked man.

- Over my dead body — Refuse to allow something to happen.

- People who live in glass houses should not throw stones.

- Pick your battles.

- Pick your poison.

- Rub someone the wrong way.

- Setting hens don't hanker after fresh eggs.

The Tree of Love Gives Shade to All

. She flew the coop. — All hell broke loose.

. She's got her habits on — A person has a negative attitude.

. She is in the right church, but the wrong pew.

. The mob has many heads but no brains.

. The rooster does all the crowing but it's the hen that lays the egg.

. Throw dirt enough and some of it will stick.

. To steal someone's thunder. — Taking credit for something someone else does.

. Two bulls can't reign in one fence.

. Two cocks can't crow in one yard.

. Two is company and three is a crowd.

. Two wrongs don't make a right.

. What goes around comes around. — We reap what we sow.

. When I told her that, she like to have had a duck fit. — She became angry.

. You're barking up the wrong tree.

. You can hide the fire, but what are you going to do with the smoke?

. You can't spit in my face and call it rain.

. You can saddle me, but you can't ride me.

. You know he done pissed in the church now. He has offended someone who has been helpful to him.

. You reap what you sow.

. You would rather run through hell in gasoline drawers than fool with me..

DISTRUST

. A leopard doesn't change its spots

. Crooked as a barrel full of fish hooks

. Don't trust a bush that quivers. — There is some danger lurking there.

. Everybody that grins in your face isn't a friend to you.

. Feed them with a long- handled spoon. — Be cautious of that person.

. He/ she is crooked as a dog's hind leg. — A person is dishonest.

. He/she has sticky fingers. — A person will steal.

. He/she is phony as a three-dollar bill.

. He/she is slippery as snot on a door knob.

. He sits on both sides of the fence. — A person cannot be trusted as he wavers in both directions.

. He that hides is not better than he that steals. — Concealing information is a form of theft.

. He who accuses too many accuses himself. — Accusations are self-accusations.

. If you dig a ditch for your brother, dig two.

. If you lie, you will steal.

. It's dangerous to let some folks fool with a gun if the gun's any count.

. It is like buying a pig in a sack. — Caveat: Beware of what you buy.

. Looks like a boll-weevil looking for a home. — Someone looks for a handout.

. Old goose is sort of suspicious about the feather bed.

. One may smile and smile, and be a villain still. — Smiles attempt to mask wretched behavior.

. On the take

. Pull someone's leg. — Trick someone as a joke.

. Something isn't clean in the milk. — Something is not right.

. Take it with a grain of salt. — Accept it but maintain a degree of skepticism.

. That is too much sugar for a penny. — If it is too good to be true, then be cautious.

. The man could talk a possum out of a tree. — Talk a big game without results.

. There is a dead cat on the line.

. The worm doesn't see anything pretty in the robin's song. Every living thing is cautious.

. Throw dust in somebody's eyes.

. Under a cloud of suspicion

. When a stranger wants to do too much for you, watch out! Beware of strangers offering assistance.

. When you dig one grave, dig two. When a person attempts to destroy another, he destroys himself.

. You're a low-down dirty dog. — A person is no good and lacks character.

. You can run but you can't hide.

 **DREAMS**

Our parents and elders had great dreams for their children. Their dreams were considered to be goals that could be achieved through hard work, persistence, and spirituality. Our elders did not half-step in their efforts to achieve their dreams. Each day they walked quickly with their vision and worked hard to reach their goals. They believed that those who walked slowly toward their goals could be easily distracted and fail to reach their goals. Dreams without vision were considered folly. Our parents were filled with stamina and effort, never saying they were tired. They knew a tired person could be controlled, enslaved and a liability to society.

. Anything is possible.

. Believe in your dreams and they may come true, believe in yourself and they will come true.
   Faith is a special tool to achieve dreams.

. Don't dream your life away. — It is good to dream but dreams only come true from actions.

. Dream as if you'll live forever, live as if you'll die today.

. Follow your dreams. — Aspire to become what you wish to be.

. Follow your own star

. If a man wants his dreams to come true, he must wake up. — Achieving dreams require actions.

Otha Richard Sullivan

EDUCATION

Education was a top priority in our culture. Our elders believed passionately in education. During slavery, it was a crime to teach a Black person to read. Slave masters knew that individuals who were literate could not be controlled. While our ancestors were physically shackled, their minds remained free to think of freedom. Consequently, they knew that education was something that nobody could take from them. After the Emancipation Proclamation, there were few schools for African Americans in Mississippi as well as the South. Whites did not view education as a priority and continued to focus on denying African Americans equal rights and opportunities.

Our ancestors knew that education was an answer to many of the problems they faced. As Black children, we were told, "You've got to be two to three times better than others." Our elders were aware of the racist research and activities of eugenicists, phrenologists, craniologist and Social Darwinists. They espoused views that blacks were innately inferior to whites. Consequently, our parents and elders refuted these claims and constantly told us that we were as brilliant as any white person.

The first school for African Americans in the Old Hopewell community in Covington County was founded and funded by freed slaves started in 1870. School was held in the Old Hopewell Missionary Church, which was founded about 1864 or 1865. Isom Booth, one of my ancestors, gave the land on which the church was built. The first building used by the church was a log cabin that served as the church and the one-room schoolhouse.

After the Civil War, education for African Americans was not a priority by the state of Mississippi. The first schools for African Americans were started by Northern missionaries. By 1896 the Plessy v. Ferguson case was heard by the U.S. Supreme Court. The Court decided that states could require separate public facilities for blacks and whites. White dominated school boards concentrated their efforts on the construction of schools for white children rather than for African Americans. Schools supported by the state of Mississippi for African Americans were held in churches, lodges and poorly constructed buildings. White children were advantaged by having better school buildings and resources. Schools for African Americans were inferior in construction, fewer books, and equipment. The Smith Robertson School was the first public school funded by the state of Mississippi for black students. This school opened in 1894 in Jackson, Mississippi.

The Rosenwald Fund came to the rescue to support the construction of schools for African Americans in Mississippi and other parts of the South. By 1922, this fund had built 141 Rosenwald schools in Mississippi. By 1921, there were only two state supported high schools for blacks in Mississippi. Eureka School, located in my hometown, was the first public school in Hattiesburg, Mississippi. It opened in 1921 and housed grades 1-12.

More than sixty years after the Emancipation Proclamation, Mississippi did not support or fund public education for African Americans. In 1909, Mississippi governor James K. Vardaman, speaking on education for African Americans shared the sentiments of whites regarding education for African Americans. He said, "Money spent today for the maintenance of public schools for Negroes is robbery of the white man, and a waste upon the Negro." From 1900 to 1901, Mississippi provided $8.20 for the instructional cost per white child and $2.60 for the instructional cost per black child. From 1929 to 1930, white children continued to receive more funding. White children received $40.42 while African American students received $7.45 and by 1949-1950 white children received $78.70 and African American students were $23.83 by the state. Salaries for African American and white teachers were not equal.

As late as 1915, no public high schools for blacks existed in Mississippi, South Carolina, North Carolina and Louisiana. Elementary schools for African Americans were one-room buildings where a teacher taught several grades. Booker T. Washington, founder of Tuskegee Institute described these schools "as wretched little hovels with no light or warmth or comfort of any kind."

The dismal state of education for Blacks in the South prompted Julius Rosenwald, president of Sears, Roebuck and Company, to start the process of building schools for African Americans. With the assistance of Booker T. Washington, founder of Tuskegee Institute, schools were built in 15 states between 1912 and 1932. Six-hundred, thirty-three schools were built in Mississippi. In my hometown, Eureka School in Hattiesburg, Mississippi, became one of the first African American high schools in the state in 1921, a right that took more than 58 years from Emancipation to establish

Ten times as many white students attended high school as did African American students. A report of the Mississippi State Education Superintendent in 1930-1931 shows that 4 percent of African Americans were enrolled in grades 9-12, while 46 percent of whites were enrolled in these grades. By 1940-1941, 56 percent of whites were enrolled in grades 9-12, while 11 percent of African American students were enrolled in these grades. These dismal statistics are reflected in the state superintendent's report in 1950-1951 of secondary enrollment in Mississippi. Sixty-two percent of whites were enrolled in grades 9-12 and only 25% of African Americans were enrolled in these grades

By 1920, the schools for African American students were elementary schools. By 1940, nearly half of all African American children enrolled in public schools were in grades one and two. White Mississippi school board members who were in charge of funding for schools failed to provide African Americans' education beyond elementary school. These officials believed that African Americans were incapable of advanced learning. They believed African American students would become educated and thus become harder to relegate them to second class citizenship.

Discriminatory practices continued to be apparent in teacher salaries for white and African American teachers. In 1915, the average monthly salaries for white teachers were $42.00 and $25.00 for African American teachers. During 1939-1940, white teachers' annual salaries were $750. African American teachers were paid $237. This disparity in salaries for African American teachers continued to exist until the late 1960's.

In Mississippi, the majority of African American students were denied a full school year of attendance as white children. This was especially true of children whose parents were sharecroppers on land owned by white people. White students throughout Mississippi started school in September and finished in June. African American children attended split sessions during their school year. They started school in mid-November after cotton was harvested. Schools were closed in March or April when cotton fields needed tending and chopping. This type of interruption of African American students' education demonstrated that learning was subordinate to the demands of the cotton field and further sent a message to African Americans that they were inferior to whites.

Some African American parents who were more financially advantaged at the time enrolled their children in private schools where they knew their sons and daughters would receive a well-rounded education. One popular school was Piney Woods near Jackson, Mississippi. Piney Woods School was founded by Laurence C. Jones in 1909. For those who were unable to pay school fees, students worked and parents often supported their children's education at private schools by offering animals, vegetables and other products.

As late as 1940, Mississippi's spending per pupil for white children was 7.2 times the spending on African American students. I recall as a student in the 1950's and 1960s, we were given used books, furniture and supplies that had been discarded from white schools.

Segregation continued to be the order of the day in Mississippi where whites felt that African Americans should not enjoy the same rights as them. The Supreme Court announced its decision on May 17, 1954 in the case of *Brown v. Board of Education*. This decision declared segregated public schools in the United States were unconstitutional and inherently unequal.

Mississippi white people were not going to adhere to the Court's decision. In response to this decision, the White Citizens Council was founded on July 11, 1954, in Indianola, Mississippi. The name changed to the Councils of America in 1956. In a pamphlet prepared by the Council, their reason for being was outlined: "The Citizens Council is the South's answer to the mongrelizers. We will not be integrated. We are proud of our white blood and our white heritage of sixty centuries." The membership of this group was composed of plantation owners, bankers, doctors, lawyers, preachers, teachers and merchants. Their purpose of this group was to maintain the "Southern Way of Life." U. S. Senator James Eastland (Dem. Mississippi) in a speech given in Senatobia, Mississippi, on August 12, 1955 said, "On May 17, 1954, the Constitution of the United States was destroyed because of the Supreme Court's decision. You are not obliged to obey the decisions of any court which are plainly fraudulent sociological considerations."

White people used economic tactics against African Americans who belonged to the NAACP and supporters of voting rights and desegregation. The Sovereignty Commission, Ku Klux Klan and White Citizens Councils labeled the NAACP as a subversive organization. which was instigated by Northern outsiders. Members of the NAACP had their mail read, office bugged, phones wiretapped and cars were followed. Most whites in Mississippi accepted the false accusation that the NAACP was a communist organization and its members were considered traitors.

Economic reprisals against African Americans were expressed by denying loans, business credit and jobs. While the Council "publicly" renounced violence, their activities incited violence against African Americans. The Council posted the names of African Americans in newspapers who tried to vote.

The Council and the Mississippi Sovereignty Committee would go to any length to prevent integration of public schools and colleges and punish any African American who attempted to desegregate its schools. One individual who attempted to change the "Southern Way of Life" was Clyde Kennard, an African American civil rights pioneer and martyr. He was born in my hometown of Hattiesburg, Mississippi. Kennard tried to enroll at Mississippi Southern College (now known as University of Southern Mississippi) over a period of three years from 1956-1958. On December 6, 1958, Kennard published a letter in the *Hattiesburg American* newspaper. He wrote that he was a "segregationist by nature" but integrationist by choice." In response to his quest for integration and his letter, the Mississippi State Sovereignty Commission conspired to have him framed for a crime. He was charged for having five pints of whiskey in his car and later charged as an accomplice for the theft of $25 worth of chicken feed. Kennard was convicted and sentenced to seven years at Parchman Penitentiary, a high security prison in Mississippi. Although he was terminally ill with cancer and denied treatment for this disease, the governor refused to pardon him. He was finally released from prison in January, 1963, and died in Chicago on July 4, 1963.

This heinous treatment of Kennard and the denial of his rights served as the impetus for my father, Benjamin Franklin Sullivan, to have me leave Mississippi after graduating from high school. Dad had information that Lawrence, Kansas was founded by Amos Adams Lawrence, a key figure in the United States abolition movement in the years leading up to the Civil War. Lawrence was against slavery and supported John Brown's abolitionism. Dad was impressed with Lawrence's financial support of the Massachusetts 54th Infantry Regiment, the first African American regiment raised in the North. This infantry saw extensive service in the Union army during the American Civil War. Dad insisted that I enroll at the University of Kansas in Lawrence, Kansas, where he believed that I would be safe and enjoy equal protection and deliver me from the fate of Clyde Kennard. I recall arriving in Lawrence, Kansas, in August of 1960. My Dad had booked a hotel room for me at the Eldridge Hotel, founded in 1925, for three nights before my registration at the University of Kansas. This stay at the Eldridge Hotel was the first time I had stayed in a hotel that welcomed African American customers.

The University of Kansas has a wonderful history of being a free-state university. African Americans were admitted to this school early in its history. Founded in 1866, the University of Kansas admitted Lizzie Ann Smith in 1876 as its first African American student. Dad was also aware that Blanche K. Bruce (not Senator Blanche Kelso Bruce) was the first African American to graduate from the University of Kansas in 1885. I am convinced that my Dad who was not formally educated had done careful research in finding a safe place for me to pursue a college degree and sending me to a state and a university where African Americans enjoyed the same rights as white people.

Governor Ross Barnett of Mississippi a rabid racist was supported by the Council as a leader who would maintain white supremacy in Mississippi and keep the "Southern Way of Life." He spoke disparagingly about African Americans by saying, "The Negro is different because God made him different to punish him His forehead slants back. His nose is different...." This governor was the one who refused the admission of James Meredith to the University of Mississippi in 1962.

Mississippi totally ignored the decision to integrate schools. The state did not begin integration of its K-12 schools until 1970. Some school systems continued to resist integration and classrooms were almost entirely segregated by race.

Our parents and elders placed a high premium on education. To them, education was the only answer to overcome discrimination. They always told their children and those in the community that they were smart and worthy of enjoying a prosperous life. I recall that all of the men and women in the community would rub your head at church, in the barbershop, at the ice cream parlor and at school and other places and say, "You are going to finish high school and go to college." Their constant reminders that we were worthy inculcated the belief that we could accomplish anything we pursued in life. Our parents and elders were aware that most whites still held racist views that African Americans are inherently less intelligent than whites. Consequently, education was a major priority and everyone in the community instilled a strong desire in youth to achieve and be the best they could be. They constantly worked to dispel any negative perceptions and stereotypes about the abilities of African Americans.

When we finished high school and were ready to enroll in college, we were asked to stand up in church and be acknowledged by the congregation. Young children were asked to look at the graduates and were told, "You are also going to college one day." Our parents and elders were filled with pride about our achievements. They also held a special collection to help us defray our college expenses. This gesture demonstrated their desire to be active participants in the development of children in the village in which we were raised.

Our elders always introduced us to college graduates in the community. They were so proud of them. My parents and others in the community were strict and made education of their children as their top priority. They supported teachers and reinforced learning after school. They attended PTA meetings and took an active role in school activities. I recall every night was filled with homework. My parents did not allow us to be involved in play activities. When the sun went down (there were no street lights in my neighborhood.) every child was expected to be in the house. Darkness was our curfew.

Many of today's youth spend an inordinate amount of time watching television, shooting hoops, listening to music and hanging out with their peers. They are tethered to technology for most of the day. African American children spend more time watching television and video games than other children. The proliferation of personal electronics, cell phones, I-pads, I-phones, Wii games, and other gadgets consume more time than being involved in reading and educational pursuits.

As a child, we were fortunate to not have the many distractions of today's youth, which impact learning. While we had a radio in our home, it was only on rare occasions that we were able to listen to the radio in the living room and when we did, it was usually religious programs and gospel music.

. A little knowledge is a dangerous thing.

. Better untaught than ill taught   It is better not to be taught at all than to be taught badly.

- Cover a lot of ground.

- Education is something nobody can take from you.

- Have a one-track mind.

- He/she is wet behind the ears. — A person lacks knowledge.

- He who sleeps much learns little. — Those who sleep a lot gain little knowledge.

- Hit the books.

- Learn others' mistakes because you do not live long to make them all yourself.

- Look before you leap.

- Mistakes aren't haystacks, or there would be more fat ponies than there are. Repeating mistakes never lead to abundance or success.

- Old man Know-All died last year.

- School of hard knocks

- Still waters run deep. — People who are calm on the outside often have a strong personality.

- Study long, study wrong. — To overthink something can be a mistake.

- Take someone under your wings.

- The poorest education that teaches self-control is better than the best neglects it.

- When a man is educated, a family is educated. When a woman is educated, a nation grows and is educated.

 **EFFORT**

A great emphasis was placed on effort. We were taught that sloth was a deadly sin and African Americans could ill afford to not make progress. Our ancestors were known for their effort, strong determination, and sacrifice. A person who never tried and failed was sorry and lazy. We were always taught that there were higher hills to climb.

. Buckle down.

. Good, better, best; never rest till good be better, and better, best.

. It is a poor dog that won't switch his tail.

. It takes a heap of licks to strike a nail in the dark.

. None are as blind as those who won't see. — Those who have no vision have no promise.

. Nothing beats a failure but a try.

. Strike while the iron is hot.

. There is no harm in trying. — Effort is a prerequisite for success.

. To climb a tree, you have to start at the bottom. Completing a task, one must start at the bottom.

. When the bait is more than the fish, 'tis time to stop fishing.

. Wishes won't wash dishes. — Hoping will not complete a job.

EPIPHANY

Countless individuals look back on their lives and feel disconsolate for the time wasted, the pain inflicted on others, the violation of others' rights, the commission of crimes, the abandonment of family, the addiction to drugs and a lack of respect for self and others. Feelings of If-I-could-have or If-I should-have thoughts play on their minds like a sharp and touching rhapsody. We can never go back to the past and recapture the time and change the events in our life. However, our strengths and weaknesses of the past can serve as a light in the highway of our minds and teach us invaluable lessons that prepare us to recognize and respond proactively to the cautions and warnings and that assist us to be more focused in realizing our dreams and fulfilling our goals.

As a former school counselor of adolescents in an urban public school, I realized that the greatest advice given to some youngsters about their negative opinions, thoughts, and beliefs can fall on their deaf ears. Gone are the days of the nuclear family and the commitment to the philosophy that "It takes a village to raise a child." Many of these youngsters have not had a parent to love, guide and teach them values that will help them rise above the hopelessness they manifest. I suppose as with any generation of youth, most lessons learned are the result of experiencing mistakes and resulting suffering, which hopefully leads to an epiphany. Unfortunately, many of today's youth grow into adulthood, become age thirty, forty and fifty, before realizing that their mind, filled with negative thoughts, opinions, beliefs and hopelessness, prevented them from achieving social, emotional, educational, physical and financial success.

Many of today's youth face more social, emotional, health and spiritual challenges than previous generations. The traditional strength and involvement of the family is lacking thus providing inadequate and unhealthy support for youth. They are influenced by multiple sources of negative lessons, mass and print media, peers, and overt expressions of rebellion and socially unacceptable behavior. Unfortunately, television, rap music, and videotapes consume more of their time in the absence of adult instruction, supervision and parenting.

The Tree of Love Gives Shade to All

Too many of our children are pregnant and become teen mothers. These are children having children and woefully lack emotional, social, financial, and spiritual skills to raise a child. In some families, four generations may range in age from one month to forty-five. Each generation has perpetuated the conception of a baby at an early age and out of wedlock and bringing children into a world of poverty. Intergenerational poverty in the broadest sense continues to affect the lives of family members.

. He who can give thanks for little will always find he has enough. Give gratitude for blessings.

. Change comes from within.

EQUALITY

To our elders, equality meant economic, social, educational, political, and industrial equality.

. A white man knows when you're right, he sees, but acts like he doesn't.

. A white man will recognize a smart Negro but he won't tell the Negro; he'll tell some other white man.

. Be yee equally yoked.

. Don't marry a pig in a poke. — Always examine an item before purchasing.

. Every man is for himself; and God for us all.

. Fingers are not equal.

. Garbage in; garbage out — Garbage begets garbage.

. If slavery isn't wrong, nothing is wrong.

. In the South, they don't care how close you get, as long as you don't get too high. In the North, they don't care how high you get, as long as you don't get too close.

. One monkey doesn't stop any show.

. What's good for the goose is good for the gander.

. You can't make a silk purse out of a sow's ear. — Inferior materials never produce superior goods.

 EVIL

We were taught to avoid evil and when confronted with evil, we were challenged to transcend evil. Our elders believed in the teachings of Ptah Hotep, 'If you wish to be free from evil, guard against the vice of greed for material things." Our elders often quoted the words in Proverbs 5;14; "Enter not into the path of the wicked, and go not in the way of evil men."

. Evils that are passed should not be mourned. — Let go of evil deeds and move on.

. It's an evil wind that blows no good.

. Never do evil that good may come of it. — Doing evil is always counterproductive.

. Repay evil with kindness. Kindness overpowers evil.

. Who doeth no evil is apt to suspect none.

EXPERIENCE

Our elders believed in the value of experience and the lessons learned from experience.

. A bird in the hand beats two in the bush.

. Blind horse doesn't fall when he follows the bit.

. Dirt shows the quickest on the cleanest cloth.

. Don't let the dog bite you twice.

The Tree of Love Gives Shade to All

- Easy come, easy goes.

- Every dog has its day.

- Experience is the best teacher.

- If it doesn't fit, don't force it.

- If it isn't broke, don't fix it.

- If you always do what you've done, you'll always get what you've always gotten.

- If you lay down with dogs, you'll get fleas.

- It's a poor dog that won't praise its own pond.

- Little hole in your pocket is worse than a big one at the knee.

- Ole used-to-do-it-this-way doesn't help anyone today.

- Once bitten, twice shy.

- One person can thread a needle better than two.

- Only a squeaky wheel gets the oil.

- Quit while you're ahead.

- Set a cracked plate down softly.

- The darkest hour is before dawn.

- There's a lid for every pot and a key for every lock.

- There is always a person greater and lesser than you.

- The steel hoe that laughs at the iron one is like the man who is ashamed of his grand-daddy.

- Water seeks its own level.

- What goes around comes around.

- What you do in the dark will come to the light.

- Where there's smoke, there's fire.

- You can take a horse to water, but you can't make it drink.

- You can't cry over spilled milk.

- You can't get blood from a stone.

- You can't hurry up good times by waiting for them.

- You have to eat a peck of dirt before you die.

- You have to take the bad with the good.

FAILURE

Failure has most often been regarded by some as a negative word. It is only negative and a state of being when we make a decision to stop trying. Success was never supposed to be easy. It requires hard work, persistence, and determination to move forward in the face of adversities. Overcoming these obstacles prepare individuals with spiritual lessons that endow them with life-long skills to deal with any suffering, pain, disease, hardship and challenge in life. I am convinced that a noble failure serves the person as faithfully as a distinguished success. Failure is no more than a personal bulletin that we should keep on trying until we are successful.

When we believe in ourselves and work hard, we always overcome failure. Individuals who succumb to failure most likely will defer their dreams. We succeed when we have faith in God who dwells within us. It gives us vision and fosters a belief in our ability to achieve and do well in life. Jan Matzeliger, the inventor of the shoe lasting machine, gives us a lesson in the power of one's vision and faith and belief in God. Matzeliger followed the guidance of God and found solace and strength in Proverbs 3:9: "Honor the Lord with thy substance, and with the first fruits of all thy increase." He believed that he would develop a machine that would completely revolutionize the shoe industry.

Matzeliger was met with opposition and criticism from coworkers who doubted the abilities of this African American man. He was undaunted with their comments and each time he was told, "Jan, you are just a dreamer. You will never be successful in inventing that machine. Why it has been tried before and folks failed!" Matzeliger did not listen to these comments and persisted in his dream to invent his machine.

The road to the successful invention was not an easy one for Matzeliger. He was faced with many adversities. His health suffered, spending only a few pennies a day for food. He became poor in his work to invent the shoe lasting machine. These conditions did not deter him from success in creating his invention.

Some people fail because they find a plethora of excuses for their failures. Excuses are easy to find, invent, create and use. Excuses only satisfy the maker and keep them living in the uncomfortable house of denial. Failure and synonyms for failure should not be in our vocabulary. They don't exist in the Divine Presence in us. Think success, claim success, exalt success, feel success, surround yourself with successful people and experiences, sleep success, dream success, wake up with thoughts of success, and live with successful thoughts. Success is a seed that is placed in the mind, nurtured, and treated with the good stuff that promotes achievement. We must abandon negative thoughts. Much like landfill trash develops methane gas and becomes combustible, our mental garbage becomes destructive in our speech and explodes into negative thoughts and actions.

. A word of encouragement during a failure is worth more than an hour of praise after success.

. Dine on ashes.

. Failure is not sweet, but it need not be bitter.

. Failure is not when you fall down. It is when you don't get up.

. Fall by the wayside.

. If first you don't succeed, try and try again. (Success comes from failing and moving forward.)

. Sink or swim. — It is up to you to fail or succeed.

FAITH

Dr. Martin Luther King, Jr., in *Strength to Love*, wrote, "Faith can give us courage to face uncertainties of the future." I recall as a child growing up in Mississippi where African Americans were discriminated against in education, employment, housing, and health services. Some were lynched for their efforts to exercise their constitutional rights to freedom of speech and the right to vote and cheated, intimidated and subjected to a state of peonage in jobs as sharecroppers. We were shielded from the racism by our parents, elders, and church leaders who always taught us to have faith and that God loved everyone, regardless of race, creed or color. We believed that faith in God would free us from the persecution due to the color of our skin. We were taught that through faith, hard work, and good work, and good deeds that "Nothing is impossible for those who love the Lord."

Faith teaches us to accept adversities as no more than challenges presented to us to test our abilities to endure as we attempt to reach our goals. These tests of faith are more precious than money and treasures for we acquire skills to overcome hurdles and never become exhausted in the days of adversity. Dr. King reminds us of the power of faith, "Before the ship of your life reaches its last harbor, there will be long drawn-out storms, howling and jostling winds and tempestuous seas that make the heart stand still. If you don't have a deep and patient faith in God, you will be powerless to face the delay, disappointment, and vicissitudes that inevitably come."

Our parents and elders used faith in God and the promise of abundance as the source of their strength, determination and desire to prosper. This faith in God was passed on to them from their enslaved family members who used faith to overcome physical enslavement and free their minds. Consequently, children were raised, nurtured and disciplined based on Scripture. Our elders taught us the Biblical admonition, "If thy faint in the day of adversity, thy strength is small." Through observing our parents' ability to be proactive and problem-solve life's adversities, we learned individual lessons on how to develop and maintain control over our minds and labor to achieve emotional, spiritual, and financial abundance.

- A faithful friend is a medicine for life. — A good friend is life's best prescription.

- Every path has its puddle. — Life has its obstacles.

- Faith does not make things easy. It makes them possible. Faith drives our ability to overcome.

- Faith is like electricity. You can't see it, but you can see the light.

- Faith is not about believing that God can, but God will.

- Fear knocked at the door. Faith answered. And lo, no one was there. Faith conquers fear.

- Feed your faith and your doubts will starve to death. — Faith always destroys doubts.

- For with God, nothing shall be impossible. (Luke 1:37

- Sorrow looks back. Worry looks around. Faith looks up.

- This, too, shall pass. — Life goes on and situations change.

 FAMILY

The family is the most important and primary institution to teach and instill values and morals in children. Our parents and elders are the link to countless possibilities where we first begin to have ourselves defined for us. During my childhood, family was not limited to biological members. Family included all of the individuals in the community. The entire community of elders and adults felt a responsibility to serve as positive role models and inculcate the kinds of values that would promote success and independence in children and youth.

A primary problem which has caused some African Americans to fail is the family structure and the absence of support offered by an entire community. Since 1960, the proportion of African American children living with a single parent more than doubled from 22% to 53.3% in 2000. This statistic is a reflection of the number of young females having children without the support of a spouse and an extended family to help teach and guide children in positive directions.

. A family that prays together stays together.

. Apples don't fall far from a tree. — Children are similar to one or both parents.

. Blood is thicker than water. — Family relationships are stronger than other relationships.

. Every crow thinks his is the blackest. — Every parent feels his child is the best.

. Everyone gets their just desert. — Receive that which is deserved.

. Family must look out for family.

. He/she is a chip off the old block. — A child resembles one or both parents in behavior.

The Tree of Love Gives Shade to All

. It's a sorry house where the hen crows and the cock is silent.

. Keep the home fires burning — Take care of home.

. Kin folks shouldn't have run-ins.

. Sisters are different flowers from the same garden.

. We may not have it all together, but together we have it all.

. You can tell a tree by the fruit it bears. — We can tell a lot about a person by its roots.

 **FARMING**

Many of us grew up on farms, which made families self-sufficient. Our elders believed that those who worked the land were closest to God. Booker T. Washington spoke of the importance of farming. He said, "No race can prosper till it learns that there is as much dignity in tilling a field as in writing a poem."

. The good farmer keeps acquainted with the daybreak.

. A bad tree does not yield good apples.

. A crow is a first-rate hand to thin corn.

. A snow year is a rich year.

. Change of pastures makes fat cows.

. Colt in the barley patch kicks high.

. Cussing the weather is mighty poor farming.

. Early sow means early mow.

. Heap of cotton stalks get chopped up from associating with the weed.

. He that sows thistles shall reap thistles. — We reap what we sow.

. It doesn't rain every time the pig squeals.

. It's a mighty deaf field hand that doesn't hear the dinner horn.

. One rain won't make a crop. — A crop requires care, rain and assistance.

The Tree of Love Gives Shade to All

. Small axes fall great trees

. The fruit must have a stem before it grows.

. The tree must be bent while it is young.

. The wheat crop can't fool you when it comes to the thrashing.

. Weeds need no sowing.

. When the frost sends you word by the north wind, you better get the pumpkins.

Otha Richard Sullivan

FATHERS

I was fortunate to have a loving father and mother who viewed their major responsibility to be an example for their children. I learned early on in life the meaning of the proverb: "Anyone can be a father, but it takes a real man to be a daddy." Benjamin Franklin Sullivan was my father and my daddy. This man I called father and quite often daddy was a man who fostered a positive relationship with my mother; spent time with his children; nurtured his children; disciplined his children; served as a guide to us to the outside world; protected and provided for his children; and served as a positive role model for his children.

Growing up, I recall that there was a father and mother in every home in my community in the 1940s throughout the 1960s. Our fathers and their fathers were taught by example to play a significant role in the family, a role that was discouraged and forbidden during slavery. Therefore, our parents believed that every child should know his father and be legally recognized as the child of the father by bearing his name. Unfortunately, in the late 1970s and beyond, many fathers absconded their responsibilities and duties. Few men failed to marry the mother of their child and have the child bear their legitimate name.

Millions of men worldwide are biological fathers. While it is relatively easy to father a child, but taking on the responsibility of being a father is a formidable challenge. Fathers are with their children from the day they are born and provide for them until they reach adulthood. President Barack Obama, speaking about his father who left his family when he was a 2-year-old, said: "Though his mother and grandparents poured everything they had into me and my sister, I still felt the weight of that absence. It is something that leaves a hole in a child's life that no government can fill. We need fathers to realize that responsibility does not end at conception" (*USA Today*, 2010). About 80% of African American children will spend part of their childhood in a single parent home.

Singer O. C. Smith profoundly describes a wonderful picture of the person we call father. He sings, "There is a man in my house/He's so big and strong/He goes to work each day and stays all day long/Comes home at night, looking tired and beat…I think I will color him Father…I think I'll color him love." This is the memory I have of my father and this must be the painting of millions of fathers.

The Tree of Love Gives Shade to All

Children view their father as the best and the greatest of all fathers. Fathers are the most commanding figures to their children, larger than life itself. Whatever a friend's father can do, the other child thinks his father does it better. They tower above their sons and daughters and every child thinks he has the largest fathers. Fathers are always the most handsome man in the eyes of their daughters. In the eyes of a father, the daughter is the loveliest girl in the world. While she may grow up and marry, her heart always belongs to her father. She is always reminded of her father's teaching about dating and marriage to get a hero and never deal with a zero. Fathers also encouraged their daughters to get an education and be sufficient so they would never have to depend on a man.

Fathers are comforting and caring. They have smiles that are as bright as the light that beams from a lighthouse. Their smiles and tender touch make them healers, soothing an injured finger or making a scraped knee feel better. Fathers are geniuses whose talents span the spectrum of ability. They can put a bike together without reading the directions; drive a car with one hand and embrace a child with the other; and control the behavior of children in the back seat. To the child, the father always makes the complex task seem effortless. Children view their fathers as being stronger than Hercules, Samson, and Frederick Douglas.

Fathers are the personification of love, constancy, confidence, courage, compassion, patience and understanding. A real father is above the old "do as I say, not as I do" credo. Their sons and daughters learn how to express these qualities for a lifetime from their parents. Fatherhood is a serious responsibility. It is a job that does not provide a vacation or offer a 401K plan. Fathers can be the most important role model for the child, especially boys. Boys mimic their fathers. They want to talk like him; walk like him; shave like him; and drive like him. This need is shared in the Ashanti proverb: When you follow in the path of your father, you learn to walk like him."

Fathers and mothers teach their sons and daughters lessons that promote success and develop positive self-esteem and know they are loved. Parents are proficient in teaching their children the real meaning of love.

. A father lives after the death of his son.

. A father loves his children in hating their faults.

. Anyone can be a father, but it takes a real man to be a daddy.

. Chip off the old block.

FEAR

. All fear is bondage. — Fear enslaves an individual.

. Don't let fear stand in the way of your dreams.

. Fear is the poison of the heart.

. He/she is on pins and needles. — One is anxious and nervous.

. He who forecasts all perils will never sail the sea.

. If you worry about what might be, and wonder what might have been, you will ignore what is.

. Like a cat on hot bricks. — A person is very nervous or restless.

. Only your mind can produce fear.

. We must act in spite of fear, not because of it

FLOWERS

I grew up surrounded by flowers that dotted the bucolic countryside of the piney woods of southern Mississippi. They grew in abundance everywhere. There were lilies in the ponds, wildflowers in the country, surrounded by thickets, bushes, and lush trees, along railroad tracks. Flowers flourished in the rich Mississippi soil and abundant rain. Practically every yard, some without grass, was covered and bordered with annuals and perennials that brought considerable joy to those who took the time to stop, look, listen, communicate and appreciate the special beauty and strength of flowers. They offered each person wonderful lessons in planting healthy seeds that developed into aesthetic beauty. Growing flowers taught special lessons in how to care for others in our lives.

The Tree of Love Gives Shade to All

Growing up on a farm I learned how to grow flowers. These experiences provided me with invaluable lessons in gardening and using the same tools to grow healthy relationships. It is important to sow healthy seeds and take care of them. The seeds require sunshine, water, tender loving care to keep the weeds away. Gardening much like growing relationships requires commitment to make sure seeds germinate, grow and produce. Our relationships need the same commitment. Sometimes our relationships, like gardens need additional sunshine and watering. We need to show forgiveness when our relationships falter much like plants and we need to water our relationships with patience and cultivate them with love, time and effort and "pest control" when disagreements and quarrels threaten friendships and relationships. Our "pest control" requires patience and a willingness to get the relationship working again.

Some people are not interested in growing flowers and planting a garden for they believe these activities require too much time and attention. Unfortunately, these individuals have this attitude when it comes to developing and maintaining positive relationships. Special and lasting relationships are not easy but they are important in developing a healthy and spiritual life. I recall my elders often saying, "Nothing worthwhile comes easy."

My mother, a self-taught horticulturist, loved flowers and treated them with the tender love and care for which she was known for by her children, family members, and friends. I am convinced that she found every living thing to be a part of God's kingdom. Mother believed that flowers, like love should be shared. She got a special pleasure from knowing that her flowers and plants were found in many homes around Forrest County, Mississippi. She was touched with the same compassion and kindness for an injured bird, a stray cat, or a three-legged dog. Mother visited the sick, cooked for the annual dinner-on-the-grounds at the Hopewell Missionary Baptist Church, and shared her abundance of fruits and vegetables from our farm to strangers. Mother always admonished me at an early age to treat others with the special care that beautiful flowers required. She taught me that the essence of flowers could be found in perfume, dyes, sachet, potpourri, and perpetual bouquets. I am convinced that my mother had a special wish for all people to be like flowers, beautiful in their appearance, strong in their roots, fragrant and inviting in their communication and strong in their life cycle.

Flowers teach us much about the good stuff that we should instill and exalt in our minds such attributes as hope, beauty, peace, joy and abundance. We were taught that flowers were resilient, strong, and capable of surviving and persisting during the harshest of winter and the drought of summer and rise to blossom with the brightest colors and strongest stems. Flowers are the product of the seeds planted much like the good seeds we plant in our relationships.

The tulip, a flower that endures and comes to life each year, reminds us of life and the stages of development we undergo to find the truth that we have dominion over our lives. Planted as a bulb in early fall, the tulip is firmly planted below the earth and gently covered. It goes into a dormant stage for several months and pierces through the earth with strength and excitement as spring approaches. Over a period of weeks, the tulip blossoms burst forth, ever so carefully and gently, taking its time to bask in the sun, and blossom in the most magnificent colors in spring. After a few weeks of beauty, the flower of the tulip sheds and still stands majestically as a plant.

We can learn much about life and our relationships by observing that it is important to cut the tops of the tulip to support its growth and development. With a short blooming cycle, the plant falls, and the strong bulb that produces such pleasure remains. We are only asked to enjoy the beauty of the tulip and respond in a positive manner. Much like caring for the tulip, we show our compassion with others by nurturing our relationships.

The observation of plants and flowers offer us invaluable information on how we should turn to the Divine Power within us to show us the light and illuminate our path to grow in a healthy and spiritual manner. Our mind is a perpetual garden. To protect this garden, we must constantly meditate, pray and contemplate about the riches of the Holy Spirit. As we meditate, claim and affirm richness in our lives, we are able to express this richness in all aspects of our lives. Plants give us lessons on the respect and attention flowers, plants and trees give to the energy of the sun and the rain that helps them to grow. We should view the sunlight in our lives as a special spirit to share joy with others. We are able to face adversities and overcome them for the fruits of the Spirit empower us with peace, joy, beauty, harmony, faith, goodness and balance.

Nurturing plants require daily efforts and attention. Plants and flowers encourage us to shift from darkness and misunderstanding to light and understanding in our relationships with self and others. Sunlight is a key factor in photosynthesis which helps flowers to grow. Much like photosynthesis, we need to bring sunlight into our relationship with others. Plants and flowers require water to grow and prosper. We water our relationships with others by being patient, communicating, and expressing kindness. Much like flowers, we must weed out the influences that stunt our growth and the growth of others. We must be like plants and flowers, constantly directing our mind to the positive energy of the Divine Presence that illuminates our thoughts, opinions, beliefs, and truth. When we draw near to God, He will draw near to us.

Flowers nurture our spirit and encourage us to give attention to the needs of others. Flowers often need fertilization. This same fertilization is important in our relationship with others by providing richness in their lives. We must be like flowers in our lives to offer hope to the infirmed and jumpstart the seeds of peace in our relationships. Flowers stand as a symbol of beauty and mirror the attractiveness and strength of our hearts. They encourage us to be still, thoughtful and affirmed in our faith during periods of misfortune, isolation, and abandonment and triumphs over difficulties. We are like flowers and other living things, constantly changing, learning, renewing, and evolving as we deal with others.

God's will is for us to share and express abundance and bring peace and happiness in our journey in life. We are like flowers when we express positive thoughts and opinions, attracting positive people and experiences and being kind to those who need kindness the most. We must be like flowers where insects and flowers are interdependent. Flowers coexist among a variety of plants and flowers, sharing and posing no threat to other plants and flowers. They teach us the special value of all people.

Roses inform us about life, its beauty and its vulnerability. The bud offers us beauty, balance, form and goodness. Its thorns acquaint us with the source of life adversities, irritations and challenge us that we must overcome suffering. Roses urge us to snap the dead buds to enable them to rejuvenate and reproduce. We can learn much about dead heading the roses in our relationships. We accomplish this by supporting each other and demonstrating commitment. We often refuse to abandon stems of discontent and buds of negative experiences which thwart our growth. When we hold on to unhealthy experiences, people and circumstances, we give others control over our lives. We must forgive and let go of pain and suffering to go forward. Holding on to bad stuff creates and perpetuates disease.

Tending flowers offers us a special communion with nature and understand how to nurture our relationships. Flowers teach us how to treat others with love, goodness and kindness. They teach us the importance of the love and care needed by plants to the love and care needed by people. Individuals who work in their flower gardens receive a special fulfillment in their effort to provide a positive and healthy environment for their flowers. Much like flowers, we must give special care to ourselves to affirm, exalt and lean on the Divine Presence that dwells within us. It enables us to have good health and positive relationships with others.

Nature has been given to us as a special laboratory to learn the good stuff that enables us to survive, prosper, and grow spiritually in the light of God. Dr. George Washington Carver in *How to Search for Truth*, wrote, "...Nature in its varied forms are the little windows through which God permits me to commune with Him, and to see much of His glory, majesty, and power by simply lifting the curtain and looking in." Our lives are enhanced when we give the same care, attention, and love to flowers to our relationships with others.

. All flowers are not in one garland.

. Give me my flowers while I live.

. If you enjoy the fruit, pluck not the flower.

. It is bad soil where no flowers will grow.

. The handsomest flower is not the sweetest. — Appearance can be deceiving.

FLY

Do you believe you can fly? According to the theory of aerodynamics, the bumble bee is unable to fly. This is due to the size, weight, and shape of its body in relation to the total wing spread which makes flying impossible. But the bumblebee, being ignorant of these profound scientific truths, goes ahead and flies anyway and manages to take a little honey every day.

Our elders always taught us to reach for the stars. Their beliefs in our ability to achieve were poignantly stated by Harriet Tubman, an African American abolitionist, humanitarian Union spy and conductor on the Underground Railroad. She said, "Every great dream begins with a dream. Always remember, you have within you the strength, the patience, and the passion to reach for the stars to change the world. "

History is filled with many accounts of individuals who were told that they would never rise above poverty, negative circumstances and conditions. Countless research studies, medical prognoses, scholarly reports, and other studies have suggested that some individuals will not be healthy, prosperous and make lasting contributions to the world. Scientific studies cannot adequately measure one's persistence, strength and determination to overcome incredible odds and rise and fly above their circumstances. There are too many examples of individuals who were able to "fly" above their conditions. Our elders are a prime example of rising about incredible circumstances and inequality.

Universally, individuals achieve greatness because they have internalized and set their vision on universal truth that they can do anything they desire if they dream it, possess a positive spirit, claim health and prosperity and identify a purpose on which to focus positive energy. Much like the bumblebee, these individuals have ignored some research about their potential and have flown to great heights in their lives.

Our mind is the most powerful source of thoughts, beliefs, opinions and actions. The spirit within successful and healthy people teaches them that no one or any circumstance can oppose or thwart their ability to achieve. Those who are successful in life have filled the vessel of their mind with the good stuff of positive thoughts that help them achieve harmony, peace, abundance and security.

Focused individuals see opportunities when others see obstacles. They believe there are limitless opportunities when other are filled with lack and exalt external forces and circumstances. Frederick Langbridge illustrates how two individuals can have different thoughts and expectations. He wrote, "Two men look out through the same bars, one sees the mud and the other stars." We must constantly look upward, onward and Godward to find the truths that enable us to fly.

There are many individuals who are a testament to the affirmation found in the Latin Proverb: "Believe that you have it, and you have it." To paraphrase, "Believe that you don't have it, and you don't have it." To believe in one's ability to soar about circumstances is the first step of expressing faith in the spirit. Through our willingness to accept the spirit of God that dwells within us, we learn that the Infinite One fosters an ability to achieve.

Bessie Coleman, an African American woman, grew up with the dream of flying an airplane in the early 1900's. To most individuals, her aspiration was dismissed with such expressions as, "Her elevator must not go to the top" and "Lights are on, but nobody is home." Essentially these individuals were saying that she could not achieve her dream and was silly to even have this dream. Much like the bumblebee, she ignored the beliefs that African American women did not have the ability to fly.

Coleman claimed flying and focused all of her energies toward fulfilling that dream, which others viewed as impossible at the time for an African American, especially an African American woman. Day after day, she looked into the sky and was in awe of airplanes. "One day I am going to fly," she said, as planes buzzed over her head. While most people dismissed her thoughts as flights of fancy, she was not going to be distracted by their beliefs or the racial discrimination she faced as an African American woman.

Coleman could have abandoned her dream for she knew the odds were against her in receiving flight training in this country due to the color of her skin. Her tenacity was exciting and a sterling example of the power of determination and perseverance. Undaunted and convinced that no laws, people, their thoughts, and expectations, she knew these circumstances could not destroy her dream or limit her possibilities in life. She saved every penny she made to pursue flight training in Paris, France. She took flight training there and received her pilot's license in 1922, becoming the first licensed African American pilot in the United States. Coleman's persistence, tenacity and determination are a testament to one's belief in being able to fly and achieve.

Henry Ossawa Tanner's dream of becoming an accomplished artist was unheard of for an African American man at the time. At best, his destiny, prescribed by others for an African American man, was to become a domestic servant, blacksmith or possibly a preacher or teacher. Tanner refused to accept the poverty labels and stereotypes of the time and was steadfast in knowing that no external person, condition or circumstance could define him and control and relegate him to any level of mediocrity. Knowing that he, and only he, was in control of life, Tanner kept his eye on becoming an artist.

Friends and a generous benefactor helped Tanner raise enough money to travel to Paris to work and pursue art. In Paris, Tanner was quite an oddity to other artists who confronted him with prejudice. Fellow students attempted to intimidate him on a daily basis. They sought to discourage him and have him leave art school. The taunting and destruction of his canvas and art supplies did not deter him from following his dream. The negative comments and malicious actions of students only served to inspire him more to reach his goal.

Tanner knew his oppressors were disadvantaged and incapable of destroying his dream. While they destroyed his art materials, they could not extinguish his determination. His detractors had no control over his ability to know, understand, and practice the richly honed skills borne of oppression and discrimination. His ability to overcome adversity and achieve at the highest level did not go unnoticed by his peers. A few students eventually began to talk with him, hoping to learn his skills and ability to develop confidence under pressure.

Tanner persisted and became one of the world's greatest artists. His distinguished work can be found in the permanent collections of the Metropolitan Museum of New York, the Chicago Art Institute, the Los Angeles Art Gallery and other prestigious museums around the world. Tanner's life provides valuable lessons to all of us in the power of reaching for the stars. His strong will instructs us that we can achieve anything in life if we only believe, work hard and persist in our endeavors.

Oprah Winfrey, a product of humble beginnings, played in bare feet on dirt roads that bordered forlorn shotgun houses and outhouses of Kosciusko, Mississippi. Social scientists and other researchers would have labeled Oprah and her family members as being poor and never being able to "fly" above their economic and social conditions. Much like Harriet Tubman, she believed that every great dream begins with a dream and there is an ability to reach for the stars.

Oprah refused to believe she was impoverished. She ignored all of the stereotypes about the ability of African Americans. She was rich in Spirit and had a strong belief that "God can do anything but fail." She also knew that her forefathers and foremothers who were freed from slavery did not faint in the days of adversities and return to bondage seeking a handout, which some former slaveholders expected of emancipated slaves. She would not be relegated to second-class citizenship due to the color of her skin nor would she be influenced by the sociological and psychological studies of the time that forecasted that she would fail in life. Much like the bumblebee, she and other African American were able to fly. She and so many others rose above the "outhouses" to the white houses of opportunity.

We must teach our children at the earliest ages that they can achieve greatness in the face of obstacles. It is important to introduce them to books on African American History that share the stories of how they became achievers. They should be introduced to African American inventors, entrepreneurs, authors, entertainers, politicians, and other history makers.

. God gives us dreams a size too big so that we can grow into them.

. The road to success is always under construction. — Meet the challenges as you approach goals.

FOLLY

. It is a mark of wisdom to dislike folly. — Wise people don't deal with foolishness.

FOOD

Our elders believed that food was a way of expressing love. They believed in the admonition of Proverbs 15:17: 'Better is a dinner of herbs where love is, than a stalled ox and hatred therein.'

. Appetite doesn't regulate the time of day.

. A thin pan will get hotter quicker than a thick pan.

. A watched pot never boils.

. Better the gravy than no grease at all.

. Blind horse knows when the trough is empty

. Eat high on the hog.

The Tree of Love Gives Shade to All

. Eat like a horse.

. Empty smokehouse makes the pullet holler.

. Fat hens make rich soup.

. Fire won't crack a full pot.

. From great rivers come great fish.

. God provides food but does not cook it.
. He/she is stuffed to the gills. — A person is very full.

. Hunger finds no fault with moldy corn.

. I am so hungry my stomach thinks my throat is cut.

. If the meat is on top of the table, then you have to stand up where it is.

. If you don't open your mouth you won't get fed.

. One man's meat is another man's poison.

. Pigs get fat, but hogs get slaughtered.

. Take all you want, but eat all you take.

. Thank the Lord and bless the cook.

. The closer to the bone is the sweeter the meat.

. The sweetest nuts have the hardest shells.

. The way to a man's heart is through his stomach.

. Tis God's blessing that makes the pot boil.

. Too many cooks will spoil the stew.

. Troubles are seasoning. — Simmons not good until the frost bite.

. Waiting on the table is a powerful way to get up an appetite.

. Your eyes are bigger than your stomach.

. You have to eat a peck of dirt before you die. — Everyone experiences some adversities in life.

FOOL

. A fool and his money are easily parted. — A foolish person usually spends money carelessly.

. Every fool will be meddling. — Fools spend their time in counterproductive behavior.

FORETHOUGHT

We have all had the experience of making a decision without fully thinking about it or relying on the special light of the Infinite Presence in us, which guides us in making good decisions. We refuse to forgive others for their human frailties and choose to take on an omnipotent attitude of burning bridges and destroying the possibilities of improving interpersonal relationships. When we choose to terminate relationships based on mistakes or the unforgivable sins you have identified, we don't help ourselves and others. When we speak without thinking, we often say things that are hurtful and negative.

Negative thoughts and opinions quite often invite us to destroy marriages, friendships, jobs, and family. There are individuals who respond to negative behavior with negative responses. When we do this, we are just as guilty and unthinking as the perpetrator. We all have seen how some arguments get started and exacerbate the situation. It usually starts with some unkind words and personal attacks on an individual and can lead to a physical confrontation. It takes two people to argue. It takes two people to fight.

Differences are never settled by hurling profanities and other obscenities, and by saying the first thing that comes to mind. Forethought expresses a respect for self and others. When we carefully think about issues, we learn that another person's battle does not have to become our battle. Forethought enables us to choose our battles and understand that 99% of the battles in which we engage are not worth it. Our elders often told us that a soft answer turns away wrath and grievous words stir anger. In Proverbs 16:24 we are given instruction in the importance of goodness; "Pleasant words are as an honeycomb, sweet to the soul, and health to the bones."

When we are filled with the good stuff of the Divine Presence in us, we make good decisions quickly for we are aware of the words, thoughts, opinions, beliefs and action that support the fruits of life: life, peace, happiness, love and joy. When in doubt of what to say or do, always think before acting as our elders warned us to look before we leap.

. Forethought is better than after thought.

. He who fails to plan- plans to fail.

. Hindsight explains the injury that forethought would have prevented.

FOREWARNING

Forewarned is forearmed. — Advance warning provides an advantage.

FORGIVENESS

Forgiveness is something we all struggle with at times. We struggle with forgiving those that have hurt us. We often struggle with forgiving ourselves when we fail. Our elders taught us that when we forgive others, it is like writing off a debt much like a bank writes off debts that unsecured and individuals refuse to pay. We must write off emotional debts that others are unable to pay much like banks. In forgiving others we call in these uncollected debts and let them go. We are taught in scripture in Matthews 6:12 "And forgive us our debts, as we forgive our debtors.

Forgiveness allows us to dump the garbage that clutters and overwhelms our minds. Too many people live a lifetime and refuse to let go of emotional scars, which we permit others to inflict upon us. To maintain our mental and physical help, it is better to let go and let God.

. Forgetting of a wrong is a mild revenge.

. It is nobler to pardon than to punish.

. The more a man knows, the more he forgives.

. We are most like God when we forgive. — It is Godlike to forgive.

FRIENDSHIP

One of the greatest lessons in growing up was you have to be your own best friend and that friends are few. My first understanding of the term, friends, was at the age of four in the Mount Zion Missionary Baptist Church in Hattiesburg, Mississippi. Hymnal 124, *What a Friend We Have in Jesus*, was prominently placed on the board that presented the order of hymns for that Sunday's church service. We believed that Jesus was our best friend.

Friendship can be a statistical rarity. Many individuals whom we meet in life and share our lives are no more than acquaintances and associates. They are only around when the sun shines and life is filled with bounty. True friends are loyal. They dare to tell you the truth when others lie to you. Friends are with you when life is sunny and when life is filled with storms that toss and turn us. True friendships tend to last longer than courtships and marriages. Friends are mirrors of our being.

W.E.B Du Bois once said, "He has nothing but 'friends'; and may the good God deliver him from most of them for they are likely to lynch his soul." The reality of life is that we have few friends and as the old saying goes, "We can count true friends on one finger and have some fingers left over." Invariably, we must be our own best friend.

. A best friend is like a four-leaf clover, hard to find and lucky to have.

. A false friend and a shadow stay only when the sun shines.

. A friend in need is a friend indeed. — True friends are with us in difficulties.

. A friend is one who walks in when the rest of the world walks out. Friends are always with you.

. A friend is someone who knows the song in your heart and sings it back to you when you forget the words.

. A false friend is worse than an open enemy.

. A friend to all is a friend to none. — A person cannot be a friend to everyone.

. A good friend is with you through thick and thin.

. A long spell of rheumatism is apt to point out your best friends.

. Any friend of someone is a friend of mine.

. A seldom visitor makes the best friend. — Real friends are not constant visitors.

. A true friend is the best possession. — A friend is a rich asset.

. Best friends are the siblings God forgot to give us. — Best friends are like siblings.

. Books and friends should be few but good. — Choose friends and books carefully.

. Cheerful company shortens the miles. — Companionship eases our journey.

. Don't let a little dispute injure a great friendship.

. Everybody who grins in your face is not your friend. Smiles can be deceiving.

. Everyone hears what you say. Friends listen to what you say. But friends listen to what you don't say.

. Friends are few and far between.

. Friends are God's way of apologizing to us for families.

. Friends are kisses blown to us by angels.

. Friends are the flowers in the garden of life.

. Friendship is a plant which must be often watered. — We must nurture and care for our friends.

. Friendship is like a bank account. You cannot continue to draw on it without making deposits.

. Friendship isn't a big thing – it is a million little things.

. Good friends are hard to find, harder to leave, and impossible to forget.

. He is my ace boon coon. — Colloquial: Best friend

. Help yourself and your friends will help you.

. He who has no enemy has no friend.

. I know if I want a friend I must first be a friend.

The Tree of Love Gives Shade to All

. Insolence puts an end to friendship. — Abuse destroys friendships.

. Keep your friends close and your enemies closer.

. Lend your money and lose your friend.

. Love your friend with his faults.

. One hand washes the other.

. Tell me who you're with and I'll tell you who you are. We are known by the company we keep.

. The best mirror is an old friend. — Friends will always reflect our being.

. The journey to a friend's house is never long.

. There is no physician like a true friend.

. They are not all friends who grin, showing their teeth. Everyone who smiles in your face is not a friend.

. They are thick as thieves. — Friends stick together.

. True friendship is seen through the heart not through the eyes.

. When friends meet, hearts warm. — A good friend makes our hearts beat with joy.

. You can count your friends on one hand and have fingers left over. There are few friends in life.

. Your friend is the man who knows all about you and still likes you.

. You've got to be your own best friend. — The best friend one can have is self.

GENEROSITY

Treat yourself to the special joy of always giving from the heart. Take time each day to give a gift from the heart. We are taught a special lesson about generosity in 2 Corinthians 8:7-8, "Excel in this grace of giving. I am not commanding you, but I want to test the sincerity of your love." —

. It's better to appreciate things that you don't have than to have things that you don't appreciate

. Don't bite the hand that feeds you. — Don't hurt those who help you.

. Don't look a gift horse in the mouth. — Don't offend those who provide assistance.

. Giving alms never lessens the purse. — It is important to give to charity and the less fortunate.

. Remember the poor and needy. It costs you nothing. Charity is a virtue.

. Those who give to us teach us how to give.

GIFTS

Each year and on a daily basis, we are faced with seemingly endless celebrations and holidays,, which are established by commercial organizations whose sole purpose is to push the sale of items that supposedly speak to one's appreciation for another. Billions of dollars are spent annually on Mother's Day, Father's Day, Christmas, New Year's Day, Grand-mother Day, Grandfather Day, and an endless of holidays where we feel we have to give others a gift. Have we really thought about the real gifts that we should be giving each day? Are these gifts shared from the heart such as love, appreciation, joy, peace and forgiveness?

Countless individuals spend more than their budgets allow at Christmas time, birthday, anniversaries, and other "special occasions," and forget that the most special occasions occur on a daily basis when we reach out to others in love. Sadly, many of us overemphasize the material aspects of holidays and other celebrations, believing that the only way to celebrate these events is to purchase material things. Most often, we feel that it is easier to go out and purchase a gift than to express ourselves through love, generosity of time, friendship, and compassion for one another.

Our elders always gave gifts from the heart that expressed their goodness and sharing what they had for they knew these gifts were pleasing to God. I recall the Christmases of my childhood were filled with special and enduring memories. Christmas, like any other holiday, was a celebration if we had food to eat and a place to sleep. As a family, we were thankful for that. It was a time that we were happy to receive some things that families could not afford during the year. There were oranges, apples, tangerines, pecans, peanuts and oh, yes the large peppermint candy on Christmas day. These special treats were carefully placed in a newspaper lined shoebox. Sometimes, a special treat among the fruit and various nuts was a quarter, carefully tied in a piece of a flour sack. Getting this quarter, which we called two bits made us feel like we were rich.

There was a special caring that went into the few toys we received from our fathers, uncles, and other elders in the community who fashioned these handmade toys were made from loving hands. They painstakingly took the time to hand-carve toys and other practical items. Sometimes there was a wooden wagon made by a relative or a sling shot that we used as a rubber gun. Girls were often treated to a home-made corn husk doll or a rag doll stuffed with cotton. There were other animals made from feed sacks and stuffed with cotton. Added to this occasion was the gesture of love of Christmas, birthdays, and other events expressed by our mothers, grand-mothers, and other women in the community. They prepared the most delectable cakes, pies, and other foods, which was the ultimate expression of love and caring for loved ones. These were simple times where we gave thanks for the most basic needs.

Other gifts from my childhood that brought joy to me included the bleached-washed feed sack shirt that my mother made for me to wear to Christmas service. It was mandatory that we attended church on Christmas day. Sometimes, businesses in town would donate toys and other items for those who did not receive anything for Christmas. Of course, our father would never permit us to take anything that was donated. He was so proud and felt that his family was content to enjoy the traditional joy of being alive and being with family.

Our parents were guided by the motto of repair, reuse and make do. Nothing was thrown away. Another gift for the family was the quilt stitched by my grand-mother who knew that the small, un-insulated "shotgun" house would get cold in winter and she wanted to make sure that I did not get cold. While the quilt helped ward off the cold, it was so heavy that there were times I felt I was in bondage from the weight.

As children, we were creative in making toys for ourselves. Girls made dolls out of Coca-Cola bottles and used pop tops and ice string for hair on the doll. Pieces of fabric were used to make clothes for the bottle dolls. We boys would put wire through tin cans and used them as stilts. We also made games of checkers out of discarded bottled tops and recycled wood. And, there were plenty of paper airplanes we made from the pages of catalogs. Other favorite activities included the marbles we used to play games. A group of us would use discarded wood to make wagons and use wheels we found in the community.

Special holidays were time for spending time with family. There were no televisions, few radios, and limited advertisement for toys and other items. Of course, we could not afford those things advertised in the newspaper or catalogs. The Sears-Roebuck and Alden catalogs became our dream books, page upon page of items that took our bright eyes on a trip through fantasy. And of course, the pages of the catalog were always recycled, serving as the toilet tissue which we used on our visits to the outhouses.

Ted Turner, media mogul, once said that in the United States we have 2.5% of all children in the world, but we purchase 60% of all the toys in the world. While other cultures tend to give gifts as a tradition on Christmas or on birthdays, they are practical and something children need. Quite often, the individuals who are less able to afford expensive toys and clothing are the individuals who spend an inordinate amount of money at Christmas time. I have often heard some mothers and fathers say, "While we may be poor, I want my children to have the best Christmas possible."

The Tree of Love Gives Shade to All

Each day is an opportunity to share the special gifts of love for one another. Each day is a special birthday, which is given to us when we awaken to a new day. Each day is a special time to give the gift of expressing our love to our children by listening to them, talking with them, correcting them, teaching them values, and help to lead them through the plethora of life's challenges. We can express our love for family members and others by taking the time from our busy schedules to show compassion by listening to another person's problems.

The most special and lasting gifts are not purchased in department stores but those that come from the heart. These gifts keep on giving and touching the hearts of others and teaching them how to give the most important gifts. These types of gifts are usually remembered and cherished above those that did not require any emotional involvement. Precious gifts are those that show love, attention, friendship, caring, guidance, counseling, compassion, kindness, generosity and time.

Can you recall gifts in your life that represented all of the above-qualities? It was evident in the quilt that your grand-mother made, attentive to design, fabric, and more importantly, each stitch was her ultimate expression of love. The special gift may have been the woodcarving of your favorite animal that your grand-father made, using the skills of many generations of woodcarvers who were craftsmen in Africa. Your special gift may have been a hand-made shirt, dress, coat or other garment that your mother or grandmother fashioned from flour sacks or other fabrics. My special gifts that continued to bring special joy are letters from my mother, the quilt that was made as a gift when I went off to college, and more especially the love and values that she and my father instilled in me.

. Every day is a gift, that's why they call it the present. We should claim each day as a special gift.

. Your time is the greatest gift you can give someone. — The best gift to share is time with loved ones.

GOALS

Our elders were goal-oriented and expected children and youth to have goals. As teachers and mentors, they demonstrated characteristics that would help their children reach goals. The goals that our parents and elders expressed for their children and youth were to become law abiding citizens, independent adults and a contributing member of society. They expected their children to be honest, have personal integrity and know their self-worth. Parents imparted these qualities by being examples to their children.

Our elders had special dreams that their children would fare better educationally and financially than them. They did not half-step in their efforts to achieve their goals. Each day they quickly walked with their vision and worked hard to reach their goals. They believed that those who walked slowly toward their goals could be easily distracted and fail to reach their goals. There was no time to be involved in folly. They were filled with energy and effort, never saying they were tired for they knew a tired person could be controlled, enslaved and a liability to society

My father often told us that you could not stroll through life hoping to find success and wealth. He practiced what he preached in his fast gait, special discipline and impatience with trivial matters. We children were required to walk quickly, proudly and with purpose.

A goal is the easiest thing to set. Reaching a goal is difficult, requiring hard work, determination and spirituality. We are taught about planning in setting and achieving our goals in Proverbs 21:5 - "The plans of the diligent lead to profit as surely as haste leads to poverty." A goal is an end that one strives to attain. We all have goals in our life that range from achieving personal peace through unlocking the Spirit that dwells within us. Our goals may be work related where we aspire to reach the top of the career ladder. Some have goals to find a special soul mate they can share wonderful feelings of the heart. Other goals in life are related to humanity, goodness, humility, generosity, truth, faith and tolerance.

I have often heard some individuals say that they did not reach their goals because they were poor, discriminated against, and lacked opportunities. They fault others but themselves for their failure to rise above the valley of despair and begin scaling the mountain of personal triumph. They bemoan the feeling that life has dealt them a deck of cards that destined them to failure, contenting them to be in a state of inertia. Those who fail become experts in giving others responsibility for their station in life. Their lack of faith is about as arid as a desert. Faith is the substance of things hoped for, the evidence of things not seen. Those who question the importance of faith and work are in denial. A person can achieve anything that he chooses to do if he works hard and accepts the formidable challenge that they will inevitably face on their road to success. I once read, "Great victories come, not through ease but by fighting valiantly and meeting hardships bravely."

Individuals who fail usually spend their time, talking, blaming, complaining, and failing. Any excuse is convenient to them but it does not change the truth that those who fail just give up trying. Successful individuals fill their life with planning, working, and being responsible. They do not permit dissonance and denial to get in their quest for success. Reaching a goal requires eliminating external individuals, forces and circumstances from our being. We must not give others the power to control our goals.

When we give the power of reaching goals to others and circumstances, we deny the great power we have in achieving goals. As a teacher and counselor, I often heard some high school graduates, who were bright students, say that they were not able to attend college because of money. In most cases, they did not prepare themselves for college admission, taking college admissions examinations, completing college applications, completing financial aid forms, and more importantly believing that they could not succeed in college. Sadly, some were consumed with fear of succeeding for it required moving from their comfortable acceptance of mediocrity, familiar surroundings, and experiences. They lacked discipline, persistence, commitment and a greater vision to rise above their self-imposed circumstances. Settling for less, some of the students took jobs paying minimum wages that did not require any expression of creativity. I always told these students that if they wanted to attend college, it didn't take money. It took brain power, discipline, excellent test scores, a positive attitude and persistence. These qualities would ensure that they would be provided scholarships and grants to pursue their education.

Goals require setting priorities, preparation, discipline guidance and will. Some individuals spend more time in leisure activities than developing their minds. Mundane activities don't require effort and commitment. Success does. If more youngsters would spend as much time reading and in creative, problem-solving activities as do shooting hoops, shopping for the latest rage in apparel, and watching videos, they would be eligible to receive financial assistance in the form of scholarships and grants to attend college. Successful individuals are avid and proficient readers, competent at mathematical functions, adept in interpersonal relations, proficient in written and communication skills, and possess effective study habits.

Reaching goals require knowledge of what one wants to do in life. It requires identifying an individual's passion. It entails finding answers to the simple question: What can I do in life that will contribute for all and make lasting contributions to the world? Success in reaching goals requires setting up objectives that enable us to meet our goals. The hard work involves establishing critical tasks that must be performed to achieve a goal. These activities cannot be assigned to others for only we must learn to do them effectively.

We must be willing to move from the simplest activity to the more complex tasks. True mastery comes from practice. There is the necessity of having benchmarks and evaluation points on the road to success. For example, if a person's goal is to complete college with 120 credits within four years, it is essential to evaluate performance at the end of the first semester. The assessment of success requires answers to the question: Did you complete fifteen credits? If the answer is no, then it is essential to identify what were the factors that prevented the attainment this milestone.

We live in a country where every person has the potential for achieving any goal he desires. Each person is capable of developing a plan and working that plan to achieve the goal. There is an abundance of role models of all colors who have overcome formidable challenges and reached their goals. They did not permit disappointments or setbacks to affect their success. In fact, disappointments can serve to develop a greater motivation and strength to achieve.

Harriet Tubman, abolitionist and a conductor on the Underground Railroad, and a person with the will of steel did not let adversities get in her way of leading slaves to freedom. She was a fugitive slave and had a $40,000 reward for her capture. She eluded her captors and returned many times to the South to help other slaves escape to freedom. Tubman knew that freedom never was a reality for the fearful.

Jesse Brown, the first African American naval aviator, was born in Hattiesburg, Mississippi, on October 13, 1926. He spent his early life watching airplanes dust cotton crops. He was fascinated by these flying machines and dreamed of becoming a pilot while achieving his goal of earning a degree in engineering. While Brown and other African American boys and girls had never touched or sat in an airplane, he set his goal of being a pilot. He knew he could achieve his dream. Brown was aware of the Tuskegee Airmen who were the first African American military aviators in the United States during World War II. He was also aware of Lt. Quitman C. Walker of Indianola, Mississippi who graduated from flight training on January 14, 1943, at the Tuskegee Army Air Field in Alabama.

Brown was blessed to have parents who worked hard and encouraged young Jesse to dream. They told him, "Jesse you can be anything that you want to if you set your mind to it, work hard and get your education." He persisted and completed high school at the top of his class and went on to Ohio State University where he earned his engineering degree, becoming one of the first African Americans enrolled there.

Brown did not permit racism and discrimination to deter him from achieving his goal. He enlisted in the U. S. Navy in 1956 and became a midshipman. Sometime later, he took the test to become a pilot. He was told that no 'N*gger' could pass that test. He persisted and finally passed the test after about five attempts. Brown earned his pilot wings on October 21, 1949. He became the first African American Naval aviator to be involved in combat. On December 4, 1950 while on a close air support mission near the Battle of Chosin Reservoir also known as the Chosin Reservoir Campaign in North Korea, his plane was hit by enemy fire and crashed. He could not be rescued and died in his aircraft. Brown achieved his goal and his achievement provided hope for other African Americans that they could become a pilot and reach their desired goals.

Individuals who don't achieve their goals fail to believe in themselves. They often extinguish their special abilities to be and do great things. Our elders always taught us, "The easiest thing in life is to do nothing." Those individuals who were overwhelmed by adversities failed to achieve their goals. They perceive detours as reason to travel the road of least resistance and cease to reach their goals. They fail for they give up trying. Successful individuals view the valley of adversities as a light that guides them to their goals. We must persevere and not defer our dreams.

. Don't limit your challenges, challenge your limits.

. Don't quit. — A person should not give up when facing adversities

. Failing to plan is planning to fail. — The lack of planning is a sure way to fail.

. Follow your own star. — Set your sights on your personal goals.

. Hard work pays off.

. If there is a will, there is a way.

. In order to succeed, you must be willing to fail. — Failure is often the first step to success.

. Keep the faith. — Faith can move mountains.

.When God closes a door, he opens a window. — Faith in God always opens an exit to situations.

. You cannot soar with eagles when you are running with ducks.

 GOD

Our ancestors and elders had a special relationship with God, for He historically delivered them through life's obstacles. During slavery, our ancestors sang spirituals, which expressed their deep religious beliefs. Through songs, they were able to speak of life and death, suffering and sorrow and weary hearts. Spirituals such as Deep River, Roll, Jordan, Roll, Go down Moses, Didn't my Lord Deliver Daniel, Steal Away spoke of freedom and a place where they, as slaves, would be delivered from trials and tribulations.

The Tree of Love Gives Shade to All

We were taught that 'He guides us through the pathless sky.' Poet Gwendolyn Brooks captures the faith of our elders in God in these words: "He's the comfort/and wine and piccalilli for soul."

Some of us treat God like we treat family members, friends, and associates, calling on Him when we feel disconsolate, in need of emotional and financial assistance, and someone to listen to our troubles, and when we are sick. Convenience and circumstances seem to dictate their communication and relationship with God. More people appear to call on God when they are confronted with illness, failed relationships, economic difficulties and obstacles that seem to be insurmountable. Some people are like the Ethiopian Proverb: "One who recovers from a sickness forgets about God."

Our hearts should be filled with an ever-present special healing presence of God at all times. While some fail to acknowledge the presence of God in their lives and the healing power of His presence, He never abandons us but waits for our communication and supplication.

. Begin each morning with a talk with God. — Every day offers a special opportunity to talk with God.

. Don't ask God to guide your footsteps if you are not willing to move your feet.
  While we ask God to help us, we much make some efforts.

. Every evening I turn my worries to God. He is going to be up all night anyway.

. Every man should live under his own vine and fig tree.

. God can do anything but fail.

. God delays but does not forget.
  We may not get an immediate response from God, but He is always on time with his response.

. God does not bless mess.

. God does not have any stepchildren.

- God does not like ugly.

- God does not sleep.

- God's answers are wiser than our prayers.

- God gives bread to those who have no teeth.

- God gives food but does not cook it.

- God gives us two ears but only one mouth.

- God has no grandchildren.

- God helps the sailor, but he must row. — God expects us to follow His teachings and act upon them.

- God helps those who help themselves.

- God loves the buffalo.

- God makes three requests of his children. Do the best you can, where you are with what you have now.

- God moves in mysterious ways.

- God takes care of babies and fools.

- God said it. I believe it. That settles that.

- God tells us to burden Him with whatever burdens us.

- God willing and the creek don't rise.

- Help yourself and God will help you.

The Tree of Love Gives Shade to All

. I am sending up timber for my Lord. — I am offering prayers to God.

. If God had meant for us to go to the moon, he'd have given us wings.

. Live innocently. God is watching.

. Nothing is impossible for those who loves the Lord.

. Only one life, 'twill soon past. Only what's done for Christ will last.

. Our thanks to God should always precede our requests.

. Thank the Lord and bless the cook.

. The Lord helps those who help themselves.

. The Lord wants our precious time, not our spare time.

. The man who walks with God gets to his destination.

. Those who start the day on their knees generally go through it on their toes.

. Want to make God laugh? Tell him you've got plans.

. What God intends for you, you'll get.

. When God says today, the devil says tomorrow.

. When we lose God, it is not God who is lost.

. You've got to take God at his word. If you can believe it, you can receive it.

GOODNESS

. A clear conscience is a good pillow. — We rest easy when we do the right thing.

. Do all you can to be good and you'll be so. — Goodness is a virtue.

. Good works will never save you, but you cannot be saved without them.
Salvation is dependent on following God's teachings about good works.

GOSSIP

There are many synonyms for those who gossip: snoop, busybody, meddler, tattler, newsmonger, scandalmonger, muckraker, backbiter, and chatterbox. There is no other negative activity that consumes so much of a person's time as gossip. Gossip is always an unproductive activity and contributes absolutely nothing to one's personal health. Our elders used the proverb to teach us how to mind our business: "You have six months to mind your business and six months to leave other people's business alone."

Attending to the affairs of others demonstrates that one attempts to escape from his/her insecurities. The thoughts and opinions we have of others are no more than the deepest thoughts we have of ourselves. It is easier for some to criticize and talk about others rather than looking into their unplumbed mind and identify the 'garbage' that clogs their minds. Positive people are busy thinking healthy thoughts than to take the time to be concerned about the affairs of others. We must vanquish the negative feelings we have of others and work on ourselves.

. A dog that will bring a bone will carry a bone.
Be aware that those who bring us bad news will carry bad news.

. A gossiper is like an old shoe. Its tongue never stays in place.
A babbler incessantly wags his tongue.

. A groundless rumor often covers a lot of ground.

. Everyone that repeats it adds something to the scandal.
  A gossiper fancies himself in adding additional information to rumors.

. Gossiping and lying go together. — Truth is foreign to one who gossips.

. Gossip has been well defined as putting two and two together and making it five.

. Gossip needs no carriage.

. The difference between gossip and news depends on whether you hear it or tell it.

. Whisper something around.

GRATITUDE

. If you can't be thankful for what you receive, be careful for what you escape.

. Much obliged

. Thanks until you are better paid.

GREETINGS

. I have not seen you in a month of Sundays. — It has been a long time since we met.

GRIEF

. Don't cry because it's over, smile because it happened. We learn from adversities.

. Grief is satisfied and carried off by tears. — Tears soften our heartaches.

. Grief pent up will burst the heart. — It is important to express grief.

 **HAPPINESS**

. A cheerful countenance betokens a good heart.

. All happiness is in the mind. — Happiness is a state of mind.

. A happy heart is better than a full purse. — Money cannot buy happiness.

. Be happy for this moment. This moment is your life.

. Happiness is appreciating what you have; not getting what you want.

. Happiness is not having what you want, but wanting what you have.

. Happier than a pig in slop

. He who leaves his house in search of happiness pursues a shadow. Happiness is not found abroad.

. Some pursue happiness, others create it.

. The really happy man is one who can enjoy the scenery on a detour.

. You cannot always have happiness, but you can always give happiness. — Always share joy.

HATRED

As a child growing up in Mississippi, I was faced with love and hatred. Love was always evident in the African American community while hatred for African Americans was quite pronounced among white people. I recall asking my parents how were they able to love those who persecuted them and tried to treat them less than a human being. As church-going people, they did not hate people for it was not God-like. They believed that love was always the way to respond to ignorance and hatred. My parents directed me to the Bible in the passages of Proverbs 6: 16-19, which reads, "There are six things that the Lord hates, seven that are an abomination to him; haughty eyes, a lying tongue and hands that shed innocent blood, a heart that devises wicked plans, feet that make haste to run to evil, a false witness who breathes out lies, and one who sows discord among brothers."

Our ancestors had every reason to abhor those who enslaved them and treated them like animals. Somehow they were able to deal with servitude and have faith that one day they would be free. I believe their faith was the ultimate response to faith. I am not sure that I could have come through physical slavery without having a great desire to destroy those who persecuted me. My rebellious behavior would have certainly cost me my life.

I was a witness to the virulent hatred that some whites expressed toward African Americans during my childhood. The hatred and inequality heaped on African American goes back to slavery and was expressed in the adoption of Jim Crow Laws (enacted from 1876-1965) that established a racial caste system in the South and other parts of the country. Jim Crow was a pejorative expression which meant Negro. These laws were rules of racial etiquette where African Americans were required to demonstrate their inferior status to whites by actions, words and manners. The African Americans who "violated" these laws or rules of conducts were often lynched by a mob of white individuals. These mobs attacked and killed African Americans who sought the right to vote, work, and acquire an education. Statistics provided by the Archives at Tuskegee Institute reported nearly 3,500 African Americans were lynched in the United States between 1882 and 1964.

While lynching was prevalent throughout the south and the north, it only became a crime when the Civil Rights Act was passed in 1964. However the law was not always enforced in a number of cases.

There were injustices and punishments heaped on African Americans throughout history. African Americans were lynched for crimes that were no more than trumped up charges. Ku Klux Klan members terrorized black neighborhoods in their efforts to destroy the rights of black people. They were forbidden to vote although they had the constitutional right to vote.

African Americans lived in constant fear of being charged for their behavior toward white men and white women. Jim Crow laws required that African Americans step off the sidewalk when meeting whites. African American boys and men were expected to remove their caps and hats when talking with a white person. They were forbidden to look a white woman in the eyes, which could be construed as intimacy. Signs were prominently placed in public places and businesses that directed African Americans where to drink from a fountain; where to enter a café or restaurant; separate rest room facilities; and separate entrance for public transportation. Some establishments posted signs that read: "No Negroes and dogs are allowed in this business."

As a teenager in Mississippi in the 1950s and an adult in the 1960s, so many African American lives were lost at the hands of white men who were so fraught with anger. There was the murder of Rev. George Lee in Belzoni, Mississippi who was killed on May 2, 1955 for his effort in voter registration. On August 13, 1955 Lamar Smith of Brookhaven, Mississippi was murdered. Emmett Till was killed on August 28, 1955 in Money Mississippi for reportedly flirting with a white woman in a store. Willie Edwards of Montgomery, Alabama was mistaken for another man whom they believed was dating a white woman. Mack Charles Parker was lynched in Poplarville, Mississippi on April 25, 1959 by a white mob on who accused him of raping a white woman. Cpl. Roman Ducksworth, a military police officer was killed in Taylorsville, Mississippi on April 9,, 1962 when a group of whites mistakenly accused him of being a freedom rider. Medgar Evers, the director of the Mississippi NAACP operations, was assassinated in Jackson, Mississippi on June 12, 1963. Addie Mae Collins, Denise McNair, Carole Robertson, and Cynthia Wesley were killed in Birmingham, Alabama on September 15, 1963 when the Sixteenth Street Baptist Church was bombed by members of the Ku Klux Klan. James Earl Chaney, Andrew Goodman and Michael Henry Schwerner, civil rights workers, were killed by members of the Ku Klux Klan in Philadelphia, Mississippi on June 21, 1964. Vernon Dahmer, a wealthy African American businessman in Hattiesburg, Mississippi, died from the firebombing of his home on January 10, 1966. Dr. Martin Luther King was assassinated in Memphis, Tennessee at the Lorraine Motel in 1968. And the list goes of martyrs go on. The names of forty individuals (1954-1968) who lost their lives in the struggle for freedom for African Americans are inscribed on the Civil Rights Memorial, sponsored by the Southern Poverty Law Center, in Montgomery, Alabama.

While these horrible conditions existed, our parents and elders taught us to be polite, industrious, studious, good citizens, and a credit to the race. We were also taught to not hate others. They knew that the only way to overcome these adversities was to achieve at the highest level, leave Mississippi and forge a life up North where our parents and elders believed African Americans people were treated better and received more rights.

Several decades have passed since my childhood, I am reminded that hatred, discrimination, and prejudice continues to exist in Mississippi and other parts of

The Tree of Love Gives Shade to All

the country. While laws have been passed to give equal rights to African Americans, these laws did not change racist attitudes of some white people. I was distressed to discover that in 2011 there was the murder of James Craig Anderson, an African American man in Jackson, Mississippi by white teens from Brandon, Mississippi. Anderson died after he was beaten and run over by a truck driven by Deryl Dedmon. According to police, Dedmon was part of a group of seven white youth from largely white Rankin County who decided to "go f**k with some "N*ggers", after a night of partying and drinking. The teens ranged in age from 17 to 19 left their homes with the intention to harm and in this case, kill a black man." According to the FBI and federal prosecutors, "The young men made a sport of attacking African Americans because of the color of their skin and laughed about it."

Dedmon pleaded guilty to murder and a hate-crime and sentenced to two concurrent life terms. Dedmon and Dylan Wade Butler and John Aaron Rich pled guilty to federal hate crime charges. The judge in this case said, "This craven act isn't who we are." I agree with the judge's statement of this despicable crime. However, hatred of whites of blacks continues to be alive and well in Mississippi and other parts of our country. The Southern Poverty Law Center found that hate crimes were larger in Southern states. Their research indicates that there are 1,019 active hate groups in the United States. These statistics do not include the single cases of individuals who commit hate crimes.

Hate crimes against African Americans are prevalent throughout the country. Of the 7,624 hate crimes reported nationwide in 2007, the most recent year for which data is available, 34 percent (2,659) were perpetrated against African Americans. On Election Night 2008, three white men in Staten Island, New York, drove to a predominantly African American neighborhood "to find African Americans to assault." These men beat a 17 year-old African American with a metal pipe and a collapsible police baton. After this assault, they continued their hate crime spree and crashed their car into a man whom they thought was African American. The victim remained in a coma for several weeks.

During the 1990s, there were several African American churches burned in the South. According to the *Washington Post* (1996), "the people burning down black churches in the South are generally white male and young, usually economically marginalized or poorly educated, frequently drunk or high on drugs, rarely affiliated with white hate groups, but often deeply driven by racism." On November 5, 2008, three white men burned the predominantly African American Macedonia Church of God in Christ in Springfield, Massachusetts after the election of President Barack Obama.

The hatred of African Americans appears to be the cause of the recent murder of Trayvon Martin in Sanford, Florida. Martin was killed by a neighborhood watchman, George Zimmerman, who believed he was suspicious. It appears that this young man was simply walking home from a local convenience store where he bought a pack of skittles and an iced tea. Martin was wearing a hoodie at the time and it is believed that the perpetrator stereotyped him as a nuisance and a thief. Florida's Stand Your Ground Law gave Zimmerman the authority to shoot and kill this kid whom he thought was a threat. While Zimmerman was advised by a 911 operator to not follow Martin, he continued to hunt him down like prey. After 45 days, Zimmerman was charged with second degree murder.

On April 6, 2012, the African American community of Tulsa, Oklahoma was terrorized when two white men, Jake (Jacob) England, 19, and Alvin Watts, 32, shot five African Americans at random, killing three and injuring two others. According to some accounts, Jake England sought revenge for the murder of his father a few years ago. His father, Carl England, hit Pernell Jefferson with a stick and knocked him to the ground. Jefferson pulled out a gun and shot England in the chest killing him. Jefferson was convicted on May 27, 2010 of feloniously pointing a firearm and is serving a six-year term in an Oklahoma prison.

. Return love for hate.

. That which you hate is to be done to you.

. You can only love or hate about someone else what you love or hate about yourself.

HEALING

As a child, I frequently heard my mother sing, "There is a balm in Gilead, to make the wounded whole. There is a balm in Gilead to heal the sin-sick soul." She expressed the belief that for every pain, suffering, and adversity, there was a balm or salve to heal the soul.

. There is a balm in Gilead.

. There is a salve for every sore. — There is a balm for every pain.

HEALTH

. Health is better than wealth. — Wealth without health is disease.

. He/she is a bag of bones. — It is an extremely thin person.

. Like death warmed up. — A person appears very ill or tired.

. Rheumatism and happiness both get bigger if you keep telling folks about them.

. Rheumatism doesn't help at the log rolling.

. There are no riches like health. — Health is wealth.

. You'll never catch a cold if you catch the first rain of spring.

HISTORY

Our parents and elders taught their children about the history and remarkable achievements of our people. They shared stories passed on by their ancestors about slavery, the struggles African Americans faced after slavery, the period of reconstruction, and the resilience of our people who were successful in their efforts to become self-sufficient. Our elders were aware that we would never learn the positive stories about black people in any textbook or publication at the time. They were aware that our history was overlooked and the purpose of this failure was to have African Americans feel inferior to whites.

Our elders believed in the African American Proverb: "Each one teach one." Our elders knew that the knowledge and understanding and application of our history would instill pride, stimulate motivation and develop a strong desire to continue the progress of our elders. While no books in the South shared that former slaves were able to build homes, own land, construct schools, help others learn how to read and write, and create inventions to ease the tedium of farm work.

Our elders introduced us to proud stories of African American achievement to destroy the myths that African Americans never achieved greatness. We were informed that two African American men were U. S. senators from Mississippi during Reconstruction. Hiram Rhodes Revels was appointed in 1870 to serve the unexpired terms of Jefferson Davis, who was the president of the Confederacy. Blanche Kelso Bruce was the second African American sent to the U.S. Senate in 1875. Bruce was the first black to serve a full term in the U. S. Senate. John R. Lynch represented the state of Mississippi in the U. S. Congress. We were also taught that more than 225 black Mississippians held public office during Reconstruction.

Our elders became our history books as they told us about the contributions of African Americans. They were aware that these lessons were important in uplifting our spirits and never feeling less than anyone else. My paternal grandfather, a teacher and successful farmer, idolized Carter G. Woodson and his efforts to right the wrongs of writers of history. Grandpa Joe shared Woodson's profound quotation about the importance of history. Woodson wrote, "Those who have no record of their forebears have accomplished are the inspiration which comes from the teaching of biography and history." My grandfather shared the book, *Mis-Education of the Negro*, which presented the importance of teaching African American history and the knowledge of how our people made great contributions to this country — lessons that are missing from the pages of history written by the outside world.

We must teach our children and youth about their history and the contributions they have made in the development of this country. African American history must be taught throughout the year by highlighting the scope of African Americans' achievements in every subject area. While Black History month is celebrated each year, I am convinced that there is a critical need to share the contributions of African Americans daily in the schools of America.

I was reminded in the late 1990s that many of youth have no knowledge of their history when I was a counselor in a middle school in Detroit, Michigan. As an enrichment activity, I asked the students to name three African American inventors. In a group of thirty students, only two could name three inventors. I recognized that I had to do something about their lack of knowledge and begin writing books about African Americans. Consequently, I wrote three books: *African American Inventors, African American Women Scientists and Inventors,* and *African American Millionaires.*

After retiring from public school education, I became a professor of Education and Psychology at a historically African American university. One night I took my stamp collection of African Americans depicted on postage stamps and the Booker T. Washington and George Washington Carver coins. My graduate students had no idea that between 1946 and 1951, eighteen different coins were made featuring Booker T. Washington and from 1951 to 1954, a dozen coins were struck by the U. S. Mint to honor George Washington Carver and Booker T. Washington together. "I didn't know there was ever a coin portraying African American on U. S. coins," was the response of my students. Although African Americans have been commemorated on U. S. postage stamps since 1942 when Booker T. Washington was honored on a postage stamp and a number of other African Americans have been honored throughout the years, my students were not knowledgeable about these events. Their lack of knowledge is a testament to the need to write more books about our history and introduce children at the earliest ages to our sterling contributions to the world.

. History is her story, too.

. Yesterday is history, tomorrow is a mystery. Today is a gift. That is why it is called present.

HOME

. Home is where the heart is.

. There is no place like home even if it is a cellar. No matter how humble, home is a special place.

. Travel east or travel west, a man's own home is still the best. — There is no place like home

HONESTY

. An honest countenance is the best passport.

. An honest man is not the worse because a dog barks at him.

. He is the wise man who is the honest man. — Honesty is a virtue.

. Put money in thy purse, but put it honestly. — Make sure money earned is honest.

HOPE

When I was a child, my parents told me a story about hope, which has been indelibly implanted in my mind throughout life. My paternal and maternal great-great grandparents were freed from slavery in 1865 in the Piney Woods region of southern Mississippi. The plantation owner called them together and told them they had a choice to continue working on the plantation or leave. He reminded them that if they left they would be on their own with no support from him. They would have to "root, hog, or die," which meant they would suffer and eventually die. With no more than tattered clothes on their bodies, they walked barefooted with hope and an abiding faith in God to land the color of clay that whites thought was unproductive. My great-great grandfather Levin Booth led a group of slaves to the area of Hopewell in Covington County, Mississippi. As he led the group, he reminded them that "The trials awaiting us will seem like nothing to our physical enslavement." Hope broke the yoke of heartache and despair of their past lives as they walked toward freedom. I am convinced that God fertilized this barren land and made it productive for former slaves. Slaveholders believed and forecasted that within a few weeks the slaves would return meekly to the plantations and beg on bended needs to their former "masters" for assistance. The slaves were undaunted with their prophecy. Our ancestors demonstrated courage and resourcefulness and armed with the spiritual support of God they worked hard and created a community that would bring self-sufficiency for its inhabitants.

After Reconstruction in the South, a number of laws were instituted to deny the rights of African Americans. There were laws where African Americans were arrested for spitting, drinking, loitering, vagrancy, gambling and other charges that criminalize African Americans. These trumped up charges led to the incarceration of many African American men and women. Once they were sentenced to jail or prison they were used as convict laborers and were leased out to private owners.

After the Civil War, the South's predominantly agriculture economy was in shambles. Fields had been burned and the primary engine of the economy of slaves was gone. Former slave holders needed laborers to farm the land. They were desperate to get freedmen and poor whites back in the cotton fields. Sharecropping was instituted to entice former slaves to return to the land. White planters or landowners assigned each family a small tract of land to farm. Tenants were provided food, clothing, shelter, seeds, supplies and farm equipment. After crops were harvested the landowner took the cotton to market and deducted what was called "furnish" money to sharecroppers. Sharecroppers were supposed to receive half of the proceeds. Some sharecroppers who expected shares of the proceeds found themselves deeply indebted for the next year's crop. This was a ploy by whites to keep sharecroppers in a state of peonage.

The English words peon and peonage were derived from the Spanish word meaning a person with little authority who is assigned to unskilled and drudgerous tasks.

The sharecropping system bound African American families to the land. Planters often shortchanged their sharecroppers as they were uneducated and could not read or write. Some sharecroppers were taken advantage of in this situation. Sharecropping, was a form of tenancy, was like slavery without legal sanctions.

It appears that all of my maternal ancestors chose freedom and left their former slaveholders. Alf Sullivan, my paternal great-grandfather chose to stay with Pappy Tom Sullivan, his slaveholder in Mize, Mississippi in Smith County. It should be noted that for a long time there were no African Americans living in or near Mize, Mississippi. The town acquired the name "No N*gger, Mississippi." When Alf died, he was buried under a large oak tree. Alf's son Frank and Frank's son, Otho Sullivan chose freedom and left the Sullivan Plantation.

With their intense faith in God and prayers for the blessings of food, clothing, shelter, and health, our ancestors settled on land, which they named Hopewell, rooted in their belief that hope springs eternal. They chose strength and affirmed that their fortitude and spirit would see them through the transition to freedom. They prospered. With the spiritual support of God, their intense faith in prayer and hard work, they knew they would survive. Their work as slaves and skills they possessed prepared them to make a life with the most meager tools and supplies.

The former slaves grew bountiful crops, which provided food for their families and shared with their neighbors. They made clothing from flour, feed and fertilizer sacks that were as well-made and fashionable as those sold in general stores. They foraged the fields to find plants and herbs for medicine to treat and cure disease and illness. They constructed sturdy homes from logs and other materials found in nature. These former slaves were proficient in building antebellum homes for slaveholders with large Doric, Ionic and Corinthian columns and surely they were able to build houses for themselves.

A number of freed slaves were granted land under the Homestead Act, which became effective on the same day President Lincoln issued the Emancipation Proclamation. African Americans were required to start living on any land they claimed within six months of claiming it. They were also not allowed to legally own any other piece of land and could not be absent from their land for more than six months within any given year. Upon establishing residency on land for five years and meeting the requirement of developing agriculture and building a living structure, the individual became eligible to own the land. The General Land Office issued the deed to the property if all requirements were met.

My maternal great-great grandfather Levin Booth was awarded 80 acres and 9/10th of an acre on March 23, 1892 by the U. S. General Land Office in Jackson, Mississippi. My paternal great-grandmother Mary Sullivan, the widow of Alf Sullivan, was granted 79 acres and 87/100th of an acre on May 20, 1897. The land was granted pursuant to the Act of Congress approved on May 29, 1862.

It should be noted that slaves built many of the historical buildings in our country. The great majority of the construction at Mount Vernon where George Washington lived was performed by slaves. Slaves helped to construct the U. S. Capitol serving as carpenters, brick masons, plasterers, glazers and painters. These slaves were 400 of the 600 workers who helped build the U. S. Capitol. Slaves were rented from plantations in Virginia, Maryland and the District of Columbia.

The White House, the residence of our president and his family, was built by slaves. They were slaves with the names of Tom, Peter, Ben, Harry and Daniel. The historical home of Montpelier, residence of the father of the Constitution, was built by slaves. Monticello, the home of Thomas Jefferson was also constructed by slaves who worked as brick masons, carpenters, blacksmiths, brick layers and stone masons.

Hope is a special part of our being. Some accept it while others refuse it. Hope runs through the precious and life-saving vessels in our hearts and minds. Hope sparks our dreams, germinates our creativity, enriches our thoughts, illuminates our spiritual journeys, fuels our aspirations and cultivates an insatiable desire for positive thoughts, opinions, beliefs, and truth that change our lives and foster peace of mind. We need to relentlessly feed hope with actions. There are times when we might feel like giving up and abscond from challenges, but hope prevails and extinguishes these thoughts. Hope is a partner of prayer that enables us to achieve dreams, reach goals, spread joy, kindness and live healthier lives. Romans 12:12 teaches us, "Be joyful in hope, patient in affliction, faithful in prayer."

. Faith is like electricity. You can't see it, but you can see the light.

. Hope ends when you stop believing. — Faith gives us strength to have hope.

. Hope is grief's best music.

. Hope is putting faith to work when doubting would be easier.

. Hope is the last thing to abandon the unhappy.

. Hope is the poor man's bread.

. Hope sees the invisible, fills the intangible and achieves the impossible. Hope transcends adversities.

. Never deprive someone of hope – it may be all they have.

. Prepare for the worst and hope for the best

. To hope is not to demand

. When the world says, give up, hope whispers; try it one more time. Never give up on hope.

. You've got to root, hog or die.

 HUGS

Many of the perceived problems we face each day could be effectively handled or even ignored if we just took the time out of each day to hug ourselves. We need to wake up to each day with a special time to pamper ourselves, appreciate ourselves and love ourselves. I am convinced that we cannot be a comforter to others, appreciate them and love them if we don't take time to work on ourselves. We all deserve a personal hug. We owe it to ourselves and it is a special greeting to God for what He has created.

We must cease saying we are too busy to do a little something special for ourselves each day. When we practice hugging ourselves, we give quality time to loving ourselves, which allows us to hug and love others. Start your day by preparing that special cup of tea or coffee or glass of milk. Sit down in a comfortable chair and allow yourself to relax for a few minutes. Meditate and pray for personal abundance for you and others. Affirm that this day and other days will be healthier and spiritual. Put on your favorite CD or DVD and take a few minutes to listen to the soothing music. Slowly move into your day with a pampering bath with the bath salts or oils that invigorate you. Never! Never! Interrupt your hugging time to jump out of the tub to answer the phone or answer the door bell. Hug yourself after you get out of the tub or shower. Look into the mirror and appreciate everything about your body and how wonderful you are created in the image of God.

Affirm that you love everything about your personal gift from God and claim, "I am strong, good, kind, helpful, special and important and I express this goodness in the lives of others that I touch each day." Take the time to select an outfit that expresses your calmness, love and joy. Hug yourself again. Walk out the door and stop to acknowledge all of God's creation, the flowers, trees, birds, squirrels and other creatures. Notice how they are hugging themselves.

The Tree of Love Gives Shade to All

Take the time to touch that tree, which brings you the pleasant breezes. Reach out to the flowers that are bedecked in their holiday clothes. Let the fragrance of the flowers remind you of how sweet it is to rise to another day and do great and good things. Listen to the birds that are singing, an expression of how they hug themselves.

When you hug yourself, you take the time to nourish your soul, the mind where you have planted and nurtured good seeds. Each time we hug ourselves we hug God and express our love for Him and respect the wonderful and healing spirit of the Omnipotent One. A daily dose of hugging yourself embraces and nourishes your spirit and allows you to hug others with love, words, compassion, humility, kindness, meekness and goodness. Each hug empowers us to live life more abundantly. So if you haven't hugged yourself today, do it now and experience the special healing power of this gesture.

. A hug is like a bandage to a hurting wound.

. A hug is a handshake from the heart.

. A hug is worth a thousand words.

. A mom's hug lasts long after she lets go.

. Happiness is an unexpected hug.

. Have you hugged yourself today?

. Hugs are the universal medicine.

. Hugs grease the wheels of the world.

. Nobody will think you're somebody, if you don't think so yourself

. You can't give a hug without getting a hug.

. You can't wrap love in a box, but you wrap a person in a hug.

Otha Richard Sullivan

IDENTITY

Our elders told empowering stories about our ancestors. They knew that the history books and other documentations would fail to reveal the many contributions of African Americans. Our elders felt the importance of sharing with children and youth about the slaves who helped to build some of the most magnificent buildings throughout America. Their sweat and toil moved them to create inventions to lessen the tedium of work. While they were not able to receive patents for their inventions because they were considered property, many slaves created a number of inventions.

We were taught about the strength and resilience of our ancestors which made them some of the strongest people in the world. They triumphed over suffering. While attempts were made to enslave their minds, they kept their thoughts of freedom and maintained their feelings about humanity and justice. Our elders spent considerable time uplifting children by telling them they were made in the image of God and that God never made any trash. They were acutely aware of the many stereotypes and depictions of blacks, which perpetuated the beliefs by whites that African Americans were unattractive, had nappy hair, and looked like some animals.

I was blessed to have a maternal grandfather who was a school administrator in a small school in Covington County, Mississippi. Grandpa Joe gave me books by W.E. B. Du Bois, James Weldon Johnson and other African American writers. He introduced me to Dr. Carter G. Woodson's book, *The Mis-Education of the Negro*. This book highlighted the fact that the education system of America failed to present authentic Negro History in schools and there was a scarcity or complete lack of literature available of our history. My grandfather knew that the books we used in segregated schools, which were handed down from white schools, gave no space to the contributions of black people. He knew that the way black people were depicted in books showed them in menial jobs, subordinate roles, and as buffoons.

The history textbooks approved and accepted by the Mississippi textbook adoption presented numerous lies about the condition of African Americans and the adversities they faced. I recall the textbook about Mississippi I used as a high school student was *Mississippi: A History* by John K. Bettersworth, a professor and administrator at Mississippi State University. As a junior high school student, I was appalled to read that the Ku Klux Klan was portrayed in a positive light as individuals who protected people. Our textbooks provided us with little to be proud of as African Americans. The books we used in our classroom led us to believe that slaves were happy, without a care in the world.

One of the biggest lies cited in our textbooks was the South won the Civil War. And, God forbid that there was any citation that African Americans fought as Union soldiers. By the end of the Civil War, roughly 179,000 African American men (10% of the Union Army served as soldiers in the U. S. Army) and another 19,000 African Americans served in the Navy. African American soldiers were involved in the Battle at Port Hudson, Louisiana on May 27, 1863; in the battle at Fort Wagner, South Carolina on July 18, 1868; the battle at New Market Heights, Virginia in 1864; and the battle at Petersburg, Virginia.

The history textbooks presented false information of the role of African Americans in the Confederate army during the Civil War. I recall a section of one textbook that cited that thousands of southern African Americans fought in the Confederate ranks and wanted to help preserve the "Southern Way of Life." This was not true as the Confederacy banned African American soldiers from its armies until they were desperate at the end of the war.

I recall a visit to the Vicksburg, Mississippi, National Park when I was in junior high school. This field trip was funded by the all-white school board in Hattiesburg, Mississippi. I did not want to go on this field trip for I knew that there were no African Americans honored or monuments for African Americans. It would be some 45 years later that a monument was erected to honor African American soldiers when three African American figures depicted two Union soldiers representing the 1st and 3rd Mississippi Infantries. This monument was proposed by the African American mayor of Vicksburg in 1999 and was dedicated on February 14, 2004. Of the 1,300 monuments in the park, this is the first to honor African Americans and the only one in a Civil War battlefield administered by the National Park Service.

Our textbooks failed to share that a number of slave rebellions occurred in this country. Based on the textbooks I read as a school child in Mississippi told the story that slaves were treated well. From these textbooks, we were led to believe that the life of the Negro lived as a slave was much better than that which he had lived in Africa. The reality is that none of this information was true and portrayed slaves as being happy, well-kept, well-fed individuals. Textbook authors at the time were like ante-bellum defenders of plantation slavery. Ethel Knight, author of *Echo of The Black Horn* (1951) described slavery as "a benevolent institution in which masters cared for and civilized a race when their ancestors boiled and ate their sons" (284).

There was no mention of the slave rebellions in our textbooks for whites felt this information would cause blacks to rebel. There was Gabriel Prosser in Virginia in 1800; Denmark Vessey in Charleston, South Carolina in 1822; and Nat Turner in Southampton County, Virginia in 1831. This information was considered to be contraband like bringing in forbidden items to prisoners.

We were not left in the dark about our history and current events of African Americans as the *Chicago Defender* newspaper served to increase our knowledge of the contributions of African Americans. These newspapers were brought into the community by Pullman car porters on trains that traversed the south. The purpose of the falsehoods in our textbooks and lack of information was to continue to relegate African American people to a lower class.

White people did not want African Americans to know there were U.S. coins that depicted African Americans. This awareness would cause African Americans to have a great sense of pride for recognition. They preferred to have us know about the Confederate States of American dollars that depicted African Americans chopping and picking cotton in an endless field. Between 1946 and 1951, eighteen different commemorative coins were issued by the U.S. Mint featuring Booker T. Washington, founder of Tuskegee Institute. From 1951 to 1954, a dozen coins were struck by the Mint that depicted the busts of George Washington Carver and Booker T. Washington.

James W. Loewen, who first taught at Tougaloo College, a historically black college and the coauthor of *The Lies My Teacher Told Me*, wrote the first integrated state-history textbook: *Mississippi: Conflict and Change*. This book tried to right the wrongs on previous Mississippi History textbooks in 1974. Loewen's book was rejected by the state textbook adoption committee because it presented a picture of a lynching, contained too much African American history, and dealt with too much recent history. Loewen sued the state and during the trial, the Deputy Attorney General of Mississippi asked John Turnipseed, one of the board members who rejected Loewen's book, to turn to page 178 where there was a photograph of a lynching. As a defense for the rejection of the book, he said, "Now you know, some 9th-graders are pretty big...especially black male 9th-graders. And we worried, or at least I worried that teachers — especially white lady teachers — would be unable to control their classes with materials like this in the book." (Loewen, 2009)

The Tree of Love Gives Shade to All

In the First Amendment case, *Loewen vs. Turnipseed*, the judge ordered Mississippi to adopt the book for the standard six-year period and supply it to any school system that requested it like any other adopted book. The textbook was finally accepted by the state adoption committee in 1980, five years after it was published.

Our youth need to know the contributions and achievements of African Americans. This information will inform them that African Americans have made great strides in spite of the obstacles they faced. They need to know that Jean Baptiste Point du Sable was the first known settler in the area which is now Chicago, Illinois. Their knowledge of James Derham was the first African American to formally practice medicine in the United States in 1783. They can be inspired by the knowledge that Macon Allen was the first African American licensed to practice law in the United States. Our youth can be motivated to know that Alexander L. Twilight was the first African American male to receive a college degree, graduating from Middlebury College (Middlebury, Vermont) in 1823. They can be dreamers by knowing that James McCune Smith received a bachelor's degree in 1835, master's degree in 1836 and medical degree in 1837 from the University of Glasgow (Scotland). They can aspire to enter politics by knowing that Lieutenant Governor of Louisiana Pickney Benton Stewart was the first non-white and first person of African American descent became governor of Louisiana on December 9, 1872.

There continues to be lies in textbooks about the status of African Americans throughout the history of this country. Some textbooks fail to share the real horrors of slavery, the horrible treatment of slaves, the reasons for the civil war and other historical information. In 2010, the Texas State Board of Education composed of Christian evangelists and social conservatives has adopted a new social studies curriculum for students. This new curriculum rewrites history that diminishes the science of evolution as well as the civil rights movement and the horrors of slavery while glorifying the south.

Our teachers who were all African American introduced us to African American History. While this teaching was not condoned by white superintendents, they refused to adhere to this edict. These teachers were for the most part better educated than their white counterparts. They held more advanced degrees than white teachers. This was accomplished by them receiving grants in aid to study at northern prestigious colleges and universities as there were no historically black colleges that offered a master's or doctorate degree. At the time a black person could not attend a white college in Mississippi until James Meredith integrated the University of Mississippi in 1962. Through their travels and exposure to the rest of the world, they brought to the classroom so much information about the contributions of our people.

Public libraries and college and university libraries did not have books by African American writers. Most of the books were censored and banned for reading and those who read these books were considered to be subversive. During my public school education, I do not recall any books being sold by W. E. B. Du Bois, Richard Wright, Ralph Ellison and other African American authors. Richard Wright, the author of books, novels, poems and short stories presented themes about the plight of African Americans during the late 19th to mid-20th Centuries. Wright was the author of *Uncle Tom's Children; Native Son;* and *Black Boy.* Whites regarded Richard Wright as a communist and "Destroyer of the Southern Way of Life." Theodore Bilbo a U. S. Senator from Mississippi, former governor of the state, and member of the Ku Klux Klan was so incensed with Wright's *Black Boy.* On June 27, 1945, he denounced the book on the U. S. Senate floor: "It's purpose is to plant devilment and trouble breeding in the days to come in the mind and heart of every American Negro...It is the dirtiest, filthiest, lousiest, most obscene piece of writing that I have ever seen in print. I would hate to have a son or daughter of mine permitted to read it; it so filthy and so dirty. But it comes from a Negro and you cannot expect any better from a person of his type."

Bilbo was the author of *Take Your Choice: Segregation or Mongrelization.* He like other white people believed that African Americans were inferior and defended segregation. During the 1928 presidential election, he helped Al Smith carry the state of Mississippi by claiming that Herbert Hoover had a relationship with an African American woman. Bilbo asserted in an article on the front page of the *Oelwein Daily Register* (Oelwein, Iowa, October 18, 1928) that Herbert Hoover during a visit to Mississippi in 1927 insisted that his train be routed through the all-black town of Mount Bayou, Mississippi, to visit with Mrs. Mary Booze whom he referred to as a negress and as black as an ace of spade. He claimed that Hoover danced with her in an intimate manner. Despite Bilbo's allegation, Herbert Hoover won the presidential election. Some historians have alleged Bilbo had a relationship with an African American woman, which was a fact from the "Founding Father" President Thomas Jefferson to Senator Strom Thurmond and beyond.

I was the recipient of the state of Mississippi grant upon finishing high school in 1960. At the time I planned to study social work. This type of degree was not offered at a historically African American college and I qualified for this program. Other undergraduate African American students took advantage of these grants when they planned to major in a field for which there was no in-state equivalent to which white Mississippians had access.

Our elders told their children stories about slavery and how our people were able to overcome the most heinous conditions in the history of this country. The purpose of these discussions was to inform children that black people possessed tremendous intelligence and an incredible spiritual strength to overcome countless adversities. In keeping with the mission to portray blacks as inferior, white people and the books they published presented falsehoods about African American intelligence and their moral worth. Our people were incessantly demeaned and devalued. Consequently, our elders felt a responsibility in helping children and youth know their history and the many accomplishments in spite of the odds placed against them. They knew this knowledge and understanding would assist a younger generation deal with racism and instill a strong identity in them.

Segregation and stereotypes were detrimental to the development of some African Americans, leading them to falsely believe that they were inferior to white people. These beliefs were evident in the research of Dr. Kenneth Clark and his wife who conducted studies in the 1930's and 1040's with the experiment involving two dolls. African American children were shown two dolls and asked about their preference. Both dolls were completely identical except the skin color and hair color. One doll was white with yellow hair, while the other doll was brown with black hair. The child was asked questions inquiring as to which one is the doll they would play with, which one is the nice doll, which one looks bad, and which one has the nicer color. The researchers found African American children often chose to play with the white dolls more than the black ones. When the children were asked to fill in a human figure with the color of their own skin, they frequently chose a lighter shade than their own skin color. The children gave the color "white" positive attributes like good and pretty. They referred to the black doll as being bad and ugly.

The experiment showed a clear preference for the white doll by all children in the study. These findings exposed internalized racism in African American children's self-hatred that was more acute among children attending segregated schools. This study also showed how these children viewed their own identity.

This study was recreated by filmmaker Kim Davis in 2006. Despite the many changes in some parts of society, Davis found the same results as the Drs. Clark.

We can never become healthy individuals and find the special peace of mind that comes from an appreciation of the physical features that God gave us. Our people spend hundreds of millions of dollars on skin whitening creams, moisturizers, hair products, weaves and the special interest in purchasing expensive Indian Remy hair. Too many individuals fail to realize their beauty and the special beauty that resides in them.

When we feel insecure about the texture of our hair, the color of our skin, and our physique, it causes some to believe they are unattractive and less than others who they fitfully admire the attributes of others. Some individuals spend more time using beauty product, keeping hair and nail appointments, and seeking corrective measure so their physical appearance, than spending time on filling their hearts, minds and soul with positive thinking, which promote good health.

Research by Target Market News found that African Americans had a buying power of more than $587 billion. These individuals spent $7.4 billion on personal care product; $29.3 billion on apparel products and services; and $321 million on books. While some African Americans struggle to keep food on the table and buy school supplies for their children, they spend a lot of money on keeping their hairstyle "tight" and keeping the "kitchens" tamed.

The emphasis placed on hair products goes back to slavery. During slavery, slave masters and mistresses often told children to refer to their hair as wool and encouraged young slaves not to like their own hair. This feeling has been perpetuated to many of today's African Americans. I have often heard some blacks talk about "good" hair. Of course, any hair is good. "Good" hair was used to refer to the texture of a slave's hair, which was the result of miscegenation where white men impregnated black women and produced hair that was similar to the texture of Caucasians.

Chris Rock produced a moved entitled "Good Hair." He decided to make this movie when one of his daughters asked him why she didn't have "good hair." He knew what she really meant. It was "Why don't I have "white hair?"

While it is important to project an attractive appearance, true beauty comes from the pride, confidence and spirituality one possesses and share with others. We are often victimized when we permit others to define beauty for us. No cosmetic products, hot comb, hair relaxer, hair color, skin bleaching cream and hair weaves can make anyone beautiful. Beauty is inward and expresses itself externally.

The Tree of Love Gives Shade to All

Stop hating what the Good Lord gave you. He didn't create anything ugly. Your feelings of ugliness are a state of mind that desperately needs spiritually repairing with the tools of positive thoughts and actions.

. A good name is a second inheritance.

. A leopard doesn't change its spots.

. A tree is known by its fruit. — A person is judged by his actions and deeds.

. Birds of a feather flock together. — Individuals with similar interests or taste stick together.

. Blood is thicker than water. — Family bonds are closer than those of outsiders.

. Don't forget where you came from. — We should never forget our roots.

. Don't toot your own horn.

. Every man thinks his own copper gold.

. He/she is crazy as a road lizard.

. I'd rather be a lamppost in Harlem than the governor of Georgia.

. If you really do put a small value upon yourself, rest assured that the world will not raise your price.

. It is a poor dog that doesn't wag its own tail.

. It takes one to know one.

. Keep your own counsel. — Keep one's thoughts and plans to oneself.

. Never despise a bridge which carries you safely over.

. Nobody will think you're somebody, if you don't think so yourself.

. Nothing ruins a duck but its bill.

. Oil and water don't mix. — Certain people or characteristics do not go together.

. Separate the sheep from the goats. — Sort out the good from the bad.

. Separate the wheat from the chaff.

. The pot can't call the kettle black.

. Water seeks its own level. — Quality people find each other and low quality people find each other.

. What can you expect from a hog but a grunt?

. When there is no enemy within, the enemies outside cannot hurt you.

. You are known by the company you keep. — We are defined by our relationships.

. You can't make a silk purse out of a sow's ear. You can't make something superior out of inferior material.

IGNORANCE

. Don't measure my bushel by your pint.

. He can't punch one's way out of a paper bag.

. He is dumb as a glass plate.

. He is not wrapped too tight.

- He is one sandwich short of a picnic.

- He is thick as two bricks.

- His elevator doesn't go to the top.

- His shortcoming is his long staying.

- If stupid was dirt he'd cover an acre.

- Ignorance is a voluntary misfortune. — A person makes a choice to be unenlightened.

- If you buy a rainbow, don't pay cash for it.

- Lights are on, but nobody's home — A person is not smart.

- Not playing with a full deck. — A person has limited ability.

- Pigs don't know what a pen's for.

- She's up the creek without a paddle. — A person is not prepared.

- She's so dumb she has to reach into her chest to count to two.

- Stupidity doesn't kill you, but it sure makes you sweat.

- The loss that is not known is no loss.

- When the blind leads the blind, the two fall in the ditch.

- You're so dumb, you can't throw rain water out of a boot, and the directions say how.

- You can send a fool to school, but you can't make him think. One must desire an education.

ILLNESS

. He/she is kicking, but not high. — A person is not feeling his/her best.

INDEPENDENCE

Our elders taught us that we should never be beholding to anyone for to do so would mean being controlled by others. They emphasized independence. We were always taught to stand on our own feet and refuse to look to others to save us from our circumstances.

. Every tub has to stand on its own bottom. — Everyone should be independent.

INDUSTRY

. Industry is the parent of fortune. — Persistence is a prerequisite for abundance.

. Morning is welcome to the industrious.

INJUSTICE

African Americans have faced injustice since colonial times through the 21st Century. One of the greatest injustices was enslavement. After the Emancipation Proclamation, some rights were guaranteed to African Americans during the Reconstruction period in this country. After Reconstruction, these rights were taken away. African Americans were exposed to horrific conditions, particularly under the black codes that existed throughout the south. One of the injustices was the arrest of African Americans for trumped up charges for vagrancy, adultery, and incarcerated and used as convict laborers in a state of peonage. The incarceration and forced servitude was the beginning of the disproportionate imprisonment of African Americans that continue to exist today.

 INTEGRITY

Integrity has always been one of the most important lessons of African Americans and to be exemplary in their character. Our elders always taught their children to be honest and have character that represented the best integrity. I recall that dishonesty, immorality and a lack of character were considered to be the most egregious acts.

INTELLIGENCE

. He/she is a lost ball in high weeds. — A person is totally confused.

. He/she is wet behind the ears. — A person is inexperienced and naïve.

. Not playing with a full deck. — A person lacks skills and abilities.

. You don't know the half of it.
    To know some facts but don't know how bad the situation is.

JEALOUSY

. Jealousy is a disease of the weak. — Jealousy is one of the Cardinal sins.

JOY

. Abandon things that steal your joy.

. Enjoy the little things, for one day you may look back and realize they were the big things.

. Everyone smiles in the same language.

. Happiness is merely the remission of pain.

. Joy is not in things, it is in us. — Joy comes from within.

. Learn what it is that steals your joy. Find a way to remove it from your life.

. Mirth and motion prolong life. — A long life requires joy and movement.

. The sun shines for all in the world.

JUDGE

Howard Thurman wrote, "It is very easy to sit in judgment upon the behavior of others, but often difficult to realize that every judgment is a self-judgment. None of us is in a position to judge others. We are not perfect. Judgment is a job for God and according to the traditional expression, "God has no grandchildren." We are not the benchmark of what is acceptable, appropriate, right, and what promotes social, emotional, physical and financial health for others. The African Proverb, "If God made him, man can find some use for him," speaks to the importance of all individuals.

Scripture teaches us about how we are to judge others. In Matthew 7:6, we are taught, "Do not give dogs what is sacred; do not throw your pearls to pigs. If you do they may trample them under their feet, and then turn and tear you to pieces." This scripture admonishes us to be discerning and wise in how we judge. The truth is we all have to be able and willing to judge from what is right and wrong. We are cautioned to be careful about the standards we use to judge people. My grandfather taught me a lesson about this scripture which was why give advice to a friend about their sin or problem of your unresolved sin or problem is greater than their problems.

Countless individuals spend their lives filled with negative thoughts, opinions, and assessments of others that impair them and keep them in the valley filled with stones that they throw at others to disguise their insecurities. None of us is in a position to judge others. We are not perfect. This is a job for the Almighty. We do ourselves a tremendous injustice when we become the ultimate arbiter of behavior.

When we categorize individuals and sort them into little convenient boxes that satisfy our being, we sort ourselves. We can enrich our lives enormously by banishing judgmental thoughts and expressions toward others from our being. Making judgments prevent us from self-discovery.

. People will judge you by the company you keep.

JUSTICE

While Black codes were used to control African Americans during slavery, rules of conduct for African Americans continued to be enforced through the 1980's in Mississippi.

There was no justice for African Americans in Mississippi. My first sense of injustice was at age 13 in 1955. In August of 1955, Emmett Till, a fourteen year old from Chicago, was sent to visit relatives near Money, Mississippi in Tallahatchie County. He allegedly flirted with a 21-year-old white woman working in a country store owned by her husband Roy Bryant. A few days later Emmett Till disappeared and his body was eventually found wired to an old factory fan on the bottom of a river. Till had been severely beaten and shot in the head.

While Bryant and his half-brother boasted of this murder, an all-white jury acquitted them. After the trial, they sold their story of murdering Till to *Look Magazine* for $4,000.

. All the justice in the world isn't fastened up in the courthouse.

. Don't be too quick to judge. — We should not be in the business of judging.

. What goes around comes around. — We reap what we sow.

. You reap what you sow. — What we do to others, we do to ourselves.

KINDNESS

As a child, I recall one of the first lessons taught by my parents and reinforced by all of the elders in the community was, "Always be kind and nice to people." We were introduced to the instruction of the Bible, "Be kind and compassionate to one another." (Ephesians 4:32). The greatest compliment to an adult was to be told their children had nice ways. When we are kind, we reach out to others and express our God-like quality of being loving. There is always a special opportunity to be kind to others. We were taught, "Let your gentleness be evident to all." (Philippians 4:5)

I remember my Dad who was in the company of several men at a barbershop. Some of the men said disparaging things about a neighbor. Dad did not participate in this negative conversation. He said, "Well he whistles well." I was always taught, "If you can't say something nice about a person, don't say anything."

If we would put on our funeral clothes of love daily, we would be kinder, love more and express the Commandments of God. Do not wait to the death of a loved one to show your love and appreciation, two powerful agents in living and sharing a fuller and healthier life. Express your kindness, understanding, patience, and goodness toward a friend each day as if it were the last. Give your friends, family members, and others flowers while they can smell them and enjoy the special gift of joy they bring. Prepare a special meal that they can enjoy and share in love and thanksgiving. Call up loved ones and just say, "I thought of you today and want you to know how special you are as I send a hug through the phone." Hug friends and family members when you meet. Let them know how much you care. Make each day a special day to celebrate, share, respond, talk, laugh, reminisce, or just quietly sit and communicate your affection.

We are reminded by Augustine "Og" Mandino: "Beginning today; treat everyone you meet as if they were going to be dead by midnight. Extend to them all the care, kindness and understanding you can muster, and do with no thought of any reward. Your life will never be the same again."

. A forced kindness deserves no thanks.

. An open door admits many visitors.

. Be kind to unkind people — they need it the most.

- Don't mistake kindness for weakness. — Kindness is never a sign of weakness.

- If I cannot do great things, I can do small things in a great way.

- If I'd known you were coming, I would've baked a cake. A host desires to please a guest.

- It is nice to be important, but it is more important to be nice.

- Kill them with kindness. — No matter how someone treats you, continue to be kind.

- Kindness is the ability to love people more than they deserve.

- Kindness is the sunshine in which virtue grows.

- Kindness, like a boomerang, always returns. — Human kindness is always shared.

- One never loses anything by politeness.

- Provide for the soul by doing good works. — We all need to do good things in life.

- Repay evil with kindness. — Kindness is the best response to evi

- Smiles open many doors.

- Sow good works and thou shall reap gladness. — When we do good things, we feel pleased.

- You catch more bees with honey than vinegar.

- You smile and the world smiles with you. — Smiles beget smiles.

KNOWLEDGE

. A closed mind is a good thing to lose. — Let go of narrow mindedness.

. A little knowledge is a dangerous thing.
   A small amount of knowledge can mislead people into thinking they are more expert than they are.

. Always drink pure water. Many get drunk from breaking this rule.

. An ox and an ass don't yoke well to the same plow. — Do not mix unlike things.

. An idle mind is the devil's workshop. — Trouble abounds for the idle person.

. A mad horse must have a sober rider.

. A man who is his own doctor has a fool for his patient.

. A rabbit knows a fox track same as a hound does.

. A robin's song isn't pretty to a worm. — Danger lies ahead.

. A rolling stone gathers no moss.
   A person gains neither friends nor person when they move from place to place.

. A wink is as good as a nod to a blind horse.

. Barking saves biting. — Being forewarned is forearmed.

. Better an empty purse than an empty head. — It is better to have intelligence than money.

. Big blanket makes man sleep late.

The Tree of Love Gives Shade to All

. Blind horse knows when the trough is empty.

. Don't care how much you whitewash a pot, the black is still there. People's attitudes and behaviors don't change.

. Don't count your chickens before they hatch. — Don't rely on something until you are sure of it.

. Don't cross the bridge before you come to it. — Don't worry about problems before they arise.

. Don't let the left hand know what the right hand is doing. — Keep your plans to yourself.

. Don't put all of your eggs in one basket. — Do not put all your resources in one possibility.

. Don't take too big a start to jump a ditch.

. Field mouse lay still when Sparrow hawk sail.

. Get the candles lighted before you blow out the match.

. If you don't know much, you can't do much.

. It's more power in being a book than a bookend.

. Late comes early.

. Learning is better than house and land.

. Learning refines and elevates the mind. — Education sharpens the mind.

. One finger won't catch fleas.

. Quagmires don't hang out no signs. — Beware of one's surroundings.

- Repetition is the mother of knowledge. — We learn from repetition and reinforcement.

- Some smart folks can't tell a rotten rail without sitting on it. — Intelligence is relative.

- Sometimes the runt pig beats the whole litter growing. We can't determine future growth by size.

- Talent is power; tact is skill.

- The bait is worth more than the fish.

- The longest day will have an end.

- The more I know, the more I know that I don't know. — Learning is a lifelong experience.

- The more you know, the less you need to show.

- The noise of the wheels doesn't measure the load in the wagon.

- The use of knowledge is power.

- To know everything is to know nothing.
  A person who thinks he knows everything has little intelligence.

- The point of the pin is the easiest end to find.

- What you don't know won't hurt you.

- You can't get blood from a stone. — You can't get help from someone who has nothing.

- You can't make bricks without straw. — You must have the right materials to complete a job.

LAUGHTER

. A good laugh is sunshine in a house.

. If you don't laugh, you'll cry.

. Laughter is the best medicine. — Laughter has many health benefits.

. Live well, love much and laugh often.

LEADERSHIP

. No one leads the orchestra without turning his back on the crowd. We cannot lead by looking back.

. That's for me to know and you to find out.

. The horse is running, but who has the reins?

. You can lead a horse to water, but you can't make it drink.

. You can't lead where you don't go, and you can't teach what you don't know.

LESSONS

. Free advice generally costs more than the other kind.

. If you make yourself an ass, folks will ride you.

. Just let your conscience be your guide. — Always have your conscience be your guide.

The Tree of Love Gives Shade to All

. New brooms sweep clean but old brooms know where the dirt is.

. The higher the monkey climbs, the more you can see his behind.

. The higher you climb, the farther you have to fall.

 **LIES**

- Ask me no questions, I'll tell you no lies. — There are subjects I'd rather not discuss.

- Liars need good memories. — Liars must try to remember what they say.

- That is a cock and bull story. — An unbelievable tale.

 **LIFE**

    We always considered our mother as the lady who made the best six layer jelly cakes and pound cakes, called plain cakes at the time. We believed that she was the best baker in the whole state of Mississippi. After eating a piece of her cake, we gave here the highest compliment, saying, "Mom, you bake the best cake in the world!" Mom was a large lady who spent most of her waking hours that she was not engaged in other tasks, always in the kitchen making the most wonderful pastries. Her skills in this area were always evident and respected at the annual "dinner on the grounds," the concluding activity of the week of revival meetings at the Old Hopewell Missionary Baptist Church in Collins, Mississippi. Deacons wore black shiny suits that shone in the sunlight from considerable wear. Other worshippers stood patiently in line for mother's cakes and pies, which were delivered to the church in drawers from a bedroom dresser. Chocolate layer cake was my favorite, made from real Hershey chocolate. For me, it was the satisfying experience to devour a slice, eating one small morsel at a time, to extend this heavenly experience.

    But when mother baked a pound it, it was like a moving prayer meeting when the mourner's bench would call on the Holy Ghost. Her baking was love expressed in every cup, teaspoon, tablespoon, pinch and dash of ingredients. She expressed love of life for her family with every beat, stir, fold, sift and blend. In preparing for this big event in the kitchen, Mom would lay out the ingredients like Frank Lloyd Wright, developing, drawing and laying out plans for magnificent buildings in Buffalo, New York. She would carefully take out the fresh country eggs that the hens had laid that day. The hens were special as they were ordered as baby chicks from Randy's Record Mart, a mail order house at Radio Station WLAC in Gallatin, Tennessee. This was one of the first American radio stations to play what was called "race" music, the music of African Americans. Those eggs were from the full grown baby chicks that had been sent within 24 hours through the mail to our Rural Route post office in the small hamlet of Palmers Crossing, Mississippi. Those country eggs were always double=yokes and an earth-tone, brownish/tan color. They were carefully washed clean from the fresh spring water that ran beside our wood frame country house. After washing them, they were free of the feathers and showed no sign of the dry waste emitted from hens in the wire-mesh chicken coop. Mama also had a preference for the hens that laid brown eggs.

Stopping intermittently, mother would wipe the salty perspiration from her forehead with the hem of her apron fashioned from bleached flour sacks. We always believed that when Mama sweated and then smiled, the food would be the most delectable. With the proficiency of an artist, she placed fresh milk on the top of the homemade wooden kitchen counter. Kept in a Mason jar, the milk had been produced on the same day from the cows that were milked lovingly and gently by hand. Milking cows always required being careful to content, soothe and pat the cow gently, like rocking a baby to sleep, while milking. "Bossy" had been in the family since the time she was given to Dad by an uncle who showed his appreciation for Dad helping him and his four children get a fresh start when they moved from Covington County, Mississippi. This was the place where their forefathers and mothers were brought from Charleston, South Carolina from Africa to slavery.

Martha White Flour was placed beside the container of milk on the oilcloth covered table. This flour was quite popular in the south and many cooks refused to use anything but it. Women sang the Martha White theme song as they baked, a commercial performed on the country Flatt and Scruggs early morning radio show. The ditty went like this: " I can bake better biscuits, cakes and pies 'cause Martha White's Self- Rising flour is the only all=purpose flour."

Believing that "necessity is the mother of invention," the flour sacks were recycled, bleached and used at a later date as fabric for a shirt for me. I recall that Mama was resourceful in using various plants for die. A white sack became a yellow shirt after Mama used the Golden Alender, a wildflower, to dye the sack that color. Watkins flavor, an ingredient that was the preference of real, natural-born cooks was removed from the cupboard. This brand of flavor was purchased from the legendary Watkins man, who usually travelled the back roads of the countryside in an old, black Ford car with the sign prominently placed: The Watkins Man. The Watkins man provided spices, flavors, and other cooking products and recipes, guaranteeing everything he sold, always proclaiming, "Satisfaction guaranteed or your money back."

The butter for the cake was made by the arduous and time-consuming task of churning. The churn had to be firmly placed between the legs, held tightly to the base so that the stick could be manipulated by continuously pushing it up and down, much like performing sit-ups. I recall the butter was churned to mother's satisfaction. The butter was placed in a small decorative bowl to mold, and a design was imprinted on it from the Depression-pin style saucers, which were sold locally at the F. W. Woolworth Store for a nickel. Sometimes after cooling in the ice box, the butter was sculpted with a kitchen knife into designs of flowers or animals.

Having placed all of the ingredients in their proper places, the recipe evolved:

· 1 pound of butter

· 12 country eggs

· 3 cups of all-purpose Martha White flour

· 1 teaspoon of Watkins vanilla flavor

· 1 teaspoon of Watkins lemon flavor

· 1 ½ cup of fresh country white milk

· 3 cups of cane sugar

It should be noted that country cooks required that the butter be a bright yellow in color. They thought something was wrong with white-colored butter.

White butter was perceived as bad for a cake. On occasion, the deep yellow butter was mixed with half of rancid butter that had been left out of the ice box for a long time and had a strange odor.

The country butter was first creamed, using a large baking spoon and the human hand to stir, press, and beat the mixture again. Then one cup of Martha White all-purpose flour was added., followed by one egg, cracked, dropped, stirred in and one cup of sugar. Another was cracked, dropped, stirred and beaten. This process continued with the milk being placed in the center of the mixture, followed by another cup of flour, alternately, sugar was added.

Finally, the cake mixture included all of the necessary ingredients. At that point, Mama stirred and beat, seemingly incessantly, with the large baking spoon, believing that the best cake was made by hand, rather than using her old Wear-Ever mixer that had been introduced to country cooks via the Sears-Roebuck catalog. Then the mixture was poured into a large iron baking pan. The wood-fueled stove had been fired up for about thirty minutes, and you didn't need to ask Mama what the temperature of the stove was, for invariably her response would be, "I can touch the oven door and determine that it is 350 degrees. After all, I have been doing this for more than thirty years." It was much like Dad looking at the sun to tell the time of day. It was an unbearable ninety degrees in the shade, when we were chopping cotton. We believed our Dad's method of telling time, and, of course who would question your mother's ability to assess the oven temperature.

We patiently, and not too patiently, observed the whole process. The major objective of this Jobian patience was to be the first one to get the mixing bowl, after the cake was placed in the oven. Traditionally, my older brothers and sister would vie for who would get the bowl to spoon, lick, and finger the delicious remains of the ingredients of the cake. To me, this was the best part of the cake-baking process. The other joy was seeing the devout sensitivity that Mama expressed in leaving enough batter in the bowl to make a small, flat cake which could be eaten immediately. Mama used to say that this was reminiscent of slavery times, when black people would use corn, ground into meal and cooked in the form of hoecakes, cakes that were precisely baked on the end of a hoe. Perhaps, this was the first invention of the current-day pancake.

As the cake was about to be gently placed in the oven, you knew from past experience that you had to clear the kitchen and let the cake bake unobstructed by movement in the kitchen. Mama would say, "Be still! Don't make my cake fall!" Knowing that the kitchen was off-base during the baking time, we patiently waited outside under the crepe myrtle trees for the cake to be ready, cooled and sliced for serving.

From observing and silently participating in the baking process, we learned many things about life: for one, the importance of self-sufficiency. And we learned that the ingredients of a healthy life are very much like baking a cake. It requires interest, patience, thoughtfulness, caring, measuring, weighing, planning, attention, mixing, cooperation, carefully adding love to improve our being and that of others. It was also an experience in sharing with others. We learned the special love of our mother who expressed and lived the meaning of the poignant Madagascar Proverb: "let your love be like the misty rains, coming softly, but flooding the river."

While I miss my mother's cake and have not found another to compare to her cake, I learned about life and learned the special ingredients of living a healthy life. Much like baking a cake, a healthy and spiritual life requires blending ingredients that reach out to others.

. I've got a right to the tree of life.

. A long life may not be good enough, but a good life is long enough.

. Don't wish your life away.

. Every man gets his just deserts.

. Half a loaf is better than none. — It is better to have less than nothing.

. He is lifeless who is faultless. — No person is without faults.

. I am sitting here wondering if a matchbox will hold my clothes.

. In three words, I can sum up life, it goes on.

The Tree of Love Gives Shade to All

- It's six in one hand and a half dozen in the other.

- Keeping up with the Jones will keep you down.

- Life guarantees a chance, not a fair shake.

- Life is a choice.

- Life is labor, death is rest.

- Life is short and full of blisters. — Life is filled with adversities that can be overcome.

- Life is 10 percent what you make it and 90 percent how you take it.

- Live and let live. — Do not interfere in other people's business.

- Live hard, die fast.

- No matter how high the bird flies, he has to come back down to the ground to eat.

- The chickens will come home to roost.

- You can't have your cake and eat it too.

- You have to eat a peck of dirt before you die. Everyone endures some adversities in life.

LIMITATIONS

God created us with unique abilities for a planned purpose. We realize God's plan fully when we remove the limitations placed on our lives. What we focus on, we empower. There are few limitations to the types of goals we can achieve in life. The greatest limitation or barrier to the attainment of goals is the belief that we have insurmountable challenges. Limitations are psychological impediments such as feeling unworthy of material or emotional success. We can either succeed or fail based on the personal limitation we feel and become. Our quest for a better life, job, relationship, sense of self can become a reality if we believe in ourselves and identify all of the personal strengths we have to achieve our goals. We cannot become limited when we possess vision, persistence, hard work, faith, and sacrifice to reach our dreams.

We help ourselves move from the valley of discontent, deferred dreams, and hopelessness when we are able to rise above circumstances. We should never let circumstances control our possibilities and relegate us to less than our capabilities. It is mandatory that we control our lives and cease to use excuses. We must believe that we and only we can make things happen for ourselves. My parents always told me "You've got to claim your space in life." They felt there were no limitations to what I could accomplish as there were so many African Americans who had vision, determination and worked hard to take their rightful place in life.

Many people settle for less in their life, believing they are not deserving and cannot overcome adversities. Some individuals feel that their socio-economic circumstances or race dictate their opportunities. There are countless examples of individuals who have been raised in dire poverty and achieved their goals. Although, these individuals were poor economically, they were rich in their spirit and faith that one's economic status did not identify them and relegate them to failure. I am reminded of Leontyne Price, undoubtedly the most gifted opera singer of all times, grew up in Laurel, Mississippi and graduated from the all-African American Oak Park High School in 1944. Leontyne Price, the daughter of a midwife and lumber millworker in Laurel, Mississippi rose from humble beginnings to a sterling operatic career on stages throughout America and the world where she sang in fluent French, German, and Italian.

In 1955, Price was the first African American to appear in a leading role on NBC-TV Opera. Some of the southern NBC stations, including Mississippi, canceled the broadcast in protest that an African American would be given such a starring role. These individuals who opposed this broadcast were the individuals who held stereotypes of African Americans and this program certainly dispelled the stereotype that African Americans were lazy, buffoons, and inferior. I am convinced that all whites did not view Miss Price and other African Americans as ignorant people. This is evident in the January 28, 1963 performance where Miss Price performed at her church, St. Paul Methodist Church, in Laurel, Mississippi. For that one night, the audience was integrated with supporters from all faiths and races.

I would encourage any youth who feels he/she is limited in life to listen to the interviews and music of Miss Price on You Tube. Anyone who takes the time to listen to this brilliant performer will overcome any fears of being successful for she is one of the most inspirational individuals in the world.

Dr. George Washington Carver, stolen at birth by a band of thieves, was raised by foster parents. He set a goal to become a scientist and persisted in his efforts and found hundreds of uses for the sweet potato and peanut, inventions that revolutionized the agricultural industry in this country. Madame C. J. Walker, one of the first African American millionaires and entrepreneur, grew up in dire poverty in Louisiana. To make ends meet and survive, she took in laundry and performed domestic work. Her dream of inventing a straightening comb and developing hair products was undaunted by poverty, racism, and struggles. Each of these individuals demonstrated an unwavering faith that caused them to dream, to work to fulfill their dream and rise above any limitations. They all succeeded and are great examples of courage.

. Hope sees the invisible, feels the intangible and achieves the impossible.

. If you stop struggling, then you stop life. — Struggles assist us in living a full life.

. Life is a great big canvas, and you should throw all the paint on it you can.

. Life has no limitations. — Limitations are self-imposed.

. Life is the sum of all the choices you make.

. Life is what we make it, always has been, always will be. Our quality of life is dependent on us.

. The sky is the limit. — It's good to aim high in life.

 **LOSS**

. I might as well kiss that goodbye.

. Lose money hand over fist.

. The cow knows not what her tail is worth until she has lost it.

. To lose is to learn.

. When you lose, don't lose the lesson.

 **LOVE**

We are taught in Romans 13:8 about love: "We owe no one anything, except to love each other for the one who loves another has fulfilled the law." Love is never manifested in the emotions that bring feelings of fear, unhappiness, physical and emotional abuse, pain and incompleteness. We all have a basic need to love and through this need, we often involve ourselves with someone who is not worthy of our love. I have heard some individuals' plaintive cry that is as necessary as their thirst for water, say, "If I could just find someone to love, I would be the happiest person in the world." These individuals have not recognized the special joy that comes from first loving one's self. When we don't love ourselves and seek to find someone to fill that deep cavern of neediness, we place our vulnerable selves in the arms of those who don't give love but abuse.

The subject of love is the most frequent discussion among individuals throughout the world. It is talked about in songs, poems, novels, movies, soap operas, work settings, churches and schools. The word, "love," is mentioned more in the lyrics to songs than any other word. Have you stopped to be still, think and define the real meaning of love? Are you able to list those things that you love in another person? Have you written your personal definition of love? Have you pondered about the real power of self-love and the special healing benefits? Do you seek love outside yourself and fail miserably in finding love? Have you mistaken love for hormonal attraction only?

If you do not know the answers to the above questions, join the millions of people who have not looked at love as first being a special feeling of personal deep and ardent affection for self. How do we know if we are loved? We know we are loved when we are the embodiment of the Spirit of God, which is love resides within us. We know we are loved when we accept, respect, cherish, and give thanks for all of the abundant blessings we receive. We know we are loved when we look at the infinite possibilities we possess to achieve health and wealth. We come to know the real meaning of love when we develop a love relationship with ourselves and accept as ourselves as being made in the special image of God.

Love is an affirmation and acceptance of goodness, happiness, joy, prosperity, peace and abundance. When we love ourselves first we walk in the light of the Spirit of God that guides us toward personal fulfillment and the expression of it in our social, emotional, physical, financial and educational pursuits. Love is the only key that opens the door to the fruits of life, which are happiness, peace, goodwill, joy and abundance. Our understanding and expression of the real meaning of love illuminates the Spirit of God within. This love does not possess, control, envy, abuse and express jealousy, vengeance, and contempt. Love empowers us and gives us vision, purpose and direction in seeking, claiming and expressing eternal truth that provide freedom. This special feeling cannot be found outside of one's self.

. A heart that loves is always young.

. A way to a man's heart is through his stomach.

- Colder than a mother-in-law's love.

- He loves well who chastises well.

- He who falls in love with himself will have no rivals.

- If there is anything better than to be loved, it is loving.

- If you love somebody, let them go. If they return, they were always yours. If they don't, they never were.

- I love you because I need you, I need you because I love you.

- It is better to be hated for what you are than loved for what you're not.

- It is better to be loved than to be in love.

- Love all, trust few.

- Love begets love.

- Love can move mountains.

- Love doesn't love anybody.

- Love is like a butterfly, it settles on you when you least expect it.

- Love is the touchstone of virtue.

- Love knows no measure.

- Love will find a way.

- Lucky at cards - unlucky in love

The Tree of Love Gives Shade to All

. Misery loves company.

. Romance without finance doesn't stand a chance.

. Take into account that great love and great achievements involve great risk.

. Tell me whom you love, I'll tell you who you are. — We are known by those we love.

. There is a thin line between love and hate.

. The tree of love gives shade to all.

. Time goes by a lot slower when you miss the one you love.

. True love has no limits.

. You can only love or hate about someone else what you love or hate about yourself.

. You can't hide love and cough.

. You can't buy love.

. You may condemn the one you love, but you pay his fine for it.

 **LUCK**

. Bet one's bottom dollar.

. Depend on the rabbit's foot if you will, but it didn't work for the rabbit.

. Don't burn my bread. — Don't wish me bad luck.

. Even a blind squirrel finds a nut once in a while.

. I can't win for losing.

. If it weren't for bad luck, I'd have no luck at all.

. It's hard for the best and smartest folks in the world.

. Knock on wood. — Tap wood to avoid bad luck.

. My ship's going to sail one day.

. Never bet your money on another man's game.

. Nothing ventured, nothing gained.

. Scared money doesn't win.

. The sun's going to shine in my door someday. — Believing life will get better.

. You can't beat that with a stick.

. Your luck isn't always equal to the length of your fishing pole.

MARRIAGE

Marriage is one of the most sacred institutions in our society. "What therefore God hath joined together, let not man put asunder." (Matthew 19:6) It only survives, matures, and demonstrates its special quality when two individuals come together with a heart and soul that is committed to working together to deal with the challenges. Alexander Dumas once wrote, "So heavy is the chain of wedlock that it needs two to carry it sometime." While millions have entered matrimony, mouthing the words, "To death do us part," a significant number of marriages fail. Marriage, like any other serious venture takes patience, commitment, understanding, mutual trust and unconditional love.

While our ancestors and elders emphasized marriage. Marriage is not realistic today for a high percentage of African American women. In the United States, women outnumber men. In the African American population, this discrepancy is even more pronounced. The number of marriage-eligible, young African American males is alarmingly inadequate. The scarcity of eligible men is due to several factors: the high number of African American men who are incarcerated; the excessive number of deaths of young African American men due to homicide; and African American men marrying outside of their race.

. A good son makes a good husband.

. A man can never thrive who has a wasteful wife.

. A nagging woman comes to no good end.

. A prudent wife is from the Lord.

. Before you marry, keep both eyes open. After you marry, it's a good idea to shut one.

. Be sure before you marry.

- It's better to climb on top of the house and sit than to live inside with a nagging woman.

- Marry in haste, and repent in leisure.
  Individuals who marry quickly without thought may be sorry later.

- Marriage is heaven or hell.

- New brooms sweep clean, but old brooms know where the dirt is.

- Why buy the cow when you can get the milk free? Not paying for something you can get free.

In my research with several couples who have been married on an average of fifty years, the following fifty tips are offered to protect and support marriage:

1.0 Begin each day with a smile and touch each other with a special embrace of awakening to a new day.
2.0 Give each other a kiss often and daily.
3.0 Respect individual differences and appreciate the need for a personal bubble of privacy.
4.0 Always be gentle in your ways.
5.0 Take time to express compliments to each other on a daily basis for the smallest things.
6.0 Treat each day as a special birthday or anniversary by doing something as simple as a walk.
7.0 Pick up the phone and call to just say 'I love you and thought about you."
8.0 Touch each other daily and feel the special power of two, lively hearts beating.
9.0 Smile for there is always something to smile about.
10.0 Support each other in their endeavors.
11.0 Send a special hand-made card or note on a regular basis.
12.0 Create your personal celebrations and rituals.
13.0 Always forgive and go forward.

14.0 Encourage each other.
15.0 Always be generous with your time for almost anything or any other person can wait.
16.0 Admit when you are wrong.
17.0 Awaken to each day with a special prayer for each other's health and prosperity.
18.0 Talk about dreams and work together to fulfill them.
19.0 Always be kind in everything you do.
20.0 Listen and keep your mind open to new ideas and adventures.
21.0 Be committed and dedicated to your marriage.
22.0 Take time each day to communicate, listen, share, and support each other.
23.0 Share in household tasks. A little androgyny is good for the soul.
24.0 Be understanding.
25.0 Always look your best.
26.0 Be a special friend.
27.0 Always anticipate and claim goodness in your relationship.
28.0 Give thanks to God for your bountiful blessings and adversities.
29.0 Take a leisure bath or shower together.
30.0 Focus on today.
31.0 Always look forward and not backward.
32.0 Never go to bed angry.
33.0 Share the special memories of events that were loving and joyful.
34.0 Laugh a lot.
35.0 Celebrate each day like it is the last one.
36.0 Share the special healing power of communing with nature.
37.0 Be patient with each other.
38.0 Always believe that your marriage has infinite possibilities.
39.0 Speak up when there are problems and commit yourselves to finding a solution to them.
40.0 Always practice what you preach.
41.0 Consider each other as equals and special beings.
42.0 Be protective of each other.
43.0 Respect the physical desires of each other.
44.0 Never take each other for granted.

The Tree of Love Gives Shade to All

45.0 Fill your life with worthwhile activities. Be bold to try out new adventures.
46.0 Don't let your heart be troubled.
47.0 Be fair in all things.
48.0 Admit when you are wrong.
49.0 Recognize there is no perfect marriage but there are perfect moments.
50.0 Practice the teachings of Jesus, "Give and it will be given to you."

MEDIOCRITY

None of us is born to be mediocre. Each of us has the energy and personal power to make contributions to the world to make it a better place. Nikki Giovanni once wrote, "Mediocrity is safe." Countless individuals accept mediocrity for it is the easiest route for them to take in life. They accept the average and substandard, believing they are not entitled to more. Mediocrity causes individuals to be critical of their circumstances, always conveniently using their plight as reasons for not doing better. Settling for mediocrity does not require individuals to change their minds, opinions, false beliefs and negative emotions to accept and claim that persistence and positive beliefs can move individuals to do extraordinary things.

Historically, African Americans have regarded mediocrity as a barrier to freedom, justice, and racial progress. In fact, mediocrity has been traditionally viewed as a "sin and a shame," a phrase many of our elders used. Our elders have always emphasized the importance of achieving excellence in education, positive interpersonal relationships, and spiritual relationships. Children were frequently told by their elders that they must be two to three times smarter, wiser, and moral than whites. From the earliest days of childhood, African American children have been introduced to the importance of hard work and self-reliance. Every child was required to awaken to each day with a constructive list of activities and work was number one on the list. The major job of the day was to attend school and get the best education and training in academics, social skills, and values. Parents viewed teachers as their aides and supported their efforts to educate their children. Every elder in the community was a surrogate parent and involved in the education and welfare of a child.

Teachers encouraged youth to be outstanding in their decorum, appearance, diction, character and academic subjects. Parents reinforced their instruction by telling children that they had a responsibility to be the best in all of their endeavors. Our elders, parents, and teachers instilled a belief in us that we had the essence of greatness. We were convinced that expressions of slothfulness and irresponsibility of any kind would threaten our freedom and be a disgrace and dishonor to our foremothers and forefathers who made great strides. I recall that every teacher effectively managed her classroom with nonverbal gestures, the movement of her head, a piercing stare or standing near a child who appeared to act out in class. Quite frankly, discipline was never a problem as students knew that they were to exhibit the best behavior. On those rare occasions where one dared to be disruptive, a behavior considered a major offense at the time, he knew he/she would be corporally punished at school and sent home with a dreadful note. Parents responded quickly to this communication with a lecture, followed by what we called a whipping. Our parents believed in the Biblical admonition, "Raise a child in the way he should go and he will not depart from it."

We were taught how to use Standard English. Teachers stressed learning. Every child was taught grammar and could conjugate verbs with proficiency. We made sure our subjects and verbs agreed. Slang was not permissible. The use of profanity was as forbidden and was considered a reflection of poor home training. Ms. Ratliff, my third grade teacher at Third Ward Elementary School always told us, "You must learn to speak well if you plan to succeed. She taught us that lazy people speak carelessly.

Excellence was taught as diligently as reading, writing and arithmetic. We were introduced to the achievements of our people. While Black history, called Negro History at the time, was for one week until it was extended to a month. We were introduced to the strength and will of men and women who faced tremendous adversities and overcame them. We were introduced to Booker T. Washington, Dr. George Washington Carver, Madame C. J. Walker, Jan Matzeliger, Garrett Morgan and many others who became our role models. We found our own role models in our homes, our fathers and mothers who awakened each day to a breakfast with prayer. Our parents represented the emotional, intellectual, and moral qualities that made men and women successful and responsible parents. Each day was filled with meaningful lessons in self-reliance.

Today's youth must be taught the same values that our foremothers and forefathers stressed. Parents must be responsible in teaching their children lessons that encourage them to have an allegiance to high standards, high expectations, and healthy social, emotional, and moral development. While many social, political, educational and economic changes have taken place in our society, we must hold fast to the family and its significance in rearing healthy children. Mediocrity will never help African Americans to succeed and possess clout in a country that continues to expect less and give less to blacks. Parents must be diligent in their efforts to instill the importance of a good education, appearance, character, spirituality, respect for self and others. We cannot let the media, rap music, and diminished morals take the place of being good parents. Too many of today's youth have resigned themselves to failure, dependency, hopelessness and a life filled with unhealthy experiences and decisions, which are directly related to the adults they raise them.

. No great shakes.

 MEEKNESS

. The meekness of Moses is better than the strength of Samson. — Humility is a great strength to have.

 MEN

Despite the overall economic gains in the 1990's, many young black men continue to have the poorest life chances of anyone in our society. The share of young African American men unemployed has climbed relentlessly. By 2000, 65% of African American male high school dropouts in their 20's were jobless, not able to find work or not seeking it or incarcerated. By 2004, the share had grown to 72%, compared with 34 percent of whites and 19 percent of Hispanic dropouts.

. A man without guts lives on his knees.

. He is a credit to the race.

. He is as cool as a cucumber.

. He is as sharp as a mosquito's peter…and that is sharp at both ends.

. He isn't worth a plugged nickel. — A man is not self-sufficient.

. He isn't worth the salt in leavened bread. — A person is no good.

. Men are like buses. If you miss one, it won't be fifteen minutes until the next one rolls by.

. Men, like cattle, follow him who leads.

. Men! You can dress them up, but you can't take them out.

. Once a man, twice a child

. There is a funny smell in a bachelor's home.

. You can take the man out of the country, but you can't take the country out of the man.

. You have a son till he marries a wife. You have a daughter for all your life.

MENTORING

Our lives were enriched with the many mentors in the community. We were taught to be sterling examples of excellence by a diverse group of individuals in the neighborhoods in which we lived. Laws of segregation at the time dictated specific rules and codes of conduct by which African American people were expected to abide. Consequently, every black lived in one of the quarters of the town, a name that goes back to slavery. The doctor, lawyer, school teacher, ministers, undertakers, servants, domestics, bootleggers, and the poet laureate lived within blocks of each other. They attended the same church or social club, which provided a means of regular communication among teachers, parents, and elders. When we were caught misbehaving by our elders, we knew "Our parents would be informed of our infraction before God got the news."

The mentors in the quarters provided hope and direction to every child, always informing us that we were somebody and would make great contributions to the world and make our parents and elders proud. Our mentors taught us that success was the product of hard work, faith, persistence and positive thoughts and actions.

Mentors were present throughout the community. Mentorship was not based on one's socio-economic or education level. Every adult met the qualifications to be an effective mentor. Each of them shared the same struggles and personal growth stories about freedom and the need for control and responsibility in one's life.

Mentors placed a high premium on education. To them, education was the best answer to freedom. While many of our elders were discriminated against and persecuted, they had an ironclad belief that they were equal to any racial or ethnic group. Their lives were filled with adversities, trials, and tribulation, but they gained strength in facing formidable challenges. Their response to adversities was always being proactive as their parents had taught them to exercise strength and determination in the face of difficulties.

Our mentors used faith in God and the promise of abundance as the source of their strength, determination, and desire to prosper. This faith in God was passed on from their slave fore-bearers who used faith to overcome physical slavery. Their faith helped them to make sure their minds were not enslaved.

The Tree of Love Gives Shade to All

As an African American child of segregation, our elders set the highest standards for conduct, achievement and citizenship. We were fortunate to have every home in the African American quarters of Hattiesburg, Mississippi headed by two parents, most of whom were married and others who lived as common law husband and wife. All adults in the community held jobs. I don't recall any adult in the community who did not work. While most jobs were menial, paying less than $2. Per day, parents fed, clothed, and sheltered their children without the assistance of any handouts. We understood early in life that having a job was mandatory and not an option.

. Each one, teach one. — Everyone should teach another person.

 **MISTAKES**

Some individuals confuse the word mistake with habit. Growing up near the border of Louisiana, I remember a relative who often admonished us, "One time a mistake, two times a purpose." A mistake should always teach us special lessons that prevent us from repeating the same error. Through the difficulties we face as a result of mistakes, we effectively learn how to avoid making the same mistake.

. Barking up the wrong tree — Make a mistake in something you are trying to achieve.

. Don't sell the bear skin until you have caught the bear.
   Don't rely on something until you are sure of it.

. Learn from other people's mistakes.

. Learn from your mistakes. — Mistakes offer valuable lessons.

. Mistakes are proof that you are trying. — We cannot succeed without making mistakes.

. Mule that chews up his own collar is fixing for a sore shoulder.

. One time the mistake, two time a purpose.

. There is nothing wrong with making mistakes. Just don't respond with encores

. You can cut off a dog's tail, but you can't sew it back.

 **MONEY**

. A dime a dozen

. A fool and his money are easily parted. — A foolish person usually spends money foolishly.

. A good paymaster needs no security.

. A man in debt is stoned every year.

. A man who is proud of his money has rarely anything else to be proud of.

. A small coin in a big jar makes a great noise.

, Before you borrow money from a friend, decide which one you need more.

. Better buy than borrow.

. Borrowing is the mother of trouble. — Borrowing causes problems.

. Buy something for a song.

. Cheapskate

. Chump change. — It is a small amount of money.

. Closefisted with money

. Control the purse strings.

. Credit is dead; bad pay killed it. — No credit is available as a result of bad payments.

. Don't be a borrower or a lender be — Don't borrow or lend money.

- Don't let your mouth write a check that your behind can't cash.
- Don't take any wooden nickels.
- Economy is great revenue.
- Feed the kitty.
- Float a loan.
- For the love of money is the root of all evils.
- Grease someone's palm.
- Have money to burn.
- He/she doesn't have two nickels to rub together.
- He/she has deep pockets but short arms. — One who has money but does not want to pay.
- He/she is living high on the hog. — A person lives in luxury.
- He/she is strapped for cash.
- He/she is tight as Dick's hat band. — A person is cheap.
- He/she lives from hand to mouth.
- If you treat a dollar right, it multiplies, and if you don't it disappears.
- I keep money in my bra because they're the only two suckers I can trust.
- It takes pennies to make dollars.
- It will cost you an arm and a leg.

- Make a killing.

- Make the money and don't let the money make you.

- Money burns a hole in your pocket.

- Money doesn't grow on trees.

- Money is no object.

- Money makes your morals trot.

- Money soon borrowed is soon sorrowed.

- Money sticks to money.

- Money sure can't buy love, but it makes shopping for it easier.

- Money talks and bullsh*t walks.

- Much borrowing destroys credit.

- Neither be a borrower nor a lender be.

- Never let the bottom of your purse or you your mind be seen.

- Only a lizard shows its money.

- Out of debt and out of danger.

- Punctual pay gets willing loan.

- Put not your trust in money but your money in trust.

- Put your money where your mouth is.

The Tree of Love Gives Shade to All

. Scared money won't win.

. That is just a drop in the bucket. — It is a small part of something big.

. The eagle flies on Friday. — Friday is payday.

. Who pays beforehand is served behindhand. — It is better to pay up front.

. You need to put up or shut up! — Put your money where your mouth is.

MOTHERS

Maya Angelou, in I Know Why the Caged Bird Sings, provides a special description of the most precious being called mother. She wrote, "To describe my mother would be to write about a hurricane in its perfect power." I recall my mother and the other mothers in the community where I grew up were strong individuals. They had the strength of Harriet Tubman, the industry of Madame C. J. Walker, the vision of St. Martin de Porres and the intelligence of Mary McLeod Bethune.

Mothers are the special caretakers of their children from conception, development in the womb, the birth of the child, and the vigilant angel who watches over the child throughout life. Mothers are the personification of safety and security to the child from the movement in the womb to the first touch of affection and the first offering of food from her gentle breast. Mothers are the primary source of a child's development of a basic trust in the world. They meet the basic needs of the child for food, warmth, and affection.

Mothers are the purveyors of a sense of love and protection from the moment they hold the child close to their breast and bond with the child. Their wonderful and soothing heartbeat communicates security and a special support that endures a lifetime. Mothers are mind readers who magically can look at the child from infancy throughout adulthood and know exactly what he/she is thinking, needing and feeling. From their first shrill cry to the first word the child utters, mothers are emotionally connected to a child for a lifetime.

There is no individual in the world that is respected and loved as much as a mother. Mothers are more powerful than any other human being on planet earth. They can juggle the tremendous jobs of motherhood without ever saying they are tired for they believe that this is a negative expression. In their eyes, heart, and mind, a child is a special blessing from God and He has delegated many of His responsibilities to her. Mothers accept their responsibilities unconditionally, always fulfilling their Divine duty.

A mother assumes more responsibilities than any other person in a child's life. Motherhood is a job that never ends. They work, commit, teach, counsel, protect, support, sacrifice, discipline, inspire, understand, advise, listen, communicate and dream. The words burden, trouble, impatience, fear, anger, unhappiness, disharmony, boredom, and anxiety are not in their mental repertoire. Their very souls are filled with joy which they express in their relationship with their children. To achieve the monumental tasks of motherhood, they are endowed with a plethora of attributes that make them visionaries, miracle workers, mediators, counselors, advisors, mentors, spiritual leaders, breadwinners, teachers, psychologists, advocates, inventors, motivators, tutors, listeners, and protectors.

Mothers face formidable challenges head-on, and view long suffering as no more than external factors that they can overcome. Adversity is a daily visitor which mothers look straight in the eye and say with assurance, "This, too, shall pass." Mothers know that they have control over the valleys and mountains of affliction and understand that those who conquer endure. They are invigorated to overcome adversities for children imitate the ways they face and deal with life's misfortunes and battlefields. Mothers are strengthened in their will to be the best parent as they believe the admonition of the scripture, "If God be for me who can be against me?" (Romans8:31)

Mothers are the greatest lovers in the world, constantly expressing unconditional love for their children no matter what the situation, condition, trouble or self-imposed adversities of the child. Duke Ellington aptly describes this kind of love by saying, "Unconditional love not only means I am with you, but also I am for you, all the way, right or wrong…" Mothers stand resolute in their mission to criticize, complement, counsel, and guide the child, always reinforcing the lessons taught from childhood. Their actions promote cognitive, psycho-social and moral development. Mothers have a special, clairvoyant power and are never fooled by the words of their children for they listen with their eyes, ears, hearts, and mind, knowing with 100% accuracy when they speak the truth or tell a lie. They always believe, practice and demand the child's actions speak louder than words. I recall my elders often saying, "You can fool others but you can never fool your mother.

Mothers have a special ability to be in touch and stay in touch with their children if they are a scant block away or a thousand miles away. Their hearts seem to have a unique GPS that tracks the movements and actions of their children. The special powers granted to mothers by God enable them to feel their children and be in touch with their joy, pain, challenges and social, emotional, physical and financial conditions. This special skill of a mother is constant and lasts for an eternity. Their powers in communication skills are greatly enhanced when they hear a child's voice. They know them like a gifted conductor who is aware of every movement in a concerto he/she composed. Any variance in a child's voice, inflection, tone, pause or refrain is read with the greatest proficiency. Simply stated, no one knows you better than your mother.

. All mothers are working mothers.

. A man's work is from sun to sundown, but a mother's work is never done.

. A mom's hug lasts longer after she lets go.

. A mother's heart is a patchwork of love.

. A mother is a mother all the days of her life; a father is a father till he gets a new wife.

. A mother's love perceives no impossibilities.

. Mother is the bank where we deposit all our hurts and worries.

. Mother knows best.

. There is no love like a mother's love.

. There is no substitute for mother.

 ## OBSTACLES

Our ancestors did not faint in the days of adversity and became more vigilant in their faith that they would overcome slavery. The savages who sought to destroy their being forgot one empowering fact that one may shackle a person's feet, cut off their hands, savagely beat the backs of men and women, but they did not give permission to have their minds enslaved. Their power and resilience in dealing with hardship blessed them with immeasurable strength and skills to deal with emancipation and the hard times that faced them. They realized that struggles were continuous and many more obstacles would have to be overcome.

Many people don't give life their best shot. They fail in their pursuits for a better life, thinking that they can slide uphill. When they are confronted with obstacles to achieving their goals, they faint, react, and make excuses for their failure and become immersed in denial of the truth they are responsible for their failure.

. Mountain, get out of my way. — Faith can move obstacles.

. Take into account that great love and great achievements involve great risks.

. Trials are but lessons. — Adversities are great teachers.

. What is bitter to endure is sweet to remember. We remember adversities that lead to success.

. You're on the road to success when you realize that failure is only a detour.

 ## OPPORTUNITY

. Catch is as catch can.

. Corn makes more at the mill than in the crib. — Stored goods have no value.

. Don't waste all your buck shots on one bird.

- If you move, you lose.

- Jump at the sun. You may not land on the sun, but at least you will be off the ground.

- Lean hound leads the pack when the rabbit is in sight.

- Make hay while the sun shines.
  Make the most of an opportunity while you have a chance.

- Once an opportunity has passed, it cannot be caught.

- Opportunities always look bigger going than coming.

- Opportunities, like eggs, come one at a time. — Seize each opportunity.

- Strike while the iron is hot. — Seize the opportunity.

- The door of opportunity won't open until you do some pushing. Opportunity is the result of effort.

- The first in the boat has a choice of oars.

- The good farmer keeps acquainted with the daybreak. — Industry is the key to a successful livelihood

- When one door shuts, another one opens. — Opportunities often come from rejection.

 PAIN

. A hit dog will holler.

. No suffering, no growth. — Hardships lead to personal development.

. Pain is inevitable. Suffering is optional. — We all face pain but we need not suffer.

. Pain is the touchstone of spiritual growth.

 PAST

Unhealthy people live in the past and die in the present. I recall my grandfather saying, "A mill cannot grind with the water that is past." This saying shares that you cannot drive forward on the road of life if you're looking in the rear view mirror. When we live in the past, filled with negative and unfulfilling activities and experiences we die a little bit each day. Dan Millman wrote, "In every moment, the quality of your life is on the line. In each, you are either fully alive or relatively dead."

The need to cling to the past is a warning that one's mental and physical health is at risk. This choice demonstrates attention to unresolved issues, which prevent individuals from romancing and living in the present. Some individuals are bitter and mentally stuck in the past over a divorce, separation, a bad relationships, and loss of a job or dispute.

Some of us are unwilling to turn the page on our past and release the garbage that clutters the mind and impedes new opportunities and possibilities. We often waste valuable time and impair our health, dwelling on past difficulties, people, events, circumstances and conditions, which have wounded us and left unhealed scars. We must regard unpleasant experiences to teach us how to live a more productive life. In fact, we should appreciate some bad relationships because they can teach us how to not deal with these problems in the present. Everything we face in life has a purpose. Every experience has a purpose. No matter how miserable past experiences were, we were where we were in that place and time.

All of our experiences provide us, if we permit, with special skills to deal with the formidable challenges of life. They can improve our vision, amend our priorities, and make a commitment to not face negative situations in the present. We gain nothing of worth or value to our health and happiness by looking at our lives in the past. We cannot grow in spiritual and physical health if we continue to hold on to past situations with remorse, feelings of contempt, feelings of failure and bitterness.

Accept the past as a necessary detour on our journey in finding and gaining knowledge to live a harmonious and well-balanced life. Dwelling on the past does not help us on our journey to personal health. We must forgive others, transcend bad experiences, and forgive ourselves in making special mistakes that help us grow.

The present is all we have. While the past teaches us invaluable lessons, we find absolutely nothing living in the past. When we languish in the past, nursing the open wounds and scabs on festering wounds feeling that we cannot shake it, we poison our being with lack. We defer our dreams. We have no vision of the endless possibilities for a successful and peaceful life. Let the past go and choose health over disease. Check the counterproductive baggage and refuse to get a claim ticket. If you feel your heart has been broken and many of us have experienced that feeling, transcend it and start living. If you feel that you have been used, abused and controlled by others in the past, forget it and don't lessen the lesson of the experiences. Above all, make a decision that you will not give others permission to treat you in a negative manner.

Have you ever stopped to think about a situation that caused you grief and discomfort? Some individuals have been divorced for years, yet in their minds, they are still hurt, angry, and ill at ease. Most likely, your former partner has gone on with his/her life and chalked up the divorce as a special lesson to grow in a positive way.

We can release the past and promote good health by forgiving others. When we refuse to forgive others and hold onto negative experiences, we thwart our ability to achieve the special fruits of life. It is important to look at the cause of negative experiences and honestly identify and accept our shared responsibility in creating the bad conditions. We must ask ourselves the question: What role did I play in developing this situation? Why do I have this unhealthy need to nurse this wound of the heart and permit it to fester and spread like a cancer throughout my body? Honest answers to these questions provide lifelong lessons in knowing what role one played in the past conditions.

Love must be the answer to the negative actions of others. Personal love grants us the power to move on with our lives and recognize that we are not responsible for the inadequacies of others. When we are able to accomplish this feat, we refuse to be the receptacle for other peoples' garbage. Their trash is not your issue to resolve.

People don't hurt us unless we give them permission to inflict emotional pain and suffering. We permit them to cause us pain because we feel, think, act and demonstrate lack, believing that our happiness is in the hands of others. I am convinced that individuals who give power to others to control them and chart their destiny will never achieve good health and prosperity. Consequently, let go of the negative past and commit yourself to a positive present and bountiful future.

. Do not dwell in the past; do not dream of the future, concentrate the mind in the present moment.

. Every saint has a past and every sinner a future.

. Forgiveness does not change the past, but it does enlarge the future. Forgiveness is a good thing.

. If you look back too much, you will soon be headed that way. Progress depends on moving forward.

. Learn in the past, move on to the future. — Let lessons of the past prepare you for the future.

. Let bygones be bygones. — Let go of past experiences and move forward.

- Living in the past has one thing going for it, it's cheaper. We never gain by living in the past.

- Never let yesterday use up today. — Release the past problems and live for today.

- That is water under the bridge. — Something settled in the past is not relevant today.

- The beauty of the past is that it is past. The beauty of the now is to know it.

- The farther behind I leave the past, the closer I come to forgive my own character.

- The past is only something that holds you back from succeeding in your future.

 **PATIENCE**

Patience is the special foundation on which we stand to reach health and prosperity in our lives. In our journey through life, we are offered countless lessons in how to live a complete life. Through patience, we practice understanding, love, compassion, and find that our lives are greatly enhanced by expressing the Divine power within us. By treating ourselves to patience, we find daily treasures that fill us with the good stuff to live abundantly and richly. "The fruit of the spirit is patience. (Galatians 5:22)

. A watched pot never boils.

. Be anxious for nothing.

. Be patient with other folks' faults for they have to be patient with yours.

. Good things come to those who wait. — Patience is a virtue.

. He who does not tire, tires adversity. — Stamina and strength help to overcome challenges.

. Hold your horses. — Slow down and don't move too fast.

. John Time will take care of that. — Time takes care of all things.

. Jump the gun. — Do something before it is time.

. None is patient but the wise. — Patient people are wise.

. Patience is a virtue. — The ability to wait is a valuable quality in a person.

. Patience is the ability to put up with people you would like to put down.

. Patience will achieve more than force.

. Take first things first. — Be patient and do things in the logical order

 **PAYBACK**

. Every dog has its day.

. It isn't any fun when the rabbit has the gun. — The shoe is now on the other foot.

. You are getting a taste of your own medicine.
   You are mistreated in the same manner as you treated someone else.

. You reap what you sow. — What goes around comes around.

 **PEACE**

As children and youth, we were taught by elders that we must always choose peace over despair, abundance over lack, joy over pain, personal self-worth over lack, and spiritual guidance to overcome external circumstances and individuals.

. Peace begins with me.
. Still waters run deep. — People who are calm on the outside often have a strong personality.

 **POLITICS**

.Politeness floats around loose on the day of election. — Politicians are pleasant and want your vote.

 **POTENTIAL**

. Anything is possible.

. Believe in your potential. — Personal faith is a key to success.

. He is a diamond in the rough. — A person has potential.

. Never give up. — Be persistent in reaching your goals.

 **POVERTY**

In 2006, the poverty rate for Blacks was 24.3 percent as compared to 8.2 percent for whites. There is a burgeoning poverty that is affecting so many individuals in our culture. This poverty is greater than any type of poverty that has existed in our culture. The poverty is self-inflicted by the behavior of individuals and the choices they make in their everyday lives. While I was born in economic poverty, I never viewed myself as being poor. We always felt that the greatest poverty one could encounter was a spiritual poverty. I have listed some of the circumstances that are preventing individuals from overcoming lack and succeed.

- Children are living in single parent homes headed by individuals who are basically no more than children themselves.
- Teenage mothers are more likely to have lower school achievement and dropout of high school, have more health problems, be incarcerated during adolescence, give birth as a teenager, and face unemployment as a young adult. Parents must begin to help their children respect their bodies and understand the challenges and difficulties in raising a child as a teenager.
- Poverty, like a disease, has been passed from generation to generation with some individuals.
- Homicide rates soar in neighborhoods where men have no jobs, children are raised without fathers, and social institutions are in disarray. At the earli-

est age of school, youth need to be introduced to academic and vocational programs that will prepare them with marketable skills. Our girls need to learn early on the importance of making appropriate choices in their relationships and know that it takes a responsible man to be a father and support a child.
- Homicide is the leading cause of death of African American males from age 12 to 19 and the second cause of death among African American females from age 15 to 24. Conflict resolution skills among some youth are lacking and they are responding to conflict in the manner in which the adult reacts. Negative conflict resolution is a learned behavior and parents need to step up to the plate and be proactive in their response to conflict.
- Violence is devastating the lives of too many youth in America's major cities. This learned behavior is related to growing up in families where violence and adult discord are common.
- A child who cannot read by the third grade is likely to be involved with the criminal justice system. (Parents need to make reading a priority for their children at the earliest ages.) Too many children are growing up in homes where they never see anyone reading and books are missing in the home. In many cases, the parent did not read on level as a student in school. Parents must take advantage of special tutoring programs in schools and the community and find ways to budget funds for a tutor at the very beginning a child enters preschool or head start programs.
- Some social service programs are not helping families and youth. There are some adults and children who receive SSI benefits for disabilities such as asthma, learning disabilities, and other disabilities. Quite often some individuals rely on these benefits for a lifetime and will not find a job and end up living in poverty and being powerless for the rest of their lives.
- There is a lack of respect among some adults and youth for themselves and others and infringe on the rights of others. Children mimic the adults who are their caretakers and learn disrespect from them. This lack of respect contributes to poverty and negative relationships with others.
- While some individuals blame their unemployment on the lack of job opportunities, some individuals are ill-equipped to get and maintain a job.

For some, getting a job is about as foreign as a language when they grow up in homes where they never see any adults going to work. It is important to teach responsibility at the earliest ages for children to have tasks and be required to complete them with some proficiency.

- Too many adults are making excuses for their children when they are in fact the cause of their difficulties.
- There is a disproportionate number African Americans who suffer from obesity, hypertension, heart disease, cancer and other life threatening illnesses that lead to an early death. Much of the disease is caused by diets that rely on fast food businesses that dominate African American communities. There is a preponderance of businesses in poor neighborhoods that cause illness by the type of food and products sold. There are liquor stores, party stores, gas stations that offer liquor, beer, cigarettes and other products that contribute to bad health and items that some store owners refuse to use. There is a need for more markets that sell fresh vegetables, meat and other produce that are healthy.
- Many of the priorities of some individuals support poverty by conspicuous consumption of goods and services that do not enhance one's health or wealth. *Target Market News,*(2010) reported that African Americans spent $321 million on books, while they spent $29.3 billion on apparel products and services. There is an apparent addiction to sew-on and glue-on hair extensions and weaves of every color and texture and length imaginable. This desire for this fake hair or the ultimate "Indian Remy" hair has become so big that the revenue generated could sustain the economies of several small countries. There is an inordinate amount of money spent on hair care and nail care, which has become one of the most successful businesses in African American communities.
- Priorities are mixed among some families where parents are willing to shell out $300 for the latest gym shoes while their children often survive on a diet of red pop, potato chips and the "death-by-super-size-food suicide" establishments that dot so many African American neighborhoods. While the desire for the latest gym shoes has caused riots at the inauguration of these shoes, there is never a stampede to a library for a library card; fill the places of worship in their neighborhood; enroll in GED programs; and seek available employment commensurate with their skills.

- Some African Americans refuse to support Black businesses, believing that another ethnicity's products and services are better. We need to become producers rather than consumers and take a lesson from other groups who know the products and services we want. It is evident that some groups know the taste for hair, fried fish joints, chicken restaurants and Chinese restaurants, and other services are products we consume rather than produce. We need to make the stuff we use.
- Health officials estimate 1 in 22 African Americans will be diagnosed with the Aids Virus in their lifetime, more than twice the risk for Hispanics and eight times that of whites. African American women comprise 64 percent of women living with HIV/Aids at the end of 2006. There is a need for every institution in the African American community to inform and share the risks of unsafe sex. Some African American churches that appear to not want to discuss this epidemic need to step forward and begin to address and provide support for individuals. We will not stem the tide of HIV/Aids with some churches referring to a scourge by God for the sins of people.
- Too many individuals have negative priorities. While it is great to lease or make payments on a Land Rover or Range Rover while they reside with their parents pass the age of adulthood, it would be enlightenment to observe that some of the richest individuals are driving a Ford Focus and live in a million dollar home.
- Predominantly African American or Latinos have a higher propensity to play the lottery. This group generates the highest lottery sales. These individuals tend to have less education and lower incomes than the population as a whole. According to the *Chicago Reporter*, (2007), the South Side's 60619 ZIP code area, lottery players spent more than $23 million on lottery tickets in 2002. State Senator Barack Obama (2007) in addressing the amount of money spent on lottery tickets commented, "The money a family spent on the lottery could be spent on a computer for a child." This finding is representative of most urban and rural areas of this country. I am convinced that many of these individuals conjure numbers from dreams, birthdays, addresses, and other dates, For many, these are individuals who do not own a car, have health insurance, are unemployed and their children receive free lunches at schools. It should be noted that businesses that have lottery machines are generally found in poor areas of cities. Those who live in more affluent areas have to search for a store that sells lottery tickets.

- All poor people aren't black and all black people aren't poor.

- Beggars can't be choosy.

- Debt is the worse poverty.

- Hard times will make a monkey eat cayenne pepper.

- He hasn't a pot to piss in or a window to throw it out.

- He is living from pillar to post. — A person has no permanent housing.

- I have been swallowing bitter pills and chewing dry bones.

- No one is poor but he who thinks himself so. — Poverty is a state of mind.

- Poverty does not destroy virtue nor does wealth bestow it.

- Poverty is the reward of idleness.

- Poverty waits at the gates of idleness.

- Root hog or die.

- Self-pity is a drug.

- Sloth is the key to poverty.

- That is an empty purse that is full of other men's money.

- They're poor as church mice.

- Things are as scarce as hen's teeth.

 **PRAYER**

I recall our elders frequently saying, "Prayer changes things." As a child, we were taught to pray and always give thanks to God for life, family, health and even hardships. Our elders found a special balm in prayer when they were physically enslaved. They had a strong belief that prayer and faith would change their circumstances. Songs were sung that expressed their firm belief that one day they would be free.

. Be careful what you pray for, because you might get it.

. Don't shout before the spirit rises.

. Even the prayers of an ant reach to Heaven. — God hears all living things.

. He who cannot pray when the sun is shining will not know how to pray when the clouds come.

. He who kneels before God can stand before anyone. — God gives us strength to face adversities.

. Lord we aren't what we ought to be and we aren't what we want to be; we aren't what we're going to be; but thank God, we aren't what we were.

. Prayer changes things.

. Prayer is a wish turned upward.

. Prayer is food for the soul.

. Pray more and worry less. — Prayer is better than worry.

. Productive prayer requires earnestness, not eloquence.

- Seven days without prayer makes one weak. — Daily devotion to God is essential for strength.

- Short prayers reach heaven.

- The most powerful position is on your knees.

- We may not get what we ask for, but we often get what we really need.

- We need tough days to drive us to our knees. — Adversities cause us to pray for assistance.

- When you go to your knees, God will help you stand up for anything.

PRESSURE

If you can't stand the heat, get out of the kitchen
When the pressure is too great, leave the task to someone else.

PRIDE

. A man cannot ride your back unless it is bent. — We give others permission to exploit us.

. Colt in the barley patch kicks high. — We revel in good times.

. The proudness of a man doesn't count when his head is cold.

. You couldn't hit her in the butt with a red apple. — A person is extremely proud.

PRIORITIES

Our elders always taught their children to keep their priorities in order and to know what things were important to achieve an independent and successful life. We were taught to never depend on others for assistance, work hard, pray hard and never spend money foolishly. We were also taught to take every opportunity to help others who were in need for we would never know who would have to help us in a time of need. Our elders did not have much but they had the good stuff of the spirit, which enabled them to live a good life.

It is amazing that my parents who worked hard in menial jobs and paid low wages were able to afford a home, place food on the table, purchase a used car, instill spiritual values, and taught their children that the only way they could overcome adversities was to get an education or marketable skill. My mother worked sometimes seven days a week as the "help" for Dr. Theophilus Erskin

The Tree of Love Gives Shade to All

Ross III at 416 Bay Street in Hattiesburg, Mississippi. She did all of the domestic work from cooking, ironing, babysitting, and house cleaning. She never made more than $19.00 per week. This wage translated to more than fifty-six hours a week at a rate of pay of about forty cents an hour. She was frequently given clothes from Dr. Ross' two daughters, apparel that was purchased at the upscale department stores of Maison Blanche and D. H. Holmes in New Orleans and the Emporium in Jackson, Mississippi.

My Dad labored fifty hours a week shifts at the local Hercules Power Company where he worked extracting resins to produce rosin derivatives, paper chemicals and Delnav, an agricultural insecticide. He brought home approximately forty dollars a week, which meant he was paid about eighty cents an hour. This combined weekly income of fifty-nine dollars a week paid a house note, brought groceries, some clothes, and other necessities. These necessities were what the family needed. There was little money for any wants or dreams we conjured up from reading the Sears-Roebuck catalog. My mother was proficient in delivering a nutritious meal on little. I recall she could take a ham bone and turn it into one of the most delectable meals. Our parents believed in the teaching, "Waste not and want not."

After an absence from Mississippi for more than forty years, I retired from the Detroit, Michigan Public School system and moved to Jackson, Mississippi. I was so proud to return to my roots, a special place where my forefathers/mothers go back to 1782. It was the place where my ancestors were enslaved, gained their freedom and found prosperity in the face of countless adversities. I had great anticipation and expectations that the historically high standards and positive attitudes and behavior, achievement and morality would be apparent among our people.

I was appalled at the self-imposed conditions and circumstances that confronted me, borne out of negative seeds deposited and nurtured in the minds of children and adults. While there were black people prospering in their service as public officials, doctors, lawyers, pharmacists, scientists, teachers, mentors and other professions, there seemed to be a lack of progress that I witnessed as a child growing up in Mississippi. I found that many of our people, young and old, were a study of individual who permitted lack, inertia to destroy the great potential that our ancestors strived for and the special dominion over their lives that God gave them. Unfortunately the parents of many of the children were no more than children who had little or no knowledge or understanding how to become parents.

I was cognizant of the fact that some youth, unlike the youth of my days, had many unhealthy distractions, which prevented them from achieving their potential. Their world seemed to be filled and consumed with dissonance and mental stimulation from external sources and people.

Having traveled to some countries called "Third World," I felt that some sections of the city were as impoverished and unhealthy as those I saw in other parts of the world. A drive along Highway 18 from Utica, Mississippi to Port Gibson, Mississippi, land bordered by large Magnolia trees, tall pine trees, lush grass and corduroy fields, I reached areas where some people lived in impoverished conditions. Numerous mobile homes and trailers were forlorn and dilapidated, unfit for human occupancy. Satellite dishes crowned and seemed to balance these dwellings. Relatively new cars were parked on the side of the decrepit trailer. Invariably, there was a basketball goal with boys playing basketball. Children, amidst garbage and raw sewage in the slick as glass back yards as they spoke in almost unintelligible sentence fragments.

Some of the schools systems, which traditionally fostered achievement, were in shambles. A large number of students were achieving considerably below grade level in reading and mathematics as measured by criterion-referenced and standardized testing.

Many youth, some of whom were "fathers" several times viewed fatherhood with pride for less than a week after the birth of their child littered the streets, parks and public parking lots of some of the city like trash as they sat, stood and sat again aimlessly and hopelessly trapped in poverty. With no agenda, no job and focus, some spent their days and nights walking the streets and being a menace to their neighbors and society. Mutual respect seemed to be abysmally low. The use of profanity seemed to be the primary language for some. Crime was at epidemic proportions in some areas of the community. Parchman penitentiary, the state prison and detention facilities were disproportionately populated by black youth and men.

While the state suffered from a shortfall of money to support educational, social, health, and other empowerment programs, budgets for prisons and jails were increased.

. Don't let someone be a priority in your life when you are still an option in their life.

PRIVILEGE

Our parents and elders provided us with an understanding of the special privileges whites enjoyed. White privilege is defined as a special right, or immunity granted solely for while people that is beyond the common advantages of all others. It is a privilege that exempts whites from certain burdens or liabilities. Growing up in Mississippi in the 1940's I learned early on that whites enjoyed privileges and rights that African Americans did not enjoy. On a daily basis, we were confronted with the special treatment that whites received and African Americans did not. Our schools were segregated and were woefully inadequate in construction, supplies, and resources and staffed by teachers who were paid less than half of the pay of white teachers. We were not permitted to eat at lunch counters and if served, were required to use a back entrance. Signs were prominently placed in public facilities for white and blacks. Our parents and elders were not permitted to vote although they were given the right to vote. White people expected African Americans to address them as mister, sir, and in some cases captain or master while blacks were called by their first names and frequently referred to as aunt, uncle, preacher, or professor rather than ever being given the dignity of being called mister or miss. White privilege was evident in the everyday lives of African Americans. For our people, there were separate churches, separate cemeteries, separate seating arrangement on public transportation separate schools, separate neighborhoods, separate colleges, and separate laws and different penalties for breaking laws.

White privilege dates back to slave-owning colonialists in 17th Century America. The colonies of Maryland and Virginia made a distinction in the privileges of European servants and African servants. Irish, Scottish, English, and German immigrants came to this country as indentured servants to flee poverty or incarceration. They worked for several years to pay off the travel cost debt to this country. They were sold to colonists for between $25 and $50. At the end of their indenture, the "white" servant was free to leave. Blacks who were indentured servants initially enjoyed some of the same rights as white indentured servants. This changed when colonists differentiated indentured servants based on color.

As early as 1641, Massachusetts took away the freedom from black servants. Virginia followed suit in 1661 and restricted the freedom of black servants. By 1660, the institution of slavery first appeared in the statute books of Jamestown and defined blacks as slaves. Slave codes emerged during this time that denied blacks the same rights as white indentured servants. These codes were an ideology of racism, which was used to justify the subordination of blacks and keep them in bondage.

The Virginia legislature made the term "white" a legal distinction in 1691. Previously the indentured servants from Europe were called Englishmen, Irishmen or Christians. Colonial rules gave poor whites preferential treatment by allocating small plots of land, wages, the right to sue their masters in court and exemption from public whipping for punishments. White servants could buy their freedom. Blacks were not afforded this right.

The privileges given to whites and denied to blacks during colonial America continue to be the norm today. In every aspect of American life, there are distinct differences in the rights of whites and blacks. This is evident in the almost century fight for African Americans' rights to vote in the south; the denial of equal protection under the law; the disproportionate number of black youth and men incarcerated; the refusal of equal educational opportunities prior to the landmark Supreme Court decision in *Brown v Board of Education* and beyond; the profiling of African American by some law enforcement agencies; the perpetuation of negative stereotypes of African Americans persist; the lack of access to health care; discounting the worth of an individual of color, his comments, and behavior; the denial of promotions for blacks; whites view themselves as central and not marginal in society; controlling what others know about their own history by presenting only parts of a story; viewing whites as normal and all others as different from normal; robbed of the chance to achieve economic parity; the primary presentation of whites in all media.

. Everyone is a product of his own experiences.

. Everything you say and do is a reflection of the inner you.

. Laundry is the only thing that should be separated by color.

. Our prejudices are our robbers; they rob us of valuable things in life.

. Prejudice is being down on something you are not upon.

. Privilege is a special advantage or immunity or benefit not enjoyed by all.

. Racial superiority is a mere pigment of the imagination.

. You've got to be two times better and smarter than them.

PROMISES

. A promise is a debt.

. Don't promise what you cannot perform.

. Promises are like babies; easy to make, hard to deliver.

. Promise only what you can deliver: then deliver more than you promise

PURPOSE

Many of life's enduring lessons come from experiences we regard as painful and emotionally costly. When we are faced with difficulties, we take it personally and wonder, "Why me?" The challenges are so personalized that we think that others are not confronted with similar experiences. When we lose a love relationship, we grieve. We regard the loss of a job as a failure. We grieve at the loss of a loved one. Each of these losses offers us a challenge to overcome and learn from the experiences for everything there is a purpose.

Hardships test our skills in confronting adversities. If we give up trying to overcome difficulties, we fail. If we fight back and feel that we are in control of the situations, we succeed. Invaluable lessons are the purpose of our suffering.

The Tree of Love Gives Shade to All

Each of us has a special purpose in life to express the gigantic excellence that God has given to us. We are all gifted with a special talent that can help to improve the circumstances in our lives. Many of us live, parent, teach, and work a lifetime not knowing our real purpose in life. When we discover ourselves, we know and understand our purpose as Val Grey states, "I have purpose and a direction/because yesterday/ I discovered me."

. If you can only find it, there is a reason for everything.

. See a man about a dog.

REASON

. Everything happens for the best. — It is important to recognize the importance of events.

. If you can only find it, there is a reason for everything

RELATIONSHIPS

The way we treat other people is a mirror of how we treat ourselves. Our relationships with other people are determined by the way we perceive ourselves. The Navajo Proverb: "Treat all people as though they were related to you," admonishes us to relate to others with respect and appreciation.

We are taught in the Bible to "Love thy neighbor as thyself." When we acknowledge the Divine Presence in us, we love and respect ourselves and we love and respect others. When we relate to individuals with positive expectation, we get positive responses. When we love God and follow his commandments, we receive and treat each person as a spiritual brother and sister.

. Aren't you a sight for sore eyes?

. Better be alone than in bad company.

. Don't cast your pearls before swine.

. Don't cry because it's over, smile because it happened.

. Don't expect a knight in shining armor to sweep you off your feet.

. Don't fatten frogs for snakes.

. Don't let him tell you to play like Jack and Jill; go up the hill for no damn water; water doesn't run uphill

The Tree of Love Gives Shade to All

. I want let that bee sting me twice.

. Lay down with dogs and you will get fleas.

. Like two peas in a pod.

. One monkey doesn't stop a show.

. Out of sight and out of mind.

. Remember that the best relationship is one in which your love for each other exceeds your — need for each other.

. She got knocked up. — She became pregnant

. The best relationship is one in which your love for each other exceeds your need for each other.

. Thick as fleas on a dog's back

. What's fair for the goose is fair for the gander.

. Worry less about what people think of you and more about what you think of them.

. You can't build a relationship with a hammer.

 # RELIGION

. A Christian is the highest style of man.

. A good sermon leaves you wondering how the preacher knew all about you.

. A profitable religion never wants proselytes.

. Be careful how you live. You can be the only Bible some people will ever read.

. Better come late to church than never.

. Better to be in heaven in rags than in hell in embroidery.

. Born once, die twice; born twice, die once.

. Everybody's got to deal with his own sins.

. Going to church doesn't make you a Christian any more than standing in a garage makes you a car.

. Hell is truth seen too late.

. It is better to live in hope than to die in despair. — Hope triumphs despair.

, The belly hates a long sermon.

. The Devil can cite scripture for his purpose.
    Bad people can appear to be good to achieve their objectives.

. The road to hell is paved with good intentions.

. When the devil cannot come he will send.

REPUTATION

. China and reputations are hard to mend.

. If you take care of your character, your reputation will take care of itself.

. No use singing spirituals to a dead man. — It is better to lift up praise to the living

. Your reputation is only as good as what you did yesterday. — Our honor/esteem is cumulative.

RESPONSIBILITY

Our elders, fraught with oppression, controlled in their movement and speech, and regarded as less than human beings, set a high benchmark for character, conduct, and work. They learned that freedom for themselves and family members and the special rewards of liberty was contingent on being responsible and examples to be followed. They were determined to dispel the stereotype that African Americans are not responsible.

. A stitch in time saves nine.

. Aren't but two things I have got to do – stay black and die.

. Bull's horns are never too heavy for its head.

. Every tub must sit on its own bottom. — Everyone has to be independent.

. He/she is a day late and a dollar short.

. He/she is in for a penny, in for a pound. — Once you start something you might as well do it well.

The Tree of Love Gives Shade to All

- Hoe your row. — Take care of your responsibilities.

- If it is to be, it is up to me. — Success is based on one's efforts.

- If the shoe fits, wear it.

- Oh, Lord help me to understand that you aren't going to let nothing come my way that you — And I cannot handle.

- On his own saddle one rides the safest. — Self-sufficiency is the best quality.

- Step up to the plate.

- Take up the torch.

- There isn't any use asking the cow to pour you a glass of milk.

- Tote your own skillet.

ROLES/BOYS/GIRLS

How many times have you heard some individuals say, "That's a man's job or that's a woman's job?" Have you heard men call for their wives when the baby is crying, needs feeding or a diaper change? Children are socialized from the earliest age by their parents into the expected roles/chores/values and behavior for boys and girls. Children do not grow up in a cultural vacuum unaffected by what they see and hear around them.

Girls tend to score higher than boys on standardized tests in verbal areas. One reason for this disparity is girls are encouraged more than boys to read. The lessons that are imparted about specific gender roles are as subtle as hugging girls to the admonition to boys, "Boys don't do things like that. It's a girl thing." Girl are most often expected to express emotions, show affection and to be emotionally dependent, and at the same time called upon to serve and care for everyone in the family.

We need to teach boys that it is okay to cry and it is good to express their emotions. They need to know that health issues are important, even if society tells them that only the weak see a doctor when they are suffering. This is an important lesson which can ensure their longevity. Generally, females live longer than males because they seek medical care and are more attentive to their health issues.

Quite often parents try to instill brute strength in boys and shy reservation in girls. Boys are expected to excel in sports, hunt with the proficiency of early settlers, endure pain and suffering and have more freedom. Fathers tend to view their role in the father-son relationship as ensuring that the boy is all-boy and learns to be assertive and adept in physical activities.

Today, more parents are realizing that boys need the same types of common skills to help them be successful in having effective interpersonal relationships and meeting their own personal needs. Both boys and girls need to have an understanding that cooperation and sharing are essential ingredients to a successful relationship and marriage. Secure men share in domestic activities such as cooking, washing, cleaning, and child-rearing. They don't feel that there masculinity is threatened by helping a wife do domestic chores.

Today more women are working outside the home and more males are becoming involved in perceived female roles. The traditional dichotomy between male and female roles is weakened as women are doing the same jobs as men.

We need to examine the expectations that we have for our boys and girls. Ultimately, they need to be taught the many skills to achieve and succeed in life. A little androgyny will help them live a better life.

. Be a man about it.

. Good example is half a sermon.

. Take it like a man.

. There are two things we should give our children. One is roots and the other is wings.

Otha Richard Sullivan

SACRIFICE

Our elders learned how to sacrifice during economic challenging times. They had experienced slavery, emancipation, World War I, the Great Depression, World War II and economic recessions. These events taught them about being self-sufficient in difficult economic times. They were accustomed to making do with little and be resourceful in planting gardens, farming, and raising livestock to supplement their livelihood.

In 1942, a year after I was born, the government began a strategy focused heavily on limiting domestic consumption. The federal department responsible for the rationing program was the Office of Price Administration, which was started in 1941. One method our government employed to enforce control was to forcibly reduce its citizen's consumption through the implementation of rationing, a program that allowed the government to equally apportion a certain amount of a particular resource to many people. The War effort required huge amounts of metal, paper, rubber and other materials. Individuals were encouraged to plant victory gardens in vacant lands throughout the community. More than 20 million victory gardens were started during World War II. These types of gardens were not new to our African American elders for they always had gardens to raise vegetables to support their families.

More than one hundred million ration books were printed during World War II. There was rationing of different foods, gas and clothing. Ration stamps were issued to all Americans. This measure was taken as soldiers needed the items to aid them in fighting the war. The stamps came in books much like postage stamp books. Colored coded, red and blue stamps were worth 10 points. Red and blue tokens were worth 1 point each. Red stamps were used for meat, butter, fats, cheese, canned meat and canned fish. Green, brown or blue stamps were used for canned vegetables, baby food, and dried fruit. These tokens were used to make change for red and blue stamps only when a purchase was made. Ration books sold for between $3.00 and $10.00. Individual ration stamps were only a few cents each.

Rubber, sugar, coffee, meat, butter, canned goods, shoes, clothing and other items were items rationed. Examples of the points for various items included one pound of hamburger, which was 12 points; one pound of butter required 16 points; one pound of American cheese, 8 points. To illustrate the scarcity of some items during World War II, you were required to have ration stamps to buy anything at the store. One pound of sugar was allowed every two weeks for each household.

Gas was also rationed. The typical car owner received an "A" gas ration coupon booklet, which allowed 150 miles of driving per month. A "B" gas ration coupon booklet was for those who had to drive further to their jobs. The "C" gas ration books were for ministers, doctors or people working directly with the war effort. Of course, many African Americans did not receive gas ration coupon booklets because they could not afford cars and either took public transportation or rode with others who had vehicles.

 SECRET

. Alcohol will preserve anything but a secret.

. Don't let the cat out of the bag. — Keep it as a secret

. He/she can't hold water. — One cannot keep a secret.

. Just between you and me.

. Keep it under the belt.

. Keep it under your hat. — Keep it as a secret

. Keep it zipped.

. My lips are sealed. — A person will not talk about what is shared in confidence.

. Put a sock in it.

. The cowbell can't keep a secret.

. You are only as sick as your secrets.

 SELF-ACCEPTANCE

Our failure to accept what the good Lord gave us has spawned and supported the development of multi-billion dollar businesses that promise self-acceptance and healing from depressed self-esteem. The promises of these businesses are expressed in the availability of diet plans, fat reducing pills, full body corsets, and other products to lose weight within two weeks. For the individuals who detest their ebony skin, there are skin-lightening creams such as Artra Skin

Tone Cream and Nadinola. For those who don't like their eye color, there are various colors of contact lenses, which come in shades of blue, green, violet and hazel. There are products to change the color of hair from its natural color to hues of blond, auburn, red and other colors.

To those individuals who hate the texture, color and length of their hair, there are varieties of wigs, faux hair extensions, weaves (sewn or glued onto the hair) Indy Remy hair (the latest craze among some African American women). Korean beauty supply businesses have become billion dollar industries in providing false hair, hair that can be purchased in inches, feet and yards. For those who feel their natural hair is unattractive and inferior to that of others, there are chemicals, gels, and more chemicals to change the texture of their hair. And to those who believe that powder and paint enhance their beauty, there are endless possibilities for powder, paint, cream and moisturizers.

And for those who dislike their bodies, there are numerous procedures available for cosmetic surgery, silicone implants for breasts, face, calves and other parts of the bodies. Some cosmetic surgeons have even begun a special "blue light" special sale of two- for the price of one procedures for clients.

There is no quick fix to enhancing one's self-acceptance and lack of appreciation for what the Good Lord gave them. I am reminded of a woman who fought hopelessly for decades and endless, costly and unsuccessful battles to lose weight. She bought into every diet plan, diet book, state-of-the-art exercise equipment, body wrap, and the services of a trainer who left in disgust because she was always too tired to exercise. Her quest for a quick fix to an internally based problem doomed her to failure with each tool of denial she used to overcome her obesity. She, like any other person, will only be successful in losing weight or any other perceived dissatisfaction with her body until she begins to identify the garbage she has injected into her mind and replace it with positive thoughts and conscious efforts to change the root cause of her addiction to food.

Khalil Gibran, in *The Voices of the Master*, provides a powerful lesson about truth and how individuals do not acknowledge truth. He wrote, "Truth calls to us, drawn by the innocent laughter of a child, or the kiss of a love one; but we close the doors of affection in her face and deal with her as with an enemy." We learn how to gain control of our lives and accept ourselves when we exalt the Spirit within and permit it to guide us and support us in our journey toward health and prosperity. That special relationship enables us to find personal freedom. We begin to understand that liberation from external people, external corrections. and circumstances enrich our lives by providing peace of mind and harmony. When we make the connection with the special relationship with the Divine Power within us, we have the creative power to remove denial from our being and face our frailties, disharmony and overcome them. We are then able to answer the basic questions about why we fail to accept ourselves and glorify ourselves. Why do I hate myself? Why do I destroy myself? What are the inner needs that drive me to feel inadequate about my body and appearance?

. If I train myself to suit others, I will soon whittle myself away.

. If you really put a small value upon yourself, rest assured the world will not raise your price.

. Love and you shall be loved.

. No amount of self-improvement can make up for a lack of self-acceptance.

SELF-ESTEEM

Every individual greets and responds to life in the manner in which he or she views self. This self-esteem or self-concept is a person's perception and appraisal of his or her strengths, weaknesses, abilities, attitudes and values. The development of self-esteem begins at birth and continues to be developed throughout life experiences. We all need a good dose of self-concept to live a happy and healthy life. The choices we make in life are directly related to the degree to which we feel mentally strong or weak. Negative or low self-esteem is one of the leading causes of mental health problems, which leads to physical problems.

Self-esteem generates our thoughts and actions and is a personal report card of how we view ourselves. I am convinced that many people never realize their true potential to achieve success in social, emotional, financial and health due to their self-perception.

Are you responding to life by making a cameo appearance? Are you the supporting actor in your life? Are you the leading actor in your life? Individuals who make a cameo appearance always give and receive less in life. These individuals constantly seek and accept "bit" parts in the theater of life. They appear to be comfortable with the crumbs of life and are frightened of having the full loaf. They are woefully lacking in self-esteem, dependent and give others control over their lives and never expect to see their names on the credits of life. These individuals are void of hope and believe their negative circumstances would never change.

The supporting actor lives a life of struggle, attempting to find self, but becomes impatient, loses the precious gift of hope, and decides to spend a lifetime helping others at the risk of losing his/her identity. Supporting actors tend to focus more on their regrets, losses, and failures that their dreams and goals. Those who make the powerful connection with the Spirit within and follow its counsel respond to life as the leading actor. They accept, claim, and respond to life in a positive manner and know that they have dominion over their lives.

Leading actors face adversities head on and realize that hope and work fosters and sustains a joyful and successful life. They know that their lives have infinite possibilities for health, happiness, abundance and service. From the casting call of life, what roles have you decided to play in your life? I believe that every individual was born to be the leading actor in his/her life.

Millions of people are ill at ease, poor, un-productive and fail because they appear to be chasing rainbows in the dark and fitfully searching for self-discovery and personal empowerment in the wrong people, places and substances. They are deficient in recognizing the caution signs that warn them that their identity and potential for health, wealth, and abundance come from the Spirit within. Unfortunately, many individuals permit lack to extinguish the powerful Spirit within, which jump starts the creative potential with which they were born. Their quest for a meaningful life is never fulfilled, as they are confused about their personal identity. They are impulsive with their word and actions and are unable to make appropriate choices when faced with moral dilemmas, adversities, and lessons that teach skills in becoming the best they can be.

There are millions of people worldwide who are fighting an endless battle in their quest to know who they are and why they do the things they do to become vulnerable victims. These battles include low self-esteem, deferred dreams, obesity, poverty, abuse and other forms of lack. Incredibly we often permit food, hopelessness, drugs to have more power over us than the mind the good Lord gave us and the special Spirit to guide us in making healthy choices.

When we think we are not worthy, it becomes a self-fulfilling prophecy. Simply stated, we fail to value ourselves and seek others to validate us who don't value you or themselves. When an individual feels powerless to change negative thoughts and behaviors that cause poor health, he/ she has not made the most important discovery of his/her life. The answer to any of life's challenges is found in the knowledge, acceptance, understanding and related actions that God dwells within us and desires for us to live a healthy and fulfilled life. His omnipresence provides us with every tool to achieve a meaningful life.

. Believe in yourself. — Have faith in your abilities.

. If you really put a small value upon yourself, rest assured that the world will not raise your price.

. Love yourself; for if you don't. How can you expect anybody to love you?

. To wish you were someone else is to waste the person you are.

SELF-SUFFICIENCY

Our elders' triumph over slavery taught them the importance of self-sufficiency. I recall our elders teaching children at the earliest age that they needed to depend on themselves and work to achieve a good job, a home and provide for their children.

I was born in an apartment in the projects of Hattiesburg, Mississippi in the early 1940's. Many individuals viewed the projects as the place where affluent black people lived. There was no stigma in living in a project for the apartments were far superior to the dilapidated homes that many blacks and whites lived in during these difficult economic times. The projects offered the kind of amenities that were missing in most homes. There was a modern heating system, indoor plumbing and a gas burning stove. An indoor bathroom was almost a statistical rarity in the homes of most people. At the time a number of black and white families lived temporarily in segregated projects. My parents always knew this type of housing was temporary and they would purchase a home once they saved enough money to make a down payment. Most parents at the time shared this same value of home ownership and realized that dream of a home within a few years. Their dream was a testament to the teachings of their parents of "God bless the child that's got his own."

My parents eventually saved enough money to make a down payment on a house when I was age two. A humble abode would be an understatement of the appearance of this forlorn house, which was an unpainted shotgun house with an outhouse. A shotgun house was the type of structure where one could take a shotgun and shoot straight through the entire house. My brothers and sister were shocked upon seeing our parents' dream house. They thought our parents had lost their mind, choosing a place with an outhouse and a well for water. Of course, Mom and Dad were not crazy. They knew this house was a big start toward self-sufficiency. They knew home ownership would enhance their self-esteem and promote independence.

To our parents owning a home, no matter how humble, was a great symbol of achieving the American dream. Home ownership gave them and their family members a sense of dignity, honor, stability and security and knowing they were making an investment in their future. It was a testament to their elders who owned a home and property just a few years out of slavery. To our parents, it was wonderful not to share walls.

Our parents at the time recognized that dependency on others for assistance caused spiritual and moral decay. Dependency would have caused them to accept subsidized housing and financial assistance. Men and women who depended on others were regarded as sorry individuals and a disgrace to the race. Our elders believed that irresponsibility was like a disease. They believed that a man was not a man when he denied his family the most basic needs of food, clothing and shelter. Our people were determined to defy the stereotypes of whites and one of the stereotype of black people, especially black men was they were lazy and neglected their family. My parents' beliefs helped to instill a sense of pride in us children. We learned to never expect others to provide for any of our basic needs.

Acceptance of food at a neighbor's house was grounds for discipline at the time. I recall my error in judgment at Christmas time at the Antioch Missionary Baptist Church. The church invited poor kids to the church every Christmas to receive a toy, which was donated from Sears-Roebuck store. I went to church on that special day because my friends had talked about the event for days before Christmas. When the minister asked the children, "How many of you did not receive a toy this Christmas?" I made the cardinal mistake of raising my hand which demonstrated that I was lying and especially lying in church in the presence of the Lord. I was given a Greyhound bus and was quite excited as the other children who received various toys.

Upon arriving home, my Dad immediately spotted the new toy and asked, "Where did you get that toy?" Realizing I had lied enough for the day, I responded, "At Antioch Missionary Baptist Church." Immediately Dad said, "Take it back and hurry home because I have something waiting for you!" He was livid at the thought that I had publicly lied and said I did not receive anything for Christmas, a message perceived by the minister and the other adults that my Dad did not provide a toy for his child at Christmas.

Embarrassed and distressed about the pending consequences of my lie in church, I quickly returned the toy, apologized to Rev. Woullard and asked for his and God's forgiveness. When I returned home, Dad was waiting for me. He commanded me to take off my clothes and I knew this meant that my behind was about to get a whipping. (Parents at the time never beat you with your clothes on.). I recall that this was one of the worst Christmases of my life yet it was a special lesson that I held dear to my heart for a lifetime.

While most of us grew up in poverty, as defined by social and economic indicators, we did not view ourselves as being poor. In fact, our parents and elders ingrained in us the teaching that real poverty was a state of mind and the greatest poverty of all was spiritual poverty.

The lessons of self-sufficiency of African Americans have fallen on deaf ears among a number of families today. Welfare has contributed to the burgeoning social, emotional, physical and financial problems some face in coping with life's challenges. There are too many people who have intergenerationally depended on handouts from local, state and federal agencies. When an able-bodied man or woman is continuously supported by society and consistently accepts handout, he/she will never transcend mental poverty and dependence.

Too many families have continued to depend on governmental assistance and lack discipline to get a job. This is a poor example for children and sets low expectations for generations of children and youth who believe they have no control over their life

President Franklin D. Roosevelt, at the dawn of the American welfare system in the 1930's, shared his thought about welfare and the possible effects on recipients in his 1935 State of the Union message. His ominous warning was "The lessons of history, confirmed by evidence immediately before me, show conclusively that continued dependence on relief induces a spiritual and moral disintegration fundamentally destructive to the national fiber. To dole out relief in this way is to administer a narcotic, a subtle destroyer of the human spirit. It is inimical to the dictates of sound policy. It is a violation of the traditions of America."

The welfare programs instituted by Roosevelt included social security benefits for retired workers and aid to families with dependent children. Perhaps the greater of the two programs was the Social Security Act, which assured retired and disabled workers financial benefits, to individuals who had worked and made a contribution to society.

Unfortunately welfare assistance programs have not worked to move some individuals out of poverty and appear to have developed a cross-generational dependency on financial assistance. By the year 2000, four generations of some family members were the recipients of welfare. I am convinced the dependency on welfare for many is directly related to their inability to problem-solve challenges in their lives.

. God, if I can't have what I want, let me want what I have

. Man who waits for roast duck to fly into mouth must wait very, very long time.

. The first step to getting the things you want out of life is this: Decide what you want.

SEX

Our elders believed that sex should not occur without marriage. There was no talk or teachings about sex. Girls were admonished to "keep their drawers up and their dresses down." For a teenager to approach the subject of sex with a parent was almost unheard of. The culture at the time was that only married couples had sex. Parents were positive roles models as they largely were married before they had children.

I recall in the 1950's when I was a teenager that there were few girls who became pregnant as teenagers. Teenagers were involved in sex but it was considered to be a sin and a shame due to religious and cultural beliefs in the African American community. Our elders believed in the teaching of the Bible, which promoted chastity and prohibited premarital sex. Teenage pregnancy was rare in the days of my youth. In 1950, I was aware of one girl who became pregnant out-of-wedlock and remained with her family. Some parents would be so shamed that they would send a pregnant teenager up north to live with a relative until the baby was born. After delivering the baby, the child was often taken care of by the teenager's parents and other family members.

When a girl became pregnant at the time, the father of the child would insist on a shotgun wedding where the father of the child was required to marry the girl. It was considered to be the honorable thing to do. Our elders believed that a child should have the legal name of the father. He was also expected to provide for the child.

Today, there is little stigma associated with out-of-wedlock births. There are few shotgun weddings held to protect the honor of the teenager and her family. A report from the National Survey of Family Growth found that between 2006-2008 more than 42 percent or 4.3 million teenage girls have had sex at least once. For teenage boys, the report found that 43 percent or 4.5 million boys had had sex.

There are a number of reasons for teenage pregnancy in this country. For some it is peer pressure and early dating; inadequate knowledge about safe sex; exploitation by older men; socio-economic factors and school dropouts. One of the main reasons teenage sex is prevalent is due to the lack of information about the consequences of teenage sex. Sex education is not taught in some schools because some parents are opposed to having schools take on this responsibility. Several programs have been instituted to have teenagers say no to sex and take a vow of abstinence. These programs have failed miserably.

More success has been found when parents are able to have discussions about sex and the importance of protecting their bodies. There are some steps that parents can take to assist their children in avoiding teenage sex. Talk with children early and often about sex; supervise and monitor children on a regular basis; monitor what they are watching, reading and listening to; know your children's friends and their families; and look for signs that they need to talk about their bodies, dating, and sexuality.

There is a need to have more discussions and lessons on sex education. Studies have found that teen mothers who had their first child as a teenager and did not have both parents in the home were more likely to have teenagers who are sexually active.

. It isn't the size of the ship, but the motion of the ocean.

. It looks like she has swallowed a watermelon. — Girl is pregnant.

. Two clean sheets don't smut.

 **SHAME**

. He is lost whose shame is lost.

 **SHARING**

Most of us recall our parents, grandparents and other elders enhancing their lives by sharing with others. Our elders stood ready to help their neighbor from the birth of a baby, the making of a bed frame for a newlywed couple, the collective gathering and sharing of crops, participation in Friday night fish fries, the comforting of bereaved families and offering assistance in times of tragedies and unforeseen acts of God.

Our elders recognized that the greatest gift they could give to each other was their time, compassion and possessions. I recall the quilting bees that were held in my maternal grandmother's house. As a child, I would peek from the living room into the dining room and see women and occasionally men, sitting in home-made chairs under the wooden "horses" that held each quilt. Each piece of fabric was special, usable and handled with care. This activity was a highly valued ceremony that offered contentment to the participants as they stitched pieces with the greatest care. Concern for each other was expressed in their lively conversations, the sipping of coffee or tea and for some, a dip of Sweet Garrett or Tuberose snuff, indulging in the tasty teacakes, boasting about the size of their garden tomatoes or the plumpness of their prized hens, extolling the size and color of their gigantic hollyhocks, or just bringing each other up to date on the social happenings in the country. It was all about sharing.

. You share and share alike.

 **SILENCE**

. A still tongue makes a wise head.

. Be silent and pass for a philosopher.

. Put a key on your tongue.

. Silence is as great an art as speech.

. Silence puts an end to quarrels.

. Speaking is silver, silence is gold.

 **SIN**

. He/she is ugly as sin. — Unattractive person

. He washed my sins away and that old account was settled long ago.

. If you do not want the fruits of sin, stay out of the devil's orchard.

. If you want to see your own sins, clear up a new ground.

. Your sins will find you out. — Our sins are always revealed

 **SLOTH**

Our ancestors overcame their conditions and stressed industry, hard work and diligence.

Sloth, as a deadly sin, was unacceptable to them and knew that continued progress and freedom depended on effort. I recall lazy folks begging others for food, individuals who were ignorant of the lessons in Proverbs 20:4, "The sluggard will not plow by reason of the cold; therefore shall he beg in harvest, and have nothing."

Our elders, parents, and teachers instilled a belief in us that we had the essence of greatness. We were taught that slothfulness and irresponsibility of any kind would threaten our freedom as African Americans and be a disgrace and dishonor to our foremothers and forefathers who made great strides in the face of formidable challenges.

. Better to be up late and wide awake than to get up early and be asleep all day.

. By doing nothing we learn to do evil.

. Can't sit on the bucket and draw water at the same time.

. Don't sleep your life away.

. Hand plow can't make furrows by itself.

. He's got molasses in his britches.

. He/she is useless as teats on a boar pig. — A reference to a bad worker

. He who sleeps much learns little.

. Idleness is the rust of the soul. — Our minds need stimulation to be effective.

. It's a sorry house where the hen crows and the cock is silent.
    Men should take some responsibility for maintaining a home.

. It is no use asking the cow to pour you a glass of milk.

. Just counting stumps don't clear the field.

. Lazy folks' stomachs don't get tired (hungry).

. Like a bump on a log.

. Looking for work and praying not to find it.

. Old used-to-do-it-this-way doesn't help anyone today.

. Providence assists not the idle. — Fortunes and blessings do not come to lazy people.

. Sleeping in the fence corner doesn't fetch Christmas in the kitchen.

. Sleepy fisherman totes a light load home. — You can't accomplish much by being sleepy.

. Sloth is the key to poverty.

. Talking about fire doesn't boil the pot.

. The sluggard's convenient season never comes. — Lazy people never find the right time to work.

. Unwilling service earns no thanks.

. When you have not done anything, you don't have to undo.

 **SORROW**

As a child growing up in a rural area of Mississippi, I remember the prophecy of my maternal grandfather, "Into each life, some rain must fall." Many individuals regard sorrow as an un-welcomed event and would rather not be confronted with sorrow. None of us is immune from sorrow and we cannot lessen the lessons of life's formidable challenges. Some view sorrow as a question of their faith. We must know that faith and its many victories grow in the valley of despair, long suffering and discontentment. Sorrows teach us to face life's challenges with an understanding that joy most often comes from experiences of pain and suffering.

We have all faced some kind of sorrow in life. Our response to sorrow is most likely as different as the unique event. Sorrow emerges in many forms, the death of a loved one; the loss of a love relationship that we believed that our very life depended on it; the pain of losing a job; the melancholy of children who stray from our teachings; and the disconsolate feelings of seeing one's inhumanity to another. Our sorrows are special opportunities to practice the special faith that the Lord always delivers us out of them all. Sorrows teach us to face life's challenges with an understanding joy most often comes from experiences of pain and suffering.

Sorrows should never be experiences that thwart our spirit and render us helpless in being in control of our life. Accept the sorrow. Share it with a loved one or a close friend. Take the sorrow to the Lord in prayer. Life is filled with tribulations that strengthen us if we only hold on to faith and pull on the great strength that dwells within us. Those who are overwhelmed and wallow in sorrow don't lack strength, they lack will. Those who choose to live in sorrow refuse to accept that personal growth and development require walking by faith and not by sight.

One cure for sorrow is to become a means of good to others. Seek ways to be involved in work, hobbies, and share your special talents with others. Take the time to be silent, meditate and get in touch with the special spirit within you. Listen to others who are dealing with personal suffering. I am convinced that when we are aware of others sorrows, our suffering pales in comparison.

. Don't borrow sorrow from tomorrow.

. Sorrow, like rain, makes roses and mud. — We all face sorrows and learn how to overcom

Otha Richard Sullivan

STEREOTYPES

I recall growing up in Mississippi and seeing the many offensive caricature depictions of African Americans on Southern postcards and souvenirs. These caricatures showed African Americans as being lazy, dishonest, violent, promiscuous, and unclean. A visit to any of the five and dime stores in my hometown was filled with racks of postcards and souvenirs that showed African Americans in a negative light. I recall some of the postcards depicted black people with blood red, grinning lips stretched to grotesque extremes stealing watermelons and eating watermelons; some depicted children as pickaninnies (an offensive name for a black child) with unkempt hair and raggedy clothes exposing their behinds; depiction of children and adults with captions of racial epithets; and other cards showed black people picking cotton and living in dilapidated shacks in a field of cotton. Some of the souvenirs purchased by white people captioned black women as a mammy and black men as "ole black Joe."

Stereotypes are generalizations about the behavior of African Americans and others. Stereotyping shows ignorance and a lack of education. It is a learned behavior from adults, parents and others who express their prejudice and beliefs they are superior to all others. Their beliefs are rooted in one's own group is superior and other groups are inferior.

Stereotypes of black people originated in colonial America and how slave owners used to view slaves. Songs, movies, minstrel shows, cartoons and print media helped to perpetuate stereotypes. Stereotypes were popularized in the character of *Topsy* in the 1852 book *Uncle Tom's Cabin*, the 1936 Hal Roach feature starring *Our Gang Children* and the character of Buckwheat. Scott Joplin's adaptation of the lyrics of *I am Thinking of My Pickanninies Days*, written in 1902. There were books that white children read such as *The Story of Little Black Sambo*, written by Helen Brodie Banerman in 1899. This book was crudely stereotypical and hurtful to blacks. Stereotypes of blacks were promoted in *Jump Jim Crow*, *Zip Coon*, *Mammy*, *Buck* and other minstrel shows of white men painted in black faces. There was the movie *Birth of a Nation* in 1915 where African American men were played by white actors in black face as unintelligent and sexually aggressive toward white women and the Ku Klux Klan as a heroic force in America.

The Tree of Love Gives Shade to All

    The Amos n' Andy radio program which was aired from 1926 to 1960 portrayed African Americans as lazy, ignorant and buffoons. This program was widely received by whites as it perpetrated the types of stereotypes they held about African Americans. It should be noted that television programs that presented African American in a positive light were canceled in southern states. For example, the "Nat King Cole" television show, a popular program, was canceled due to outcries from white people. The television show was cancelled after one year. This type of racist behavior from some individuals who could not conjugate the verb "to be" was present in 1955 when Leontyne Price, opera star, appeared in a leading role in the NBC=TV Opera program. The program was canceled by some southern NBC affiliates in protest of presenting an African American in such a positive role.

    When I was growing up in Mississippi, there were no libraries for African Americans. We were forbidden from entering white libraries in the community. The books we used in our schools perpetuated the belief that blacks were inferior. These books did not present any of the contributions of African Americans. The purpose of this deletion in history books was to have blacks feel inferior to whites. Carter G. Woodson, in *The Mis-Education of the Negro* (1933) shares that "If you teach the Negro that he has accomplished as much as good as any other race, he will aspire to equality and justice without regard to race. Such an effort will upset the program of the oppressor in Africa and America."

    Our parents, elders, and relatives worked hard to dispel the stereotypes and provided positive books, magazines, newspapers, and poetry that highlighted the contributions of African Americans. While no bookstores included positive literature about African Americans, our elders called upon Northern relatives, local teachers and others to secure real literature about African Americans. Consequently, we were introduced to the writings of Alain Leroy Locke's book, *The New Negro*; W.E.B. Du Bois book: *The Souls of Black Folk* and other writings; *The Crisis*, the publication of the National Association for the Advancement of Colored People (considered to be contraband literature by whites in Mississippi); the poetry of Langston Hughes, Countee Porter Cullen, Arna Wendell Bontemps, and James Weldon Johnson. We were introduced to three black-owned newspapers: the *Chicago Defender*, the *Jackson Advocate* (Jackson, Mississippi) and The *Pittsburgh Courier* (Pittsburgh, Pennsylvania). These newspapers presented positive articles about African Americans and their contributions. During my childhood, there were more than 200 African American newspapers in this country. Their mission was to fight injustice and highlight positive news about the achievements and contributions of African Americans and empower the African American community.

The *Chicago Defender* newspaper helped African Americans be informed of injustice and discrimination. It also served to provide objective and positive news and presentations about African Americans. The paper exposed racism and oppression that African Americans faced throughout the United States. Southern whites loathed this newspaper because it presented graphic images of lynching, assaults and other violence against African Americans. The *Defender* was the stimulus for the great migration of African Americans from the South to the North. More than 1,500,000 African Americans migrated to the North from 1915-1928. White landowners hated the *Chicago Defender* newspaper for its effective efforts in recruiting of African Americans to leave sharecropping and move north for better opportunities. This migration depleted the source of workers for white-owned farms. Pullman car porters and entertainers smuggled the newspaper into the South (Pullman car porters were members of the first labor organization led by African Americans). "Fight or Be Slaves" was the motto of the Brotherhood of Sleeping Car Porters. The paper was widely read by African Americans. Ku Klux Klan members sought to confiscate copies of the paper and intimidate its readers.

The caricatures of the past and the stereotypes promoted by whites during slavery have contributed to the current stereotypes held by some white people. These stereotypes have served as propaganda that African Americans are inferior to whites. Our parents and elders always told us to ignore the stereotypes and reverse any of the stereotypes as they were not accurate depictions of African Americans. Our elders told us that stereotypes are banal expressions used by ignorant and prejudiced individuals that project negative perceptions and are employed to relegate African Americans to second-class citizenship. We were taught that those who used stereotypes were ignorant, poorly educated and economically marginalized individuals and we were smarter to never believe their stereotypes. When the stereotype of an African American as being lazy, we were taught that we were smart. When we were portrayed as being lazy, we were told that our people were the most industrious as they worked hard to build this country.

The Tree of Love Gives Shade to All

We could all lead a more fruitful and healthy life if we followed the Navajo Proverb: "Treat all people as they were related to you." Unfortunately, many people do not follow this proverb and through their ignorance find it easier to identify, sort and select people as being less than others based on their skin color.

Our world is filled with individuals who have negative thoughts, beliefs, opinions and false truth about individuals who differ in skin color, race, creed, religion and cultural customs. These beliefs lead to stereotypes that promote discrimination and racism and only serve to disease the mind and body of those who hold such negative thoughts of others. Dr. Martin Luther King, Jr., in *Where do We Go from Here*, wrote "Racism is a contempt for life, an arrogant assertion that one race is the center of value and object of devotion, which other races must kneel in submission."

As a child growing up in Mississippi, I was confronted with disrespectful, contemptuous and insulting terms used to refer to African Americans. These terms included ape, coon, crow, darkie, jungle bunny, chocolate drops, pickaninny, tar baby, jigaboo and boy. Adults were disrespected by whites who refused to acknowledge them as equals. I recall a white person would never refer to an African American man or woman in a respectful manner as "Mister, "Miss," "Mrs." Or "Ma'am." They called some African American men by their first name or referred to them as" uncle," "preacher" or "boy." African American women were referred to as "Auntie" or were called by their first name. Blacks had to use courtesy titles when referring to whites and were never permitted to call them by their first names.

Stereotypes and discrimination of African Americans were manifested in separate facilities. There were separate water fountains for blacks and whites although the water came from the same pipe. Schools were segregated and the books and equipment for African American students were those discarded from white schools. None of the textbooks we used cited any contributions of African Americans. Occasionally there were some brief citations about Booker T. Washington and Dr. George Washington Carver. White people did not want African American children to know any positive presentations or information that would upset the status quo of African Americans. Textbooks did not present any information about W. E. B. Du Bois, as he was considered by whites to be too controversial and "arrogant."

African Americans were relegated to menial labor, serving as the help as domestics, chauffeurs, house servants and the like. Department stores forbade blacks from trying on clothes, but accepted their money with ease which was never a white or black denomination but a green bill with the appropriate dollar amount. When we went downtown, we boys were cautioned to step off the sidewalk when a white girl or woman approached to prevent an altercation or threat of being an insolent black. Some whites taught their children that they were better than blacks. On the way to school through white neighborhoods, we were confronted with being called the 'N' word, chocolate drop, pickanninny, and monkey.

Our parents and elders instilled a special feeling of pride and worthiness as they told us to ignore and not internalize the negative thoughts and beliefs of an outside world. Our teachers, the preacher, the domestic, the common laborer, the barber, and the insurance man told us over and over again that we were special and were somebody – equal to any other individuals. These teachings helped us to know and understand that we were just as worthy as anyone else. We understood early in life that we had to reject negative thoughts, opinions, beliefs and false truths held by others. We knew that God did not make a difference in people. Segregation did not thwart our Spirit to love and forgive people and understand that ignorance abounds.

While some strides have been made in providing black children and youth with positive literature about the contributions of African Americans, much still needs to be done to introduce them to their history. As a science teacher, I asked my students to name three African American inventors. Out of a class of twenty-five students, only three students were able to cite the names of inventors. This lack of knowledge, the paucity of information, and failure to incorporate Black History into the public schools curriculum, moved me to write several books on African American History. When our youth don't know their history, they are condemned to poverty and diminished aspiration on what they can become.

Stereotypes of African Americans continue to be pronounced in American society. The recent tragedy of Trayvon Martin by George Zimmerman, a neighborhood watch captain, who shot and killed this 17-year-old boy as he walked from a convenience store to his father's house in Sanford, Florida. Martin was unarmed and was wearing a hooded sweat shirt, called a hoodie. Zimmerman allegedly was threatened by this young man simply because he represented the stereotype of a hoodie-wearing black boy as a thug and a threat to white people.

. By ignorance we make mistakes, and by mistakes we learn.

. Despite setbacks and stereotypes, I'm proud of my roots and history.

. Stereotypes are devices for saving a biased person the trouble of learning.

. The greatest ignorance is to reject something you know nothing about.

. The price of ignorance is far greater than the cost of an education.

. There is no reply to the ignorant like keeping silence.

. Your ignorance cramps my conversation.

SUCCESS

The quality that separates successful people from those who are not successful is persistence. Success is never achieved by sitting and waiting for it to knock on your door. I have often heard some individuals say, "My ship is going to sail and come into port one day." Each of us is like a ship that sails on turbulent waters, attempting to reach our destination. Our ability to steer the ship and sail into the port of success is based on our skills to face the challenges. I am convinced that "a smooth sea never made a skillful mariner."

Our elders taught us the lesson that nothing worthwhile is easy. They admonished us to work hard and do our best in school. When we felt we were failing, they lifted us up and reminded us that some failure is the stepping stone to success.

. A good run is better than a bad stand.

. A quitter never wins.

. Change your mind and you will change your life.

. Corn makes more at the mill than in the crib.

. Cream rises to the top.

. He who succeeds is reputed wise. — Wisdom comes from struggles and achievement.

. If you don't climb the mountain, you can't see the view.

. If you never reach, you're never going to grab what you are after.

. Judge your success by what you had to give up in order to get it.

, Nothing beats a failure but a try. — Trying is better than failure.

The Tree of Love Gives Shade to All

. Nothing succeeds like success.

. Nothing ventured, nothing gained. — If you don't risk anything, you won't gain anything.

. Perseverance brings success. — Persistence leads to achievement.

. Success comes in cans; failures comes in can't. — When we feel we can't achieve, we fail.

. Quit while you're ahead.

. Sharp ax is better than a big mule. — Some tools are more effective than others.

. The first one to the spring gets the clearest water.

. The top of the hill is harder to find than the bottom. — It is easier to accept less than strive for more.

. The two hardest things to handle in life are failure and success.

. To reach a great height a person needs to have great depth.

. You've got to crawl before you walk. — It takes small steps to reach our goals.

 SUPERSTITIONS

Superstitions among some African Americans originated from ancient African religion and Native American folklore. Some of the superstitions that have been passed on from one generation to another:

. Animals know when you are pregnant.

. Don't cut a baby's hair before his/her first birthday.

. Don't put your purse on the floor or you'll stay broke.

. Don't talk on the phone or turn on the TV while it is thundering and lightning.

. Fish dreams means that someone is having a baby.

. Girls are carried high and boys are carried low.

. If you allow children to sweep the floor, they will sweep up unwanted guests.

. If you break a mirror, you will have seven years of bad luck.

. If you keep making funny faces, one day it will get stuck that way.

. If your ear is ringing someone is talking about you.

. It is bad luck to cross a black cat's path.

. Never buy your boyfriend or husband shoes as a gift, because he'll walk out of your life with them.

The Tree of Love Gives Shade to All

. Splitting the pole gives you bad luck.

. Step on a crack, you'll break your mother's back.

. Sunshine, raining and thunder at the same time means the devil is beating his wife.

. When you cross the railroad tracks you need to touch a screw for safe crossing.

TALK

. His mouth isn't a prayer book.

. If you can walk, you can dance. If you can talk, you can sing.

. Talk is cheap.

THIEF

. A thief thinks every man steals.

. Show me a liar and I'll show you a thief.

. Stolen fruit is the sweetest. — What is forbidden is the most tempting.

TIME

. Day's short as ever, time's long as it has been.

. He that has most time has none to lose.

. If your coattail catches fire, don't wait until you see the blaze for you to put it out.

. Little and often make a heap of time.

. Stand the test of time.

. The crawfish in a hurry looks like he's trying to get there yesterday.

. Time does not stand still.

The Tree of Love Gives Shade to All

. Time and tide wait for no man.

. Time is the healer of all wounds. — In time, pain, hurts, and grief subside.

. Turn back the clock.

. Until the cows come home. — It is a long period of time.

. When the time is right

. You can't hurry up good times.

TOUGHNESS

Our elders taught us that mental, physical and spiritual toughness was evident in our skin color and DNA from our foremothers and forefathers. The heritage of our ancestors, who overcame slavery and adversities after emancipation, expressed toughness in their spirit and soul. They did not faint in the days of adversities and never were overcome with feelings that they could not overcome barriers placed in their lives. Our history as African Americans is a sterling testament of strength and energy as tools to overcome obstacles. When we faltered and did not demonstrate toughness, our parents and elders always presented historical evidence of individuals who persisted and became successful in their lives.

. Drink no tea for the fever and wear no crepe for the dead.

. He/she is tough as nails.

. Only the strong survive.

TRAVEL

Elders constantly reminded us that life is a continuous journey as we try to reach our goals in life. They taught us that the road to success would never be smooth. As we traveled down the road of life, we were reminded that the journey would be filled with detours and hurdles that were necessary to teach us how to maneuver and reach our destination. Our elders emphasized that we could not give up when there were unexpected detours in our journey.

. If you don't know where you want to go, any road will take you there.

. The distance to the next milepost depends on the mud in the road.

The Tree of Love Gives Shade to All

. Travel is the great source of true wisdom.

. Travel makes a wise man better, but a fool worse.

. We've come a distance, but we have a distance to go.

TROUBLE

As a child, I was taught to always stay out of trouble. Our parents felt that a child who got into trouble was a reflection of their parents. During my youth in the segregated state of Mississippi, there were many codes, which our elders referred to as the new 'black codes' to control the movement and lives of African Americans. The original black codes were instituted during slavery to control the movement and lives of slaves. These laws were created to punish African Americans for violation of these laws. Our parents defined trouble as a condition that causes pain and leads to punishment. They taught us at an early age that the outside world expected black youth, especially boys to get into trouble and be incarcerated. One of the sayings that is etched in my mind from childhood was "Take care of the high chair so you don't have to worry about the electric chair." At the time, there were a disproportionate number of African American males who were imprisoned. Our parents knew that this condition was a conspiracy of the outside world to destroy black boys and men.

We were informed that we must follow our parents' teachings that were rooted in Christianity and an understanding of the Jim Crow laws. We were admonished to learn and apply the Ten Commandments as a guide to lead a trouble-free life. We were taught to do unto others as we were expected to be treated. We were constantly reminded of the scripture in Deuteronomy 5:16: "Honor your father and your mother, as the Lord your God has commanded you, so that you may live long and that it may go well with you in the land the Lord your God is giving you." The highest honor a parent could receive was from those who recognized the positive behaviors of their children. It was a compliment to be known as Mr. or Mrs. Sullivan's child.

Our parents and elders led by example and were involved in the lives of their children and other youth in the community. These individuals stressed education and were involved in our education. We were taught that getting a good education was the one way to overcome racism and limit our potential for being in trouble. They believed that while laws took the freedom of African Americans, education was something that no one could take from you. We were taught the difference between right and wrong. Parents taught us to be cautious of our associates and were always aware of the individuals with whom we spent time outside the home. Our parents demonstrated unconditional love and disciplined their children. Most often the discipline was in the form of corporal punishment. They often said, "I am going to whip you so the police do not have to whip you unmercifully." Our parents were moral models in demonstrating honesty and integrity.

. Borrowing is the mother of trouble.

. If you don't want trouble, don't go looking for it.

. Much borrowing destroys credit.

. No one gets into trouble without his own help

. Trouble always comes in threes.

. Troubles don't last always.

. Trouble follows a sin as sure as a fever follows a chill.

. Trouble is seasoning. Persimmons aren't good until they are frost bit.

. Trouble will rain on those who are already wet.

. Up the creek

. When trouble sleeps, don't wake him up.

. You can't keep trouble from coming, but needn't give it a chair to sit on.

TRUST

We often fail Trust 101 and live an unhealthy life when we place our trust in others. We are all endowed with a special power to trust ourselves. We graduate from Trust 101 when we learn and apply that life is about putting a special trust in God. Placing our trust in external sources leads to disease and disharmony. When we place our trust in God we are delivered from disease, poverty, aimlessness, hopelessness, emotional distress and other negative conditions. Trusting in God helps us to be victorious in our lives.

. If you trust before you try, you may repent before you die.

. In God we trust, all others pay cash.

. It takes years to build up trust, and only seconds to destroy it.

TRUTH

Growing up in Mississippi during segregation, we were confronted on a daily basis with laws and negative behaviors that attempted to instill a belief in African Americans that they were not as smart, capable, worthy, and less than white people. Whites held a myriad of myths, misperceptions, falsehoods, and stereotypes of African Americans, which were passed on from generation to generation. These falsehoods were first used and taught for hundreds of years to justify enslavement and dehumanization of African Americans. These beliefs continue to promote the inequality and acceptance of African Americans.

Our elders were diligent in their teachings from the earliest ages of childhood that we were confronted with racism and that we could not ever believe any of the lies about our race. We were also taught that to overcome these falsehoods, we had to be dedicated to excellence in every aspect of our lives. Consequently, our parents and elders fought to teach us that we were as worthy and capable as anyone else. Much of their teachings were based in Christianity and strongly believed that ultimate truth was found in the Bible, in Jesus who said, "I am the way, the truth, and the light...." (John 14:16)

. A good lie finds more believers than a bad truth.

, A liar begins with making falsehood appear like truth.

. A lie runs until it is overtaken by the truth.

. A lie sprints, but truth has endurance.

. A lie travels faster than the truth.

. As scarce as truth is, the supply has always exceeded the demand.

. Come clean. — Confess

. Dying men speak truth. — When people are about to die, they usually tell the truth.

. Facts do not cease to exist because they are ignored. — Truth endures.

. If I tell you a hen dips snuff, you can look under her wing. — I am telling the truth.

. It is as right as rain.

. It'll all come out in the wash. — Truth will eventually come out.

. If I tell you a hen dips snuff, look under its wing and find a whole box.

. It's too good to be true. — Be skeptical of false presentations.

. No one is always right.

. Some people handle the truth carelessly. Others never touch it at all.

. Straighten up and fly right.

. Tell the truth and shame the devil. — Stop lying.

. The greatest homage we can pay to truth is to use it.

. Truth is not determined by the volume of the voice.

. Truth is the only ground to stand upon.

. Truth is universal. Perception of truth is not.

. Truth needs no colors. — Facts are facts.

. Truth will out. — Truth will not be hidden forever.

. Truth will prevail. — Truth will always stand.

. You can take that to the bank.

. You might as well call a spade a spade.

VALEDICTION

. Let the door hit you where the good Lord split you.

. See you when the cows come home.

VIOLENCE

Violence has overtaken some urban and rural communities throughout America. Newspapers and other media provide us a daily dose of crime. There are drive-by shootings that injure and kill innocent babies; parents are afraid of their children and some incidence of children killing their parent(s); home invasions; theft of property; kidnapping and rape; stealing copper wire and other materials from homes, schools and churches; gang violence that leads to homicides; and killing an individual because he looked at a person. While the media reports who, what, when, where and how these crimes are committed, there is hardly any reporting that the cause of these crimes are directly related to the parent and how these youth were raised. The violence is never going to stop until there are frank discussions on how the environment from which these children and youth cause the violence.

The root causes of the surge in violence are not mysterious. Some causes include the family structure, single parent homes, community influences, street norms and values that conflict with the norms and values of the larger society and the lack of parental supervision.

For the most part these are black on black crimes. Black on black violence has emerged as the most significant social problem threatening the survival and quality of life among Blacks since slavery. Few people want to look at the root cause of violence and often blame it on the lack of jobs, racism, poverty, and adhere to the belief there is a conspiracy to destroy black boys. The plain truth is that these factors are not the underlying factors that cause youth and adults to become violent and prey on their communities. The conspiracy to destroy black boys and girls begins in the home where children, called parents, are woefully unprepared to teach children positive behavior. The single parent homes from which so many children grow up without involved fathers and adults are almost destined to become liabilities to society and lose their way and end up in the criminal justice system.

The homicide rate for African American males is almost ten times the rate of white males within twelve to twenty-four years of age. Homicide is the leading cause of death for African American youth in the fifteen to twenty-four-age range.

Many of the crimes are not solved due to the no snitch rule in some African American communities. Nobody ever seems to see anything and nobody decides to report a crime. In most communities, a person who sees a murder or a crime being committed is called a witness. But in many inner-city neighborhoods in this country that person is called a snitch. This message has appeared in hip-hop videos, on T-shirts, Websites, CD and album covers and street murals. Geoffrey Canada, a nationally recognized educator and anti-violence advocate says, "When I was growing up, kids used to talk about snitching….It never extended as a cultural norm outside of the gangsters. It was not for regular citizens. It is now a cultural norm that is being preached in poor communities."

While there are too many excuses for who has the responsibility for raising a child, the fact is that the mother and father have the primary responsibility. Sadly, some of these individuals relinquish their responsibilities and find it easier to place blame on society. The only person(s) who must take charge and teach the child from infancy is the parent.

As a child growing up in the 1940's in the state of Mississippi, our parents and elders taught us that we had to be exemplary citizens, respect authority, stay in school, respect self and others, mind your manners, and decorum. My parents set high standards for conduct, achievement and citizenship. They believed that these attributes would offer more opportunities in a society that relegated black Americans to second-class citizenship. Our parents taught lessons by example and viewed themselves as the primary source of teaching values. They did not shirk their responsibility in being parents and positive role models.

Discipline was always the immediate response to any child's violation of rules of respect, decorum and responsibility. Most often this discipline was equally meted out with verbal reprimands and physical punishment. Any and all adults in the community were disciplinarians and exercised their rights to serve as a surrogate parent in the absence of a parent. Children respected every adult in the community and heeded his/her counsel. A child was perceived and treated as a part of a village and every adult in the village was a role model and was accountable for assisting in rearing children.

Parents taught their children the importance of respecting the rights of others. This was not an optional lesson. There was a specific code of moral conduct in adhering to rules and laws. Those children who violated these rules and got into trouble were perceived as a reflection of their parents' negative teachings and behavior.

Our parents and elders instilled a fear in us at an early age about life in prison. One of their lessons was, "Take care of the high chair so you don't have to worry about the electric chair." This simply meant it was the responsibility of parents to teach a child appropriate behavior as a child and prevent him/her from ending up in prison or worse.

Our elders always shared horror stories about the infamous Parchman Penitentiary, referred to as the Parchman Plantation by some in Mississippi. Parchman, a prison farm, was built on 20,000 acres of some of the state's most fertile land. Cotton was the primary cash crop grown on the rich land in the Mississippi Delta. We were told that convicts were beaten brutally and worked like slaves from dawn to dusk, picking cotton, building railroads, planting, growing and chopping cotton, cutting down huge pine trees, making turpentine, clearing land, and being leased out as workers to private individuals, a condition of servitude as heinous as slavery.

One of the primary reasons for the violence in African American communities is directly related to the fact that children are having children and some so-called fathers are no more than sperm donors. Single mothers are trying to raise children and have limited or no skills in how to be effective parents. There are so many negative strikes against them that include dropping out of school early, having no marketable skills to get and maintain a job, and the belief that the responsibility for providing for children is a state responsibility. Teen mothers face poverty, inadequate support, a lack of education, cognitive immaturity and greater maternal stress, which leads to poor social and educational outcomes for the children of teen mothers.

Children born to teen mothers often do not have an even start in life and live in a life of poverty. They are more likely to grow up in a poor and mother-only family and live in a poor or underclass neighborhood. Children of teen mothers are at a greater risk of being abused or neglected. Children of adolescent mothers are more likely to drop out of high school and their children are three times more likely to be incarcerated than children born to adult mothers. The daughters of adolescent mothers are significantly more likely to give birth themselves before the age of 18. Daughters of teenage mothers have an increased risk of teenage childbearing, perpetuating intergenerational cycles.

Another reason for the violence that exists in many of our communities is the fact that violence is a learned behavior. Children who grow up in homes and experience domestic violence and observe that adults demonstrate violent behavior learn that violence is a means to deal with negative situations.

. He that lives by the sword shall die by the sword.

. Some people are only alive because it's illegal to kill.

VIRTUE

. He that spares vice wrongs virtue.

. Love is the touchstone of virtue.

VISION

. None are as blind as those who won't see.

. The first step toward creating an improved future is developing the ability to envision it.

. You can't see the forest for looking at the trees.
  Focusing on small details and failing to look at the bigger picture.

. You must be blind in one eye and can't see out of the other one.

VOTING

As a child and adult, I lived in the state of Mississippi where African Americans were disenfranchised. For more than a hundred years, millions of African Americans fought for the right to vote. During this struggle for this constitutional right, countless individuals were intimidated and lost their lives as they sought to vote. On February 3, 1870, the Fifteenth Amendment to the United States Constitution stated "The right of citizens of the United States to vote shall not be denied or abridged by the United States or by any State on account of race, color or previous condition of servitude." This constitutional guarantee did not ensure that African Americans would be granted the right to vote throughout the United States.

The denial of African Americans' right to vote was seriously egregious in the South. African Americans who attempted to register to vote were required to pass literacy tests, pay poll taxes and meet other criteria that otherwise were not required of whites. Some of the prospective African American registrants were asked to answer such preposterous questions as: How many grains of sand are in a quart Mason jar? How many fish are in the Mississippi River? How many black-eyed peas will fill a gallon jug? How many bolls of cotton will weigh 100 pounds?

Other efforts were made by whites to deny African Americans the right to register to vote. One such requirement was a literacy test where an African American applicant was given a passage of the constitution and asked to recall to memory several paragraphs within minutes or to explain the meaning of a certain passage of the constitution with 100% accuracy. It should be noted that some of the snuff dipping white examiners were illiterate and could not read at a third grade level.

The Voting Rights Act of 1965 outlawed discriminatory voting practices. This Act was signed by President Lyndon B. Johnson. It prohibited states from imposing any qualification or prerequisite to voting. Although this Act gave African Americans the right to vote, Southern states continued to enforce their illegal requirements to deny blacks the right to vote after almost a hundred years of being denied this right.

Our ancestors worked hard to give African Americans the right to vote. They were intimidated in their efforts. Economic reprisals were quite prevalent at the time as white employers fired African American employees who tried to register to vote. Some men and women were removed from the land where they were sharecroppers. Firebombs were often used to burn down the homes of African Americans. The Ku Klux Klan burned crosses, raped African American women, burned African American churches, conducted drive-by shootings and committed murder and mob lynching. The names of would-be voters were published in local newspapers so that employers, bank loan officers, landlords, and others for the purpose of intimidating men and women and retributions directed to family members, even children.

Hundreds of African Americans were murdered for trying to register to vote. There is a list of individuals who were martyrs in seeking voting rights. In 1955, Rev. George Lee was murdered in Humphreys County, Mississippi. Herbert Lee who worked with Civil Rights leader Bob Moses was killed in Liberty, Mississippi on September 25, 1961. Medgar Evers, the Field Director of the Mississippi NAACP was assassinated in his driveway on June 12, 1963. On June 21, 1964, James Chaney,

Andrew Goodman and Michael Schwerner, three young civil rights workers, were murdered near Philadelphia in Neshoba County, Mississippi. They had been working to register African American voters in Mississippi during Freedom Summer. In January, 1966, Vernon Dahmer, a Hattiesburg, Mississippi businessman, offered to pay the poll tax for those African Americans who were unable to pay. (The payment of a poll tax was not imposed on whites.) After this announcement was made on a local radio station, his house was firebombed on January 10, 1966. Dahmer was injured and died shortly after this incident. There were some arrests in the deaths of these men but they were freed by an all-white jury of their peers. In some cases, it would take more than forty years for some to come to justice and for others, justice was never served.

Civil rights leaders came in many colors, religious persuasions, and various professions. While they differed in race or religion, they were all attacked for their efforts to gain African Americans the right to vote. Although the Voting Rights Act of 1965 was to guarantee African Americans the right to vote, Mississippi dragged its feet and sought to deny African Americans this right. Much like the U. S. Supreme Court decision in *Brown vs. the Board of Education* of 1954, it would take almost seventeen years for the state to integrate schools. The Voting Rights Act did not end the problems of Mississippi's noncompliance to the law. African American voters frequently had to return to the courts to force state and local officials to fulfill requirements of voting changes.

In 1965, the only black local elected officials in the state of Mississippi were the mayor and the city council of the all-African American town of Mound Bayou in the Mississippi Delta. Since the late 1960's dramatic changes have occurred in the number of African American elected officials since the Voting Rights Act of 1965. Today, Mississippi has the highest number of black elected officials in the country. Twenty-seven percent of the members of the state legislature are African American. Thirty-one percent of the members of the country governing boards are African Americans. While these are encouraging statistics, African Americans are still under-represented at all levels of government in Mississippi. Despite the highest African American population of any of the fifty states, none of Mississippi's state-wide officials are African Americans. There continues to be a polarization of voters where whites do not vote for African American candidates.

In 2012, there continues to be efforts to suppress the rights of African Americans and others to vote as well as drafting conservative legislation for states all over the country. The American Legislative Exchange Council (ALEC) in Washington, DC, which describes itself as non-partisan organization advancing "the Jeffersonian principles of free markets, limited government, federalism and individual liberty." This organization is funded by corporate sponsors. These corporate sponsors include ExxonMobil, AT&T, Wal-Mart, State Farm and others. Membership in this organization is composed of state legislators from all fifty states, members from 300 private sector corporations, 85 members of congress, 14 sitting or former governors. ALEC has drafted and distributed model legislation for vote ID laws that disproportionately affect youth, seniors, the disabled and minorities. Recently, Coca Cola and Pepsi cola, former members of ALEC ended their relationship with this organization. ALEC also championed many of the "stand your ground" gun laws passed in states in recent years. As a result of a campaign by the National Rifle Association and ALEC, a "Stand Your Ground Law" was passed in Florida in 2005. This law has spread to more than 30 other states with various names such as the "Castle Doctrine."

Today's youth need to know the history of the struggles of African Americans in their fight for their right to vote. They need to understand that this freedom took more than 100 years to come to fruition and it is imperative that they exercise their rights to vote. They need to view voting as a priority. They need to be as diligent and persistent at the polls as some of them are at the inaugural sale of Nike Air Jordan shoes. Gym shoes will never support freedom and casting a vote will enhance the freedom of all people and support a better life for everyone.

. Always stand up what you believe in, even if you stand alone.

. In times of stress and strain, people will vote.

. Nobody can do everything, but everyone can do something.

. One vote does count.

. Protect one's right to vote.

WEALTH

. A contented man is always rich.

. He is rich who owes nothing.

. Poor without debt is better than a prince.

. The poor sit in Paradise on the first benches.

. The rich man is often poorer than the beggar.

. We're riches when we give, and poorer when we keep.

WEAPONS

As African Americans we were constantly reminded of the weapons that were used by the outside world to deny our equal rights, dignity, and opportunities. Segregation was an evil weapon whose purpose was to instill feelings of inferiority through stereotypes, poor educational opportunities, inferior housing, limited job opportunities, low wages, dilapidated schools and restrictive laws to deny the freedom and inalienable rights that others enjoyed.

To combat these weapons of denial of freedom, we were taught the scripture of Isaiah 54:17: "No weapon that is formed against thee shall prosper and every tongue that shall rise against you shall condemn. This is the heritage of the servants of the Lord, and their righteousness of me, says the Lord."

This scripture was much like the eleventh commandment for our elders, parents, and other role models in the community. We were taught that we could overcome adverse situations, inequality, hate and evil heaped upon African Americans by the outside world and overcome the conditions. Everyone in the community instilled a strong belief that we were equal to anyone and worthy of any opportunities that others enjoyed. Our parents told us, the preacher told us, grandparents told us, aunts and uncles told us, teachers told us, and our neighbors told us that we could succeed and rise above those who sought to relegate us to nothingness and nobody-ness and we believed it and persisted in keeping our eyes on the prize of freedom, self-confidence and achieving our dreams.

Our armory of defense rested in being taught to reject every insult, deny false truths, and negative conditions by being taught to be better a smarter individual, a better communicator, superior in manner, proficient in Christian teachings, and a genius in feelings of self-worth.

. Adversity is a fact of life. It can be controlled. What we can control how we react to it.

. Faith will move mountains.

. For every person who doubts you, tell you will fail, try twice as hard to prove them wrong.

. Fraud and cunning are the weapons of the weak.

. No one would ever have crossed the river if he could have gotten off the ship in a storm.

. Racism is a mere pigment of the imagination.

. The higher we reach; the longer and harder we have to try.

. The impossible is often untried.

. The tongue can be a dangerous weapon.

. Think highly of yourself for the world takes you at your own estimate.

 WISDOM

. A wise man listens to his conscience. — It is important to let your conscience be your guide.

. Experience is the father of wisdom

. Get wise.

. Keep your wits about you.

. Only dead fish go with the flow.

. When an old man dies, a library burns to the ground. Wisdom leaves with an old person.

WOMEN

. A lady's honor will not bear a soil.

. A silent woman is always more admired than a noisy one.

. A whistling woman and a crowing hen will not come to a good end.

. A woman knows what a woman needs.

. A woman who knows how to cook is mighty pretty.

. A woman who will tell her age will tell anything.

. A woman without her sisters is like a bird without wings.

. A woman's work is never done.

The Tree of Love Gives Shade to All

. I'll drop that man like a hot potato.

. It's a privilege to be ugly, but some take advantage of it.

. Tattling woman can't make the bread rise.

. Women, can't live with them, can't live without them.

WORDS

. A single fact is worth a shipload of arguments.

. Facts are more powerful than words.

. Speaking kindly doesn't hurt the tongue much.

WORK

Dr. Martin Luther King Jr., wrote, "If a man is called to be a street sweeper, he should sweep streets as Michelangelo painted or Beethoven composed music or Shakespeare wrote poetry."

. A hobby is hard work you wouldn't do for a living.

. A little hard work never hurt or killed anyone.

. A woman's work is never done.

. Bad workers always blame their tools.

. Can't sit on the bucket and draw water at the same time.

. Do first what you dread the most.

. Find a niche and scratch it.

. Fish or cut bait. — Proceed with an activity or abandon it.

. Flies can't fall in a tight-closed pot.

. Get down to business.

The Tree of Love Gives Shade to All

. Hand plow can't make furrows by itself.

. Hard work breaks no bones.

. He/she won't hit a lick at a snake.

. Ifs and buts butter no bread.

. I respect work like I do my mother and I wouldn't hit her a lick.

. It is easier to admire hard work if you don't do it.

. It takes a steady hand to carry a full cup.

. Just counting stumps don't clear the field.

. Make hay while the sun shines.

. Man who gets hurt working ought to show the scars.

. Many hands make light work.

. 'Mean to' doesn't pick the cotton.

. Nobody ever drowned in sweat. — Hard work never hurt anyone.

. One finger won't catch flies.

. Root hog or die. — Work is required for survival.

. Sleepy fisherman totes a light load home.

. The best way to get something done is to begin.

. The daily grind of hard work gets a person polished.

- When you do a job, do it properly or do not do it at all.

- Work up a sweat.

- Work your fingers to the bone.

- You can't make bricks without straw.

- You don't see an empty bag stand up.

- You have got to feed a mule before you work it.

 ZEAL

Zeal means to have enthusiasm or the zest to do something worthwhile. In Proverbs 19:2, we are taught "It is not good to have zeal without knowledge nor to be hasty and miss the day." Zeal drives us to give extra effort at work, in the family, and the community. Zeal is demonstrated in our efforts to reach out to others through volunteering and caring for others. Individuals who work on Habitat homes, advocate for the homeless, and promote justice for all people. One of the most prolific examples of a person who lived a life filled with zeal was Dr. Martin Luther King, Jr. Dr. King fought to eradicate social injustice, to build bridges of community and peace and equality. Another example of a remarkable individual who possessed ultimate zeal in her life was Mother Teresa. For over 45 years, she ministered to the poor, sick, orphaned and dying while guiding the Missionaries of Charity expansion throughout India and other countries. At the time of her death the Missionaries of Charity had 610 mission in 123 countries including hospices and homes for people with HIV/AIDS, leprosy and tuberculosis.

Sister Thea Bowman, a catholic nun from Yazoo City, Mississippi, showed her zeal by sharing the message of God's love through a teaching career. The bishop of Jackson, Mississippi invited her to become the consultant for Intercultural Awareness. In this role, she gave presentations throughout the country that combined singing, gospel, preaching and storytelling. These programs were directed to break down racial and cultural barriers. She fought evil, especially prejudice, suspicion, hatred and things that drive people apart. She passed away in 1990 from breast cancer.

While we do not have to be as well-known as Dr. Martin Luther King, Jr , or Mother Teresa and Sister Thea Bowman, we can all follow scripture and reach out to others who are less fortunate with our knowledge to help them overcome obstacles in their lives. We can offer our services to soup kitchens, help the homeless, serve as foster parents, become advocates for social justice, and improve the lives of others as the tree of love gives shade to all.

The Tree of Love Gives Shade to All

. Rest is good after the work is done.

. Too much zeal spoils all.

. Zeal is blind when it encroaches upon the rights of others.

. Zeal is fit only for wise men, but is found mostly in fools.

. Zeal is like fire. It needs both feeding and warning.

. Zeal without knowledge is a runaway horse.

www.ingramcontent.com/pod-product-compliance
Lightning Source LLC
Chambersburg PA
CBHW060641170426
43199CB00012B/1635